Compensation and Benefits

Compensation
and
Benefits

Luis R. Gomez-Mejia
Editor

Ray Olsen
George T. Milkovich
Consulting Editors

The Bureau of National Affairs, Inc., Washington, D.C. 20037

Library of Congress Cataloging-in-Publication Data

Compensation and benefits.

   (ASPA/BNA series   ;   3)
   1. Compensation management.   2. Employee fringe bene-
fits.   I. Gomez-Mejia, Luis R.   II. Olsen, Ray,
1933-   III. Milkovich, George T.   IV. Bureau of
National Affairs (Washington, D.C.)   V. Series.
[HF5549.A9574   1988 vol. 3   658.3 s [658.3′22] 89-17473
[HF5549.5.C67]
ISBN 0-87179-603-1

HF5549
.A9574
1988
vol. 3

Published by BNA Books, 1231 25th St., N.W., Washington, D.C. 20037

Printed in the United States of America
International Standard Book Number: 0-87179-603-1

Preface

It has been 15 years since the first volume of the original ASPA Handbook of Personnel and Industrial Relations was published. A great deal has changed in our profession since then. No longer is PAIR (personnel and industrial relations) the accepted acronym for the management of human resources, primarily because our roles and our accountabilities are so different.

Human resource executives have been broadening their horizons and learning new ways to make a bigger contribution to their organizations. So, too, does the focus of this new HRM (human resource management) series indicate the extent to which the field has changed and how pace-setting human resource executives have been reshaping management practice. We have tried to reflect those changes in this new series.

The original series was eight volumes with a heavy emphasis on "how-to-do-it." This new series, comprised of six volumes, focuses more heavily on the why than the how, on strategy and integration rather than the specifics of execution.

The very process we used to develop this series indicates the shift in orientation. Each of the six volumes had a different well-known academician as its editor. These individuals were supported by at least one consulting editor, a senior practitioner in the HRM field whose role was to provide the "real world" perspective so necessary to this kind of project. And the overall series was guided by an editorial advisory board made up of practitioners, academicians, and representatives of BNA and ASPA. Members of the editorial advisory board are listed opposite the title page of this Volume.

Collectively, we struggled through the development of each volume and its chapters, striving to achieve the proper balance between a macro perspective of the profession and an evolutionary approach to the material presented. Our target audience—middle to upper level practitioners and those who aspire to such positions—was a constant presence during all of our discussions.

The six volumes in this series and their key players are:

1. *Human Resource Management: Evolving Roles and Responsibilities* edited by Lee Dyer, professor at Cornell University with

JAN 0 7 1999

Jerry Holder, retired vice president of human resources for Marion Laboratories, as consulting editor. Additional consulting editors included Robert Berra of Monsanto, Leo Contois of Consolidated Foods (retired) and Garth Dimon of Bristol-Meyers.

2. *Human Resource Planning, Employment and Placement* edited by Wayne Cascio, professor at the University of Colorado with Donald Sweet of Hawkins Associates, Inc. as consulting editor.

3. *Compensation and Benefits* edited by Luis R. Gomez-Mejia, professor at the University of Colorado with consulting editors Ray Olsen of TRW and George Milkovich of Cornell University.

4. *Employee and Labor Relations* edited by John Fossum, professor, University of Minnesota, with Jerauld Mattson of International Multifoods as consulting editor.

5. *Developing Human Resources* edited by Kenneth N. Wexley, professor, Michigan State University with John Hinrichs of Management Decision Systems as consulting editor.

6. *Managing Human Resources in the Information Age* with Randall S. Schuler of New York University as editor and James Walker of Walker and Associates as consulting editor.

This new management series reflects the coming of age of human resource management. ASPA is grateful to the individuals whose work is reflected in its pages and proud to mark this professional transition with such an outstanding series.

Ronald C. Pilenzo
Alexandria, VA
June 1988

Introduction

This third volume in the ASPA/BNA series focuses on what is perhaps the most basic and ancient mechanism that employers have at their disposal to influence employee behavior: the compensation system. While much debate has taken place since biblical times about the role of money as a motivator, most HR practitioners and scholars alike agree that the way pay dollars are allocated send a powerful message to all organizational members as to what the firm deems important and the types of activities which are encouraged. Furthermore, there is general agreement that people tend to do those things that they perceive will lead to a valued reward. This is just as true at the top executive rank as it is for the lowest-paid worker. Thus pay has a deep psychological and symbolic meaning to employees that go well beyond its purely materialistic value.

The field of compensation has experienced a dramatic transformation since the mid 1970s when the first ASPA/BNA series was published. The previous emphasis on tools and techniques (e.g., point system, functional job analysis) has given way to a strategic orientation where such tools have become a means to an end rather than an end in themselves. Many of the same old issues (e.g., merit pay, internal equity, market adjustment) are still important, but these are now examined from a business perspective rather than through narrow functional lenses. The predominant concern for the 1990s and beyond is how the compensation system links with organizational strategies rather than on the development of new administrative procedures for making pay decisions. The typical question being asked of the compensation system in this new era is "Are we doing the right things?" rather than "Are we doing things right?".

This book is designed to capture this emerging strategic view of the field by bringing together in a single volume the thoughts and ideas of leading compensation scholars and consultants, and present these in a way that is accessible to practitioners in the field.

The first chapter, "Employment Compensation Planning and Strategy," by Thomas Mahoney, focuses on the major concerns, contingencies, and policy choices that HR managers should take into account when designing compensation programs. Mahoney develops a model that examines compensation strategy in terms of

viii   Compensation & Benefits

"work contingencies" and "non-work contingencies." A contingency
refers to a basis for assigning pay. According to Mahoney, the main
challenge that confronts compensation practitioners is choosing the
best combination of contingencies that most closely match organizational structures and strategies as well as HR strategies.

The second chapter, "Internal Pay Relationships," by Frederick Hills, focuses on the major issues and mechanisms that should be
considered when organizations attempt to establish internal pay
structures. Hill reviews the underlying conceptual basis for job
evaluation, the most widely used system to determine pay schedules based on each job's assessed contributions. He also examines
the key policy choices and legal constraints that should be taken into
account when implementing such programs. Hill concludes his
chapter by reminding us that there is no universally held criteria for
job worth, and that ultimately the acid test for the success or failure
of job evaluation is the extent to which decisions made under the
system enjoy the acceptability of affected employees.

Chapter 3.3, "External Pay Relationships," by Charles Fay, is
concerned with the variety of strategies available to organizations to
remain competitive in the relevant labor market. He examines three
major approaches that may be utilized to achieve external equity.
An internal labor market strategy attempts to protect the organization's salary structure from external labor market forces. An across-
the-board strategy adjusts an organization's complete salary structure by a fixed percentage. The third strategy differentially adjusts
salaries of various jobs depending on their assessed contribution to
business goals. Fay also examines the major factors influencing
external pay levels and key policy choices to consider when linking
the organization's pay structure to market rates.

Chapter 3.4, "Employee Benefits and Services," by Robert
McCaffery examines the major strategic dimensions that should be
considered in benefits planning. These include organizational
objectives, work-force characteristics, and the firm's total compensation strategy. He also outlines the major types of benefit plans,
and the key choices available under each. Finally, McCaffery discusses the most important issues involved in the management of
employee benefits.

The fifth chapter, "Pay for Performance," by Edward Lawler,
examines the strategic choices available to the designers of pay for
performance systems and how these relate to organizational effectiveness. Lawler first discusses the multiple objectives of pay sys-

tems and how strategic planning, organization design, and reward programs overlap. He then proceeds to discuss how different approaches to paying for performance and their effectiveness vary according to such factors as organizational structure, company culture, and management style. Lawler's basic thesis is that pay for performance systems cannot be analyzed in isolation; to be effective they need to be congruent with the organizational context in which they function.

Chapter 3.6, "Compensation Programs for Special Employee Groups," by Jerry Newman, focuses on strategic pay concerns related to the nature of, and contributions of, workers who are viewed as critical to the organization's mission. According to him, employees who deserve special treatment are responsible for boundary-spanning functions and these activities must deal with environmental contingencies that are strategically important to the firm. Newman discusses the unique compensation programs that have been developed for particular employee groups such as supervisors, R&D workers, and foreign service personnel, and how these separate pay plans can be integrated with the organization's total pay system.

The last chapter, "Strategic Design of Executive Compensation Programs," by Luis Gomez-Mejia and Theresa Welbourne, examines research findings, strategic issues, and current trends that influence the design of a successful executive compensation program. According to these authors, executive pay strategy is the most critical element of the compensation program. It directly and indirectly drives both the formal compensation plan for the remainder of the employees and how they perceive the reward system's link to their own performance. Gomez-Mejia and Welbourne present an array of strategic pay choices that should be considered when designing executive compensation programs. They argue that if these options are not explicitly addressed in the design phase, the compensation system may be decoupled from the organization's strategic orientation, and by implication, become less effective or even counterproductive.

I would like to acknowledge the contribution of several dozen practitioners and academics who met in Washington on several occasions to review and criticize earlier outlines and drafts of this book. I am particularly grateful to Ron Pilenzo and Cate Bower at ASPA, Ray Olsen of TRW, as well as Mary Miner and Anne Scott of

BNA, for all the hours they have devoted to this project. And there is a third group of people, the contributing authors, who must be commended for the endless patience, responsiveness, and willingness to undergo several time-consuming revisions of their chapters.

Luis R. Gomez-Mejia
Boulder, Colorado
June 1989

About the Authors

Chapter 3.1

Employment Compensation Planning and Strategy

Thomas A. Mahoney (Ph.D., University of Minnesota) holds the Frances Hampton Currey Professorship in Organization Studies at the Owen Graduate School of Management, Vanderbilt University. He previously served on the faculty in industrial relations at the University of Minnesota for a number of years. His research interests focus upon rewards and compensation, human resource strategy, and organization theory and behavior. Mahoney has published extensively in various journals and he has held a variety of professional association appointments including editor of the *Academy of Management Journal*.

Partial support for this chapter was provided by the Dean's Research Fund, Owen Graduate School of Management, Vanderbilt University. Comments from John Deckop, George Milkovich, and Donald Schwab are gratefully acknowledged.

Chapter 3.2

Internal Pay Relationships

Frederick S. Hills (Ph.D., University of Minnesota) is an associate professor of management at Virginia Polytechnic Institute and State University. He has published many articles in leading journals, and chapters within books, as well as authoring the book *Compensation Decision Making*. His current research programs are in the areas of compensation and equal employment policy.

Chapter 3.3

External Pay Relationships

Charles H. Fay (Ph.D., University of Washington) is associate professor of industrial relations and human resources in the Rutgers University Institute of Industrial and Labor Relations. Dr. Fay has authored or co-authored several books, including *Compensation: Theory* and Practice; Administering Human Resources; and Research Based Decisions. He has also published numerous compensation articles in scholarly and professional journals. Dr. Fay received an M.B.A. degree at Columbia University.

Chapter 3.4

Employee Benefits and Services

Robert M. McCaffery (M.S., Cornell University) is a human resources management consultant based in Upper Montclair, NJ. He was previously Vice President-Human Resources with Schering-Plough Corporation and has had extensive experience in employee relations, compensation and benefits, employee communications, and personnel management. He is also an adjunct professor of industrial relations and human resources at Rutgers University and series editor for the quarterly journal, Topics in Total Compensation.

Mr. McCaffery is the author of three books on employee benefits and has written a number of articles for personnel, compensation, and business publications.

Chapter 3.5

Pay for Performance: A Strategic Analysis

Edward E. Lawler III (Ph.D., University of California at Berkeley) is the director of the Center for Effective Organizations at the University of Southern California. He is the author or co-author of over 100 articles and 17 books. Among the books he has written are Organizational Assessment; Pay and Organization Development; High Involvement Management; and Designing Performance Appraisal Systems. His book Pay and Organizational Effectiveness, published in 1971, is a classic in the compensation field.

Chapter 3.6

Compensation Programs for Special Employee Groups

Jerry M. Newman (Ph.D., University of Minnesota) is associate professor of human resources in the Management Department and director of the Center for Human Resources Research at the State University of New York at Buffalo. Professor Newman is the author of numerous articles on compensation, staffing, and appraisal. He is also co-author of the book *Compensation.*

Chapter 3.7

Strategic Design of Executive Compensation Programs

Luis R. Gomez-Mejia (Ph.D., University of Minnesota) is a professor in the Department of Management at Arizona State University. Prior to this, he was an associate professor in the Department of Strategy and Organization Management at the University of Colorado at Boulder. He has had several years experience in human resource management at Control Data Corporation and the City of Minneapolis and has also been a consultant to numerous private and public sector organizations. Dr. Gomez-Mejia has authored over 50 publications in compensation and human resource management which have appeared in various journals.

Theresa M. Welbourne is a doctoral student in the Department of Strategy and Organization Management at the University of Colorado at Boulder. She has had over 10 years experience as a compensation practitioner and consultant in several firms. She has written several publications appearing in such journals as *Human Resource Planning* and *Compensation and Benefits Review.*

Contents

3.4   Employee Benefits and Services   3-101
Robert M. McCaffery

3.5   Pay for Performance: A Strategic Analysis   3-136
Edward E. Lawler III

3.6   Compensation Programs for Special Employee Groups   3-182
Jerry M. Newman

3.1

Employment Compensation Planning and Strategy

Thomas A. Mahoney

Employment compensation in the form of wages and salaries is a central characteristic of an industrial country. It is a prime concern of employers, workers, and society at large. Compensation is critical to workers since employment income determines their ability to consume goods, purchase services, and invest savings. These expenditures fuel the economy and make compensation a concern to society at large, particularly in the United States where wages and salary form two-thirds of personal income.

This chapter will focus on the importance of compensation to another segment of society, employers. Given that wage and salary payments form about 60 percent of all costs of non-financial corporations, employers have an obvious interest in compensation. Since compensation rates influence productivity and thus employment levels, the design of compensation strategy can impact significantly on profit margins and on the accomplishment of organizational objectives. This following discussion will examine the various issues, contingencies, and strategic options that HR managers can use to maximize the contribution of compensation programs to organizational success.

Philosophical Views Concerning Compensation

The term "employment compensation" readily calls to mind the wage and salary payments received by employees. Yet the word "compensation" has other, more general connotations related to the role of compensation in employment. Dictionary definitions of compensation indicate that the term refers to making whole or supplying an equivalent to something. And the verb "compensate" is applied in various settings to indicate some type of correction, adjustment, or provision of damages to an injured party.[1]

Viewed in this context, wage and salary payments are provided as an equivalent to some loss occasioned by employment. Understanding the nature of this loss, measuring the amount of loss, and understanding how to manipulate wage and salary payments so as to provide equivalence are core concerns of employment compensation theory and practice.

Because of its social as well as economic significance, compensation also exemplifies and reinforces social norms. In capitalistic societies, for example, wage and salary compensation is associated with market exchanges but not with household work performed by family members or with so-called volunteer activities, despite the net contribution of these activities to social welfare. In a similar fashion, social standards influence both the type and the amount of compensation offered for a job. Wage and salary compensation is more than a mere economic transaction; it also expresses social norms and values.[2]

Employment Contract

Employment compensation plays a key role in any employment contract. Employment contracts take many forms, ranging from a formally negotiated contract between an employer and a union, to formal statements of employer personnel practices, to less formal sets of expectations of an employer and an employee. In each instance, an employee contracts to deliver time, effort, and skill as required, within certain bounds, by an employer, and the employer in turn provides payments compensating the employee for these contributions.[3]

Contribution Costs

In theory, the valuation of employee contributions and determination of an appropriate compensating payment occurs in the contracting process. Employees contract to employment only if they judge the promised payment to be appropriate compensation for the contributions required. Otherwise, a prospective employer must increase promised payments or reduce the required contributions until a compensating balance is reached. For example, an employer might raise the wage offered, promise continued employment, or reduce demands for time and effort in order to reach a contract with a prospective employee.

Opportunity Costs

A broader view of employee contributions invokes the concept of opportunity cost. Employment contracts specify obvious contributions of time, skill, and effort, and these contributions require that employees forgo alternative applications of time, skill and effort. At a minimum, employees must give up leisure; more commonly, they must forgo alternative employment and its associated compensation. The opportunity cost of an employment contract expresses the employee's valuation of forgone alternatives.[4] In this sense, employment compensation often serves as an incentive, an offer of employment benefits such that a prospective employee will choose to forgo alternatives to the employment offer. The dual concepts of compensation and incentive become intertwined in this broader context.

Cost-Benefit Variables

Individual employment contracting is not common, however. Instead, employers usually design employment contracts to secure acceptance by a required number of providers of labor. Employment compensation strategies address the design of all elements of an employment contract and not merely the formulation of schedules of payment of wages and salaries. Wage and salary payments compensate for the less attractive elements of an employment contract, and employers can manipulate both payments and these other elements of the contract to achieve balance.

Wage and salary payments are most easily analyzed in monetary terms, yet their potential attractiveness often depends upon other characteristics. Salary, for example, typically refers to weekly or monthly payments while wage refers to hourly payments. Thus, salary connotes less variable compensation and proves more attractive to prospective employees. Other forms of payment, such as vacation, sick leave, and insurance, also vary in terms of relative attractiveness.[5] Finally, the value of monetary compensation depends not only on its consumption potential but also on the attractiveness of payments relative to other known comparisons.[6] As a result, compensation designers can manipulate the attractiveness of wage and salary payments in ways that do not increase labor costs.

Compensation Differentials

A striking feature of employment compensation in any society is the wide range of observed differentials in payment.[7] These differentials presumably serve a purpose; they must accomplish something not otherwise achievable. A major challenge for compensation theory is to provide an explanation for these observed differentials.[8] For HR managers, the challenge is to design and administer compensation differentials to accomplish organizational objectives, the design and implementation of compensation strategies.

In general, differentials in payment serve to balance other compensating differentials in an employment contract. These other differentials commonly include location, occupation, industry, employer, worker characteristics, and collective bargaining. Observed differences between any two employees may incorporate several of these variables. For example, a difference in wages between teachers in Tennessee and airline pilots in Minnesota incorporates location, industry, and occupation as wage influences. Reasons for these wage differentials are not obvious, but the following discussion illustrates several different perspectives.

Supply Theories

Explanations usually appeal to market concepts since, presumably, the exchange of labor in an employment contract is a negotiated exchange. One set of explanations addresses differences in labor supplies. This position argues, for example, that relatively scarce labor supplies command a premium in wage negotiations. A relative scarcity may arise due to the job's location or its required level of education, skill, and experience. Wage differentials associated with temporary scarcities should diminish over time, while persistent wage differentials presumably serve to remedy disadvantages associated with qualifying for a position (e.g., obtaining a college education).

These supply-based explanations imply that employers should design wage differentials to reflect relative scarcities of labor supplies and pay only those differentials necessary to attract the required supplies. However, some evidence indicates that wage differentials are not always easy to change as labor demand and supplies fluctuate.[9] Relative wage comparisons involve more than mere compensation for prior qualification. Traditional occupational wage differentials, for example, may hold steady despite significant changes in relative labor supplies. Employers faced with a labor shortage may vary the qualifications for entry and thus the real cost per unit of labor hired instead.[10] For example, a scarcity of skilled electricians would seem to require raising wages to attract skilled electricians. To do so, however, could disrupt established and traditional wage comparisons between electricians and mechanics with consequent grievances and concern. An alternative solution is to maintain traditional wage differentials and accept less-qualified applicants as electricians, thus varying differentials in entry qualifications to replace varying wage differentials.

Demand Theories

Another set of explanations for wage differentials emphasizes labor-demand considerations. According to this perspective, wage differentials arise when one industry and/or employer can afford to pay more for labor than another due to characteristics of the product market and exploits this ability.[11] In short, a particular type of labor may be worth more to one employer than to another. For example, an employer who experiences growing product demand, sells in an oligopolistic market, or uses a capital-intensive technology may value labor more than an employer in another setting.

A practical implication of these demand-based explanations is that employers should manage compensation competitively with similar producers. The primary goal of compensation strategy would be to avoid unfavorable cost comparisons with competing producers.

Interactional Factors

Market supply and demand factors no doubt influence wage differentials, but differentials observed at any point in time do not result from direct bidding in the labor market. Labor markets have institutionalized customs, traditions, and rules for behavior. Wage rates are administered prices established by an employer unilaterally or through collective bargaining. The ultimate test of an employment compensation program will be market-related—does it serve to attract, retain, and direct the requisite labor suppliers within competitive cost constraints? But the design and administration of compensation programs are management decisions made in the context of strategic goals.

Compensation Contingencies

One major aspect of variation in employment compensation addresses contingency relationships. Compensation contingencies have both motivational and cost implications. All employment compensation requires at minimum an employment relationship. Beyond that relationship, other contingencies specify the amount and, at times, the type of compensation, its cost to employers, and routes through which employees can earn increased compensation.

Details of employment compensation can vary almost infinitely, and this variation is what offers the potential for HR managers to tailor compensation programs to the specific goals of their organizations. Compensation programs can incorporate either single or multiple contingencies. Single-contingency programs, such as a straight, fixed-rate, sales commission, offer the advantage of clarity and simplicity in communicating desired employee contributions. Multiple-contingency programs, while less easily analyzed, provide the means to address each different contingency criterion. For example, in stock option programs, one criterion, usually position, determines when an employee first becomes eligible to participate. A second contingency can relate the amount of options granted to some measure of performance. Still other contingencies, such as stock performance, determine the ultimate value of options exercised.

The close linkage between employment contributions and compensation inducement sometimes obscures the underlying rationale for a particular element of an employment contract. For example, should employers view flexible-hours scheduling as an employee contribution of time or as an inducement to employment? In general, the following discussion will focus on traditional compensation contingencies and discuss variants of employment contributions only as specifically related to compensation.

Work Contingencies

Reasonable people expect employment compensation to be contingent upon work. It compensates for the opportunity costs associated with work and serves as an incentive or inducement to perform work. Making compensation contingent upon work presumably will inform employees about the work desired while controlling the labor costs of the good or service produced.

Work-contingent compensation attempts to replicate as much as possible an independent-contractor relationship in the employment setting. An independent contractor undertakes delivery of ouput at an agreed price, output of work being what an employer really seeks, and payment depends solely upon completion and delivery of a good or service. The client purchases a good or service, not work. However, an entire economy cannot operate around independent-contractor relationships, so instead large production organizations purchase labor supplies and then transform the work of these labor supplies into goods and services for sale. [12] The design of work-contingent compensation plays a key role in achieving this transformation while controlling the labor cost of outputs.

Work, simple as it sounds, proves difficult to define and measure in many organizations. In practice, three differing sets of measures for work-contingent compensation have emerged: performance contingencies, job contingencies, and person contingencies (see Figure 1). As noted later, performance-contingent compensation most closely links pay and output. Job-contingent compensation serves as a substitute when performance contingencies are infeasible, and person-contingent compensation is employed where job-contingent compensation proves unsuitable.

Performance Contingencies

Performance-contingent compensation, while conceptually simple and direct, is often difficult to operationalize and apply. In concept, performance-contingent compensation provides payment for output or outcome and most closely resembles compensation of independent contractors.

From a motivational standpoint, performance contingencies provide clear direction for and regular reinforcement of performance. Partly for these reasons, performance-contingent compensation often serves as a substitute for direct supervision. It is used for

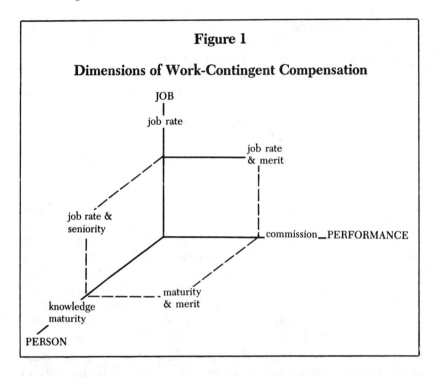

Figure 1

Dimensions of Work-Contingent Compensation

jobs involving outside sales or as a means of exercising board control over top executives.[13] From a cost standpoint, strict performance-contingent compensation also controls the labor cost per unit of performance. For example, piece rates and commissions strictly regulate the labor cost per performance unit and are favored in industries, such as garment manufacturing, that face considerable cost competition.

Strategic Issues. Strict performance-contingent compensation only works in selected situations. First, job performance must produce an identifiable and measureable output, such as the sale of an insurance policy, the stitched cuff on a shirt, or the assembly of a product component. The job must involve relatively few outputs; otherwise the variety of contingencies for payment become confusing. For example, a sales person with 100 products, each with a different contingent payoff, lacks the direction of a sales person who has only four products and contingencies. Performance level also should depend on the employee's efforts and not vary due to equipment failure, faulty materials, or cooperation of others. For all these reasons, relatively few jobs and occupations rely exclusively on performance contingencies; more commonly, performance-contingent compensation is modified and/or supplemented by other forms of compensation.

One modification provides some form of base compensation not linked to performance outcomes (such as base salary or base rate). These plans assure an employee of a minimum income, and use performance-contingent compensation to provide direction and to motivate performance beyond that base. Awards for cost-saving suggestions illustrate one form of performance-contingent compensation for unusual work contributions.

Another modification relates to the performance criterion. Instead of identifying a product associated with performance, employers often specify performance in behavioral terms. These plans outline behaviors believed to be critical to organizational outcomes and make compensation contingent upon performance of these behaviors. Examples would include bonuses for perfect attendance, payment for customer calls and not merely sales, and awards based upon courtesy.

Merit pay based upon subjective appraisals of performance bears a resemblance to performance-contingent compensation. Unfortunately, merit pay too often has only a nebulous performance contingency. Subjective assessments of performance, such as cooperation, responsiveness, and adherence to rules, are difficult to communicate and often provide little direction. Further, they prove difficult to measure and their validity may be questioned. Finally, most programs incorporate merit compensation into base compensation, thus removing the contingency relationship for future performance.

Performance-contingent compensation also can be modified to reward group performance when individual measures of performance are not feasible. Profit sharing, gainsharing, and team bonuses are examples of group performance contingent compensation.[14] While group performance contingencies lessen individual incentives, HR managers can combine group with individual pay contingencies to foster cooperation and individual performance.

Pros and Cons. Performance-contingent compensation, particularly when combined with other bases of compensation, can direct and reward a variety of performance outputs. For example, a single organization can employ individual attendance awards, individual and group suggestion awards, performance bonuses, gainsharing, and profit sharing to reward different performances. As an example of multiple contingencies, management bonus formulas link the bonus to company profit performance, divisional performance, and individual performance.

Performance-contingent compensation offers a diversity of options for application limited only by one's imagination. It does, however, require careful planning and administration to succeed. Too many organizations design performance contingencies around easily measured but less relevant performances, and reward something other than the output desired.[15] The potential offered by performance-contingent compensation comes accompanied by the challenge to design and apply it correctly.

Job Contingencies

Performance-contingent compensation is not always feasible for various reasons: Performance may prove too difficult to define or measure; desired performance may vary considerably over time; and performance may depend on factors outside the worker's control. In these situations, organizations can employ job-contingent compensation, with a job description serving as the best available indicator of desired performance.

Compensation contingent upon the job held and the time supplied by a worker is the most common single form of employee compensation. "Payment for the job" is a well-established principle of compensation practice. The concept of "job" encompasses the type and level of performance sought by an employer and the requisite skill and effort demanded from an employee. The concept of job thus serves as a proxy measure of both labor inputs and outputs. Unfortunately, this blending of performance and person lessens the potential impact of separate performance and person contingencies.

Job-contingent variations in compensation arise most strikingly in well-established occupational wage structures and in traditional approaches to job evaluation and wage-survey job pricing. Traditional organizations adhere to bureaucratic work models: Tasks are grouped into jobs independent of incumbent consideration, and people are then hired, trained, supervised, and paid on the basis of job characteristics. The job thus serves as the basic integrating concept for all HRM programs including compensation.

Strategic Issues. Job-contingent compensation bears a lesser relationship to strategy and choice than performance contingencies.

While employers and workers alike presume that different jobs receive different compensation, the specific basis for differentiation remains an unsettled issue.[16] One approach to establishing job-contingent compensation follows the conceptual model of labor-market wage determination. Job-contingent differentials are a function of relative supply and demand in the labor market, which in part reflect employer and employee valuations of the work contributions associated with different jobs. Assuming competitive labor markets, wage rates for different jobs evolve through competitive bidding of employers and prospective employees. Any employer seeking to hire for a particular job must pay that market rate to be assured of a supply of qualified workers.

Observation of market rates can presumably guide employers when determining the appropriate job rate for a position. In practice, however, virtually every wage survey reports considerable variation in compensation for any job and there is no obvious single market rate.[17] Indeed, employer practice often involves establishment of a so-called "policy line" to guide the establishment of job rates relative to the *average* rates observed in market surveys.

Job evaluation is another approach to the establishment of job-contingent differentials. Under this approach, employers use some set of comparison factors to measure jobs within an organization and to determine relative compensation for each. Advocates of so-called "comparable worth" have criticized job evaluation in recent years, charging that traditional measures do not always reflect true relative worth of different jobs and may underrate jobs staffed predominantly by women.[18] However, lacking a universally accepted set of job evaluation standards, employers must judge the validity of job evaluation by determining whether the resulting compensation differentials conform to work-force norms and serve to attract and maintain labor supplies.[19] Organizations that experience turnover, grievances, or a lack of job applicants may need to revise their job compensation differentials.

Another strategic choice related to job-contingent compensation concerns practical distinction among jobs. Jobs may be defined in gross terms, such as occupation, or in quite specific terms which distinguish among multiple jobs in a single occupation. For example, should the job of auto mechanic on the night shift be distinguished from auto mechanic on the day shift? Should the job of counter clerk at a fast food outlet be distinguished from that of hamburger flipper? Critics argue that extremely fine distinctions among jobs, coupled with pay differentials and rules for job assignment, caused lack of flexibility and productivity in past years, and many organizations are now attempting to reduce job distinctions. As job distinctions diminish, however, job-contingent compensation becomes less meaningful and employers must seek other means to recognize differences in performance within broad job classes.

Pros and Cons. Job-contingent compensation conforms to bureaucratic organizational principles, attempts to operationalize the common norm of "equal pay for equal work," and provides differentials intended to compensate for, and thus attract labor to, less appealing and less desirable jobs. However, it does not address performance motivation within individual jobs. In addition, job-contingent compensation requires a relatively stable organization of tasks into jobs since any reorganization of tasks will make prior job evaluations obsolete. Attempts to define jobs quite precisely, often result in differentiation among hundreds or thousands of jobs, each with a different rate of compensation, and create relatively inflexible employee assignments and performance levels. Job-contingent compensation, with its base in bureaucratic principles, embodies all of the advantages and disadvantages of bureaucratic organizations.

Person Contingencies

Person-contingent compensation addresses personal inputs brought to a job in line with concepts of human capital.[20] Person contingencies serve to reward employees for prior investments in human capital and to motivate future investments; consequently, these variables should be manipulable by the individual. For example, level of education might serve as a contingency variable while gender or race would not (indeed, gender and race contingencies would constitute illegal discrimination).

Person-contingent compensation is more common than might be thought. Career-entry compensation, for example, often reflects personal characteristics presumed to predict future performance; persons with MBAs typically receive higher starting pay than those with baccalaureate degrees, although both individuals may be hired as management trainees.

Person-contingent compensation also is associated with such professionals as electrical engineers, attorneys, and teachers. Qualifications such as type and level of education and experience are primary in determining compensation differentials. Pay-for-knowledge compensation schemes for non-professional employees have evolved in recent years and represent a shift from job-based to person-based compensation.[21] A somewhat similar basis for pay differentiation has existed for decades in craft trades which distinguish between apprentice, journeyman, and master craftsman.

Strategic Issues. Person-contingent compensation may offer an alternative to performance- or job-contingent compensation for individuals whose performance and job tasks defy precise definition. For example, most job analysts would find it difficult to define the daily or monthly performance expected of a scientist engaged in research and development, especially since job tasks will change in response to research developments. Instead, these types of jobs are defined broadly in terms of whatever someone with specified training and experience might be expected to do. Person contingencies thus can act as both job definitions and compensation criteria.

Person-contingent compensation seems best-suited to situations where the job is relatively less structured, more variable over time, and where performance outputs are difficult to establish. For example, maturity-curve compensation for engineers and scientists appears to have evolved due to the difficulty of identifying comparable jobs for survey purposes.[22] The operational definition of comparable electrical engineering jobs is "whatever a BSEE ten years out of school does." Craft distinctions likewise assume that higher-skilled employees will perform more varied and difficult assignments.

Pros and Cons. Arguments favoring person-contingent compensation reflect a reaction to the bureaucratic rigidities of job-contingent compensation. Person-contingent compensation abandons relatively minor distinctions for broader skill grades and provides the flexibility to assign employees among varying tasks. The introduction of teamwork to replace individual job assignments also has promoted pay for knowledge since person-contingent compensation encourages team members to acquire skills and so increase their flexibility of assignment. Relaxation of bureaucratic principles of work organization also can provoke a shift from job- to person-contingent compensation.

As for the disadvantages, compensation contingent upon personal qualifications provides little direction or motivation for performance, and requires joint use of other approaches for those purposes. It probably works best for positions in which the tasks are intrinsically motivating or the employees exercise considerable self-direction. If a pay scheme fails to exploit personal qualifications to enhance organizational performance, it will offer little value to an employer.

Non-Work Contingencies

Various forms of compensation, while based primarily on some aspect of work, also reflect some non-work consideration. Most so-called benefits illustrate these contingent forms of compensation. Certain benefits such as pension, severance pay (including golden parachutes), and life insurance provide payouts which may vary with tenure and/or level of base compensation, but entitlement to these programs is contingent upon some non-work contingency often reflecting need. For example, severance pay is contingent upon job loss, life insurance upon death, and medical benefits upon illness. A dual contingency relationship operates, reflecting both prior work variables and some condition of need.

Strategic Issues

Unlike the positive and continuous reinforcement provided by work-contingent compensation, the receipt of pension, death and medical payments is not continuous with work variables and only offsets the negative conditions associated with the qualifying contingency. Such benefits may offer security and peace of mind but they are not reinforcing in the usual sense. By eliminating the need to purchase these contingent forms of compensation independently, they may serve to raise an employee's real income, but this consideration does not affect the present analysis.

Convenience, rather than need, serves as the basis for other forms of non-work contingent compensation, such as child-care provision, purchasing discounts, and wellness programs. Again, these forms of compensation may provide peace of mind and some increase in real income, but they do not directly reinforce work behaviors. Still other types of non-work contingent compensation, such as tuition reimbursement, may be related to variables which potentially influence future work performance.

Pros and Cons. Work-contingent compensation provides some continuous reinforcement of some aspect of work through periodic payments, bonuses, and other awards. Non-work contingent compensation may reinforce preparation for future work (e.g., education), provide convenience and peace of mind (e.g., childcare), or enhance security through a promise of future reward contingent upon some event such as death, illness, or severance from employment. Non-work contingent compensation may help to attract and retain employees, but it offers little inducement for improving work contributions. In a real sense, non-work contingent compensation offers employees some security and peace of mind, which may enhance their response to work-contingent compensation.

Compensation Comparisons

The design of compensation contingencies accomplishes what is usually termed compensation structuring. It prescribes the bases for differentials in compensation among employees of an organization and it identifies exactly what is to be exchanged for different levels of compensation. The structuring of contingencies does not, however, accomplish what is usually termed pricing; it does not provide a dollar basis for calculating compensation amounts. Instead, some form of compensation comparison typically is employed in this latter process.

Compensation comparisons presumably influence employees' choices among various work alternatives, such as occupation, job, employer, training, and effort. An employment contract involves direct exchange of work contribution (costs) for inducements (rewards). But employees rarely view these exchanges singly; instead, they compare an employment exchange with other available alternatives. Thus the reward/cost exchange for alternative A is compared with the reward/cost exchanges for alternative B. For example, someone who perceives selling real estate as requiring significantly greater demands than teaching school may prefer to accept a teaching position even though it offers lower compensation than real estate sales.

External vs. Internal Comparisons

While comparisons ultimately turn on subjective personal evaluation, some general types of comparisons can guide designers of compensation systems. A key distinction concerns the choice between external comparisons, or comparisons with other employers, and internal comparisons, or comparisons with other jobs in the same organization. Which comparison an organization should emphasize depends critically upon what employees view as *feasible* alternatives. The relative weight on external versus internal comparisons also hinges on an organization's HRM strategy. As discussed later in this chapter, feasible alternatives in the craft HRM model are structured as similar jobs with other employers, while in the organization model, alternatives are structured as related jobs with the same employer.

HR managers who rely on external market comparisons for compensation pricing face a strategic choice regarding where to position their organization relative to competing employers.[23] For example, one organization might seek to lead the market and price above most other employers, while another employer may choose to lag the market and price below others. Typically, employers who dominate the labor market seek a leading position and smaller employers tend to lag, although ability to pay is a key consideration in this pricing strategy.

Organizations that emphasize internal comparisons in compensation pricing still maintain some link to the external market, often at hiring or entry jobs. Rates for other positions are determined in comparison with these so-called key rates. A strategic decision for internal comparison pricing concerns how much spread or dispersion to provide among rates.[24] Wide dispersion permits many fine distinctions among rates and the creation of highly structured differences; a narrow dispersion permits fewer distinctions and less structured differences. Choices regarding the degree of dispersion should reflect an organization's philosophy and culture as evidenced in its structuring of work. For example, various employers in the auto and steel industries currently are trying to replace traditional wage structures differentiating among thousands of jobs with simplified wage structures differentiating among only four to six grades of work.[25] The objective is to redefine work in broad terms as a means of reducing work rule barriers to task assignment and, long term, control labor costs.

Compensation comparisons in pricing are easiest to determine when compensation operates on a single-contingency formula (such as only job contingency). However, HR managers who rely on market surveys of job-based compensation without considering possible supplementary contingency compensation can be misled. The increasing use of various supplementary contingency programs seems likely to limit even further the value of job-based market surveys.

Managing Compensation Contingencies

A total compensation system is, in one sense, a network of promises of contingent compensation. In simple form, the design of a compensation system involves merely developing contingencies that will direct employees' attention to desired organizational objectives and reinforce achievement of those objectives. Given the variety of possible contingency relationships, the challenge facing compensation designers is to select the combinations that best fit organizational structures and strategies.

Table 1 illustrates the three basic dimensions or work contingencies described earlier and elaborates combinations of different forms of compensation. While some employers may use only an extreme form of these contingencies (such as strict commission or a flat job rate), most compensation systems combine these contingencies in various ways. For example, one employer might specify a job

Table 1

Forms of Contingent Compensation

Compensation Contingency	Illustrative Form	Work Characteristics	Organizational Characteristics	Prototypical Occupations
Performance	Commission, piece-rate, gain-sharing, profit-sharing, suggestion awards	Clear, measurable, outcomes expected and controllable by worker(s)	Start-up organization, cost competition, minimal supervision	Sales work, executives
Job	Salary, hourly wage	Fixed and specified duties, outcomes not always specifiable or controllable	Stable and routine technology, bureaucratic organization	Office and production jobs
Person	Skill-based, maturity, professional ladder, seniority pay	Variable tasks and outcomes dependent upon skill	Professional-craft technology, flexible and varying tasks	Scientists, engineers, professional staff

range (not rate) and vary pay within the range based on performance, while another employer might set a job rate and attach a
commission based on performance to that guaranteed rate. Other
possibilities include use of a job rate supplemented by increments
based upon seniority or reliance on a maturity-based rate with
adjustments that reflect performance ratings.

Strategic Linkages

Compensation strategy relies on some mix of reward structures
rather than a choice among the three dimensions. Any organizational strategy has quite varied performance implications for different divisions, units, and positions, and no single compensation
strategy would be appropriate for all.[26] Direct links between organizational and compensation strategies occur most commonly at the
executive level where strategic objectives have most relevance.[27]
Anayses of CEO compensation, for example, indicate that the
emphasis placed upon variable compensation varies with strategic
orientations.[28] Performance-share compensation also provides the
opportunity to link compensation with strategic accomplishments.
Other evidence suggests that the nature of performance compensation for divisional executives varies with strategies of growth
through acquisition or internal development.[29] Finally, new growth
organizations tend to emphasize compensation in the form of share
equity, a practice consistent with strategic orientation and/or cash-
flow considerations.[30]

Other Linkages

Broad strategic orientation has a less obvious influence on
compensation systems for non-executives because of the varied
strategic implications for lower-level positions. A more appropriate
linkage would tie compensation strategy to an organization's HR
strategy and management style. These characteristics probably per-
vade all organizational levels with more uniformity and prove more
enduring than, for example, a marketing strategy.

Organization culture is a popular concept that has bearing on
the design of compensation systems. Culture has been defined
variously as the set of rituals, beliefs, customs, and traditions common to an organization and which shape the behavior of members.[31]
While the concept encompasses many aspects of organizational life,
it has particular relevance to HRM policies and practices. The

criteria for selecting, promoting, and rewarding employees, the channels for movement within the organization, and the structure of jobs and authority all evidence and shape organizational culture. Systems for compensating and rewarding employees form critical components of this culture.[32] Compensation strategy cannot be separated from the broader HR strategy and organizational culture if it is to have a positive influence on an organization's performance.

HR Strategies

Analysis of HRM practice suggests three different strategic characterizations or models: craft or job strategy, organization career strategy, and unstructured strategy.[33] HR managers can apply a single strategy consistently throughout an organization or mix all three for application to different occupations or work units. Each model corresponds to a different HRM system or organizational culture and involves a different orientation to the organization of work and the compensation of employees.

Craft Strategy

The craft strategy to HRM utilizes the concept of occupation to define work and classify workers. Workers qualify for occupational employment through some sort of training or experience and are employed for immediate performance. Career mobility involves moves among employers within an occupation rather than job or occupational shifts within an organization. Examples of employees in the craft model would include aerospace engineers, skilled craftsmen, the construction industry, nurses, and teachers.

Many HRM activities in the craft strategy take place prior to employment. Schools and apprentice programs provide training and qualification; unions and professional associations may perform recruiting and administer pension and benefit programs. Jobs, defined occupationally, are relatively standardized among employers, which permits easy mobility within the occupation with immediate performance expected of workers upon hiring. Standardized expectations of occupations also facilitates work coordination.

Occupational rather than organizational commitment of employees provides both a benefit and a cost to employers. An organization invests little in employee development and can readily hire and lay off workers as indicated by production needs. Qualification for immediate performance is assumed and little supervisory

Table 2

Models of HR Strategy

	Craft	*Organization*	*Unstructured*
Job design	standardized occupation	unique	unskilled
Supervision	scheduling	coaching, counseling	monitoring
Staffing	recruit all jobs as needed	recruit entry jobs promotion	recruit as needed
Training	external	internal, on-the-job	minimal
Appraisal	performance	potential	minimal performance
Compensation	occupational markets	internal job hierarchy	unskilled market

coaching or job orientation is necessary. However, the craft model depends upon an adequate supply of qualified workers in the labor market. Shortages of labor and/or organizationally unique jobs challenge the usefulness of the craft strategy.

Compensation strategy within the craft model relies primarily on job-contingent compensation since employers are concerned primarily with their ability to recruit in an occupation. Compensation comparison concentrates on market pricing by occupation with little concern for occupational comparisons within an organization. Occupational wage surveys, not job evaluation, dominate in wage determination. An employer also might use person-contingent compensation to reflect occupational qualifications. For example, an organization may reward advanced occupational education (e.g. teachers) and continuing education (e.g. attorneys) when continued employment is expected. Tenure-contingent compensation is employed only when turnover becomes bothersome. Performance-contingent compensation, such as merit-adjusted maturity curves, is another option to encourage continued employment. However, employers apply both person and performance contingencies within the context of specific job-based compensation rather than uniformly across all occupations. Other compensation contingencies, such as rewards for cooperative group effort and innovative performance, are less common because of the occupational standardization of jobs.

Organization-Career Strategy

The organization-career strategy for HRM centers upon an employing organization rather than an occupation. Employees join an organization with the expectation of advancing through a series of job and occupational changes with that employer. Examples of this strategy include traditional practices in the banking and insurance industries and at IBM, most managerial HR policies in organizations that emphasize knowledge of the company over knowledge of the profession, and so-called Theory Z Management practices.[34]

The organization-career model requires extensive HRM activity. Individuals are recruited and selected on the basis of potential for development and performance. The employer provides training and development for the immediate job and for later career jobs through formal programs and extensive on-the-job experience. In addition, this model requires constant assessment of employees' current performance and potential for future development.

This HR strategy presumes that organizational commitment and long tenure will justify the investment in training and development. As before, this organizational commitment offers both benefits and disadvantages: Employee loyalty reduces turnover and associated costs, but it also imposes a commitment upon the organization to provide continuing employment. This strategy would prove inappropriate for employers who experience drastic changes in production demands, and it can constrain an organization's rate of growth and diversification.

Recent HRM literature suggests other benefits to employers who adopt the organization-career model. By cultivating organizational values and beliefs among workers, an employer enhances cooperation, innovation, and flexibility of task assignments. Since the organization provides training and development, it does not need to adhere to standardized occupational definitions of work and can design jobs to meet its unique needs. Further, commitment to employment and job mobility within the organization encourages flexible assignment of employees. The characteristics of organization culture advocated in the popular management press seem more compatible with the organization-career model than with the craft model.[35]

Compensation strategy in the organization-career model traditionally has focused upon job-contingent compensation. However, the lesser standardization of jobs across organizations and emphasis on internal comparison over market comparison makes job evaluation a more appropriate measure than market surveys. Person contingencies are critical in initial recruiting and in rewarding both development and tenure. Performance-contingent compensation tends to emphasize long-term performance behaviors, such as cooperation, rather than short-term output. Finally, non-work contingent compensation, such as benefits, emphasizes the importance of continued membership in an organization.

Unstructured Strategy

The unstructured strategy is, in a sense, a variant of the craft strategy. New hires enter directly into jobs designed for immediate performance and workers rarely advance in organizational careers. Unlike the craft strategy, the unstructured model is usually applied to unskilled jobs which require no training or qualification and which lack standardized definitions. Examples would include unskilled labor in many industries and counter-help in the fast-food industry.

HRM activities in the unstructured model include structuring jobs for relatively immediate performance by unskilled workers, recruiting and screening applicants, performing minor orientation, and supervisory monitoring of performance. The employer provides little, if any, training and development for future performance and disregards tenure unless labor supplies are scarce. Employees must meet some prescribed minimal levels of job performance and have little opportunity for innovative performance.

Compensation programs use a job-based strategy with a market orientation; recruitment requirements rather than market surveys provide the primary market link. Any performance-contingent compensation will likely address behaviors like attendance rather than measured output. Employers rarely offer person-contingent compensation except a tenure component to reduce turnover. Finally, employees receive little non-work contingent compensation other than legally mandated benefits.

The three models of HR strategy, while presented in ideal forms, often merge in practice, and aspects of all three may operate in a single organization. Thus a hospital might apply the craft model to nursing staff, the organization career model to administrators, and the unstructured model to unskilled workers. Choice of a model might conform to industry traditions, as in the construction industry, or it might reflect a strategic decision of an employer. For example, although the craft model traditionally determines compensation of nursing staff, a hospital plagued by excessive and costly turnover might attempt to implement the organization-career model to foster commitment. Such a change would require redesigning jobs, establishing nursing career ladders, and altering compensation programs. Regardless of the model used, compensation strategy should complement an organization's related HR strategy.

Compensation Strategies

Primary compensation strategies should reflect the HR strategy applied in a particular work unit. However, the variety of compensation contingencies permits employers to supplement primary contingencies with other approaches that promote specific strategic goals. Performance contingencies offer particularly diverse options: They can focus employees' efforts toward a specific, short-term objective, such as product sales promotion or project completion bonus; address group, department, or organizational performance; and enhance behaviors (e.g., attendance) as well as output. Employers also can alter the relative reliance upon different contingencies by changing payoff schedules. For example, individual or team bonuses can offer greater or lesser payoffs than organization-wide incentives.

The strategic design of contingent compensation obviously begins with careful study of strategy implications for performance and the potential contribution of work efforts at each level. The diversity of potential strategic contributions among business units, departments, and jobs necessitates equally diverse combinations of compensation contingencies. Production workers, for example, might be compensated largely upon the basis of job, with supplemental compensation contingent upon behavior such as attendance, seniority, or divisional performance where cooperation is sought.

Compensation for employees in operations with considerable independence, such as research and development, might primarily reflect personal competencies, with supplemental compensation contingent upon divisional and organizational performance. Mid-level managers might be compensated primarily on the basis of job contingencies supplemented again by divisional and organizational performance-contingent compensation. In each instance, the particular contingency and relative payoff should be shaped to conform to opportunities for and expectations of contribution.

Use of diverse compensation contingencies entails a decentralization of compensation planning and administration. Adaptation to unique circumstances is difficult to accomplish in a centralized manner. An ever-present issue in compensation management concerns balance between the decentralization needed to adapt to varied circumstances and the centralization required to control labor costs. A single, standardized compensation system for all employees makes budgeting and controlling compensation costs far easier, yet such standardization thwarts the alignment of compensation contingencies with strategic orientations. Decentralization of compensation management requires development of information systems and performance budgets similar to those used in other aspects of operations.

An approach often used to control performance-contingent compensation probably could be adapted for decentralized compensation management. This approach involves working backward from financial planning to determine an acceptable compensation budget. Incentive compensation then is controlled to specified amounts or is contingent upon specified financial outcomes. Decentralization of compensation planning would parallel decentralization of strategic and budgetary planning.

The management of compensation contingencies will vary with the specificity of an organization's mission and strategy; the stability of its mission, technology, and product mix; the nature of accounting controls; and the overall management style. To the extent that decentralization results in diversified compensation, it will influence compensation comparisons. Employees in an occupation or work unit who are compensated differently than others may perceive inequities in their comparisons unless the structure of compensation plans complements overall organization philosophy and culture.

Summary

While the concept of an employment contract or exchange is simple, the reality encompasses an infinite variety of exchanges which are always interpreted subjectively by the involved parties. The general characteristics of an employment exchange outlined in this chapter serve only to organize the analysis and not to limit modifications in practice.

Employment compensation, as one side of the employment exchange, is the primary inducement offered in return for labor services. Each of the three different bases for work-contingent compensation represents a different definition of work: Performance contingencies focus upon outcomes, person contingencies emphasize inputs, and job contingencies address the processing of inputs into outcomes. Each basis for contingent compensation provides a different incentive in the employment exchange.

The three bases for contingency compensation may overlap as, for example, when job evaluation factors address skill (person), effort (performance), and responsibility (job). Merged into one compensation structure, a single contingency appears to operate. On the other hand, many forms of compensation address only one or another contingency and when used in combination, these contingencies communicate multiple incentives. This possibility of designing a mix of compensation contingencies provides challenge as well as opportunity.

The choice of compensation contingencies has strategic implications, but organizational strategy encompasses more than a compensation system standing alone. Rather, an organization's HR system more readily embodies overall strategy. Strategic design of compensation systems calls for alignment with both the HR system and shorter-term operating strategies. Each of the three different types of HR systems reviewed here presents different opportunities for and limitations on organizational performance.

Finally, HR managers should remember to *manage*, not merely administer, compensation contingencies by adapting them to the changing needs of organizations. Employment contracts should undergo constant review and renegotiation to provide support to the overall business and HR strategies.

♦

Notes

1. Webster.
2. Mahoney (1987).
3. Jaques; March and Simon; Mahoney (1979).
4. March and Simon.
5. Nealey.
6. Dunlop; Thurow.
7. Brown.
8. Dunlop.
9. Thurow.
10. Reder.
11. Pierson and Mahoney.
12. Williamson.
13. Gomez-Mejia, Tosi, and Hinkins.
14. Graham-Moore and Ross.
15. S. Kerr.
16. Jaques.
17. Rynes and Milkovich.
18. Ferraro; Mahoney (1987).
19. Livernash; Bellak.
20. Becker.
21. Gupta, Jenkins, and Currington.
22. Fuller.
23. Milkovich and Newman.
24. Hills.
25. Mcmorandum of Agreement Between Saturn Corporation and UAW.
26. Ziskind.
27. Salter.
28. Murthy and Salter.
29. J. Kerr.
30. Balkin and Gomez-Mejia.
31. Deal and Kennedy.
32. Kerr and Slocum.
33. Mahoney and Deckop.
34. Ouchi.
35. Peters and Waterman.

♦

References

Balkin, D. and L. Gomez-Mejia. 1985. "Compensation practices in High Technology Industries." *Personnel Administrator* 30 (June): 111–123.

Becker, G. *Human Capital*. 1964. New York: National Bureau of Economic Research.

Bellak, A. 1985. "Comparable Worth: A Practitioner's View." In *Comparable Worth: Issue for the '80s*, Vol. 1. Washington, D.C.: U.S. Civil Rights Commission.

Brown, P. 1977. *The Inequality of Pay*. Berkeley: University of California Press.

Deal, T.E. and A.A. Kennedy. 1982. *Corporate Cultures*. Reading, MA: Addison-Wesley.

Dunlop, J. 1957. "The Task of Contemporary Wage Theory." In *New Concepts in Wage Determination*, ed. G. Taylor and F. Pierson. New York: McGraw-Hill.

Ferraro, G. 1984. "Bridging the Gap, Pay Equity and Job Evaluation." *American Psychologist* 39 (10): 1166–1170.

Fuller, L.E. 1972. "Designing Compensation Programs for Scientists and Professionals in Business." In *Handbook of Wage and Salary Administration*, ed. M.R. Rock. New York: McGraw-Hill.

Gomez-Mejia, L., H. Tosi, and T. Hinkin. 1987. "Managerial Control, Performance, and Executive Compensation." *Academy of Management Journal* 30: 51–70.

Graham-Moore B.E., and T.L. Ross. 1983. *Productivity Gainsharing*. Englewood Cliffs, NJ: Prentice-Hall.

Gupta, N., D. Jenkins, and W. Currington. 1986. "Paying for Knowledge: Myths and Realities." *National Productivity Review* (Spring): 107–123.

Hills, F.S. 1987. *Compensation Decision Making*. New York: Dryden Press.

Jaques, E. 1961. *Equitable Payment*. New York: John Wiley & Sons.

Kerr, J. 1985. "Diversification Strategies and Managerial Rewards: An Empirical Study." *Academy of Management Journal* 28: 155–179.

Kerr J. and J.W. Slocum. 1987. "Manging Corporate Culture through Reward Systems." *Academy of Management Executive* 1: 99–108.

Kerr, S. 1975. "On the Folly of Rewarding A, While Hoping for B." *Academy of Management Journal* 18: 769–783.

Livernash, E.R. 1957. "The Internal Wage Structure." In *New Concepts in Wage Determination*, eds. G.W. Taylor and F.C. Pierson, New York: McGraw-Hill.

Mahoney, T.A. 1979. *Compensation and Reward Perspectives*. Homewood, IL: Richard D. Irwin.

———— 1987. "Understanding Comparable Worth: A Societal and Political Perspective." In *Research in Organizational Behavior*, vol. 9, eds. L.L. Cummings and B.M. Staw. Greenwich, CT: JAI Press.

Mahoney, T.A. and J.R. Deckop. 1986. "Evolution of Concept and Practice, in Personnel Administration/Human Resource Management." *Journal of Management* 12: 223–241.

March, J.G. and H.A. Simon. 1958. *Organizations*. New York: Wiley.

Memorandum of agreement between Saturn Corporation and UAW, July 26, 1985.

Milkovich, G.T. and J.M. Newman. 1987. *Compensation*. Plano, TX: Business Publications.

Murthy, K.R. and M. Salter. 1975. "Should CEO Pay Be Linked to Results?" *Harvard Business Review* 9: 66–73.

Ouchi, W.G. 1981. *Theory Z*. Reading, MA: Addison-Wesley.

Nealey, S.M. 1963. "Pay and Benefit Preferences." *Industrial Relations* (October): 17–28.

Peters, T.J. and R.H. Waterman. 1982. *In Search of Excellence*. New York: Harper & Row.

Pierson, D. and T.A. Mahoney. 1982. "Labor Market and Employer Ability to Pay as Wage Contour Influences." *Southern Business Review* (Fall): 87–95.

Reder, M. 1962. "Wage Differentials: Theory and Measurement." In *National Bureau of Economic Research, Aspects of Labor Economics*, no. 4. Princeton, NJ: Princeton University Press.

3-28   Compensation & Benefits

Rynes, S.L. and G.T. Milkovich. 1986. "Wage Surveys: Dispelling Some Myths about the Market Wage." *Personnel Psychology* (Spring): 71–90.

Salter, M. 1973. "Tailor Incentive Compensation to Strategy." *Harvard Business Review* 51: 94–102.

Thurow, L.C. 1975. *Generating Inequality*. New York: Basic Books.

Webster's New Collegiate Dictionary. 1981. Springfield, MA: G & C Merriam.

Williamson, O.E. 1985. *Markets and Hierarchies: Analysis and Antitrust Implications*. New York: Free Press.

Ziskind, I. 1986. "Knowledge-Based Pay: A Strategic Analysis." *ILR Report* 24 (1): 16–22.

———— ◆ ————

3.2

Internal Pay Relationships

Frederick S. Hills

Theoretical Bases for Addressing Internal Equity

At a conceptual level, equity is readily defined by numerous scholars and writers. For example, one definition of distributive justice states that equity exists when each actor receives profits proportional to his or her investments.[1] In a similar manner, social theory views equity existing when one person's output-input ratio equals the outcome-input ratio of another person.[2] Consistent with these general definitions, internal pay equity exists when individuals feel that job differences (inputs) result in corresponding differences in pay rates (outcomes); if there are not corresponding differences (equal ratios), inequity is present.[3]

Behavioral Consequences of Inequity

Concern over internal pay equity assumes that important employee behaviors are influenced by feelings of inequity. Equity theory, in general, addresses reactionary, not anticipatory, behavior on the part of employees and sees inequity as serving to arouse a person to action.[4] Empirical evidence suggests that pay inequity can prompt employees to take one of three actions: 1) change outcomes, 2) change inputs, or 3) abandon the present exchange relationship.

An employee who feels inequitably treated in monetary terms may elect to alter outcomes. For example, when a perceived under-reward exists, employees may seek to increase their outcomes through grieving their current wage rate, asking their supervisors for pay raises, or forming a union. Anecdotal evidence suggests that in cases of overreward, employees may attempt to return a portion of their salary on the grounds that their job is not worth those earnings.

Rather than changing outcomes, employees may try to alter their inputs. Some systematic empirical evidence suggests that employees may increase their input levels under conditions of overreward. For example, employees whose piece-rate pay is too high may increase the quality of their work to reestablish equity. In the case of hourly overreward, individuals may increase the quantity of output.[5] Employees who are underrewarded in an hourly pay situation produce less quantity, and those underrewarded in piece-rate systems produce a lower quality.[6] Underpaid teachers, for instance, have been known to "work to the contract" and work "slowdowns" occur in other wage disputes.

Finally, the absence of internal wage equity can decrease an employee's motivation to remain with an organization and arouse a search for more pleasant alternatives.[7] In short, employee turnover will result from internal inequity if other employment is available. Another possible response to inequity is for employees to attempt to change the outcomes or input ratio of other employees. In most practical cases, this response will prove difficult to implement, and empirical information to substantiate this behavioral response appears to be lacking.

Historical Issues in Internal Equity

A major issue in internal equity concerns the criteria upon which perceptions of equity or inequity are based. As one analyst noted more than a decade ago, "Developments in compensation theory in recent years largely ignore a basic issue—the issue of distributive justice . . . compensation theory and administration today lack an accepted criterion of justice."[8] This same assertion regarding the lack of universally accepted standards for arriving at internal equity holds true today. This problem accounts in part for the current controversy over comparable worth and the legitimacy of traditional equity criteria.

Market-Rate Approaches

Despite the lack of universal standards, numerous criteria for determining internal equity do exist. The "market rate" approach probably ranks as the most commonly advocated method in the recent past. This classic economic model suggests that wage levels should reflect free competition in the labor market. Since market rates reflect employers' valuation of labor and employees' preferences for various wage rates, the free market thus dictates fairness.

Unfortunately, a market rate criterion is deceptively simple and may prove impractical for numerous reasons. First, the notion of "a" market rate raises debate since any given labor market offers a broad array of rates for the same job.[9] Second, large numbers of jobs within many organizations have unique configurations of tasks that make it difficult to find "comparable" jobs in the market place. For those jobs, reliance on a market criterion simply is not feasible. Because of these problems with market rates, job evaluation became the alternative method for establishing internal equity.

A Brief History of Job Evaluation

The concern over maintaining internal wage equity is hardly a recent phenomenon, and modern forms of job evaluation date back more than a century. Frederick W. Taylor's early time studies at the Midvale Steel Company in 1881 signaled the beginnings of systematic use of job evaluation in industry, and by 1909, Commonwealth Edison Company of Chicago had introduced job classification plans.[10]

The private sector was not alone in its concerns over equitable wage payments. As early as 1838, federal government clerks petitioned Congress to set wage rates equally for those who performed similar work.[11] This concern over equitable wage rates later lead President Grover Cleveland to direct that promotions within the civil service should be from one grade to another. By 1902, the U.S. Civil Service Commission had summarized and recommended changes for a reclassification of pay rates on the basis of "duties performed." Today, of course, job evaluation is thoroughly entrenched in the federal system with the General Services Schedule, and state and local governments have adopted job evaluation plans.

Industrial practice in the 1920s and 1930s reflected the value that companies saw in using job evaluation. Industry associations such as the National Metal Trades Association and the National Electrical Manufacturers Association introduced job evaluation for hourly production workers, and such plans gained a reputation as the most useful tool for setting equitable wage structures.[12] Union growth in the private sector also spurred growth in job evaluation.

In the union-management context, job evaluation permitted parties to negotiate over criteria for pay differentials between jobs and provided a vehicle for reevaluating job worth as job content changed during the life of an existing contract.

World War II further accelerated acceptance of job evaluation. During the war, Congress had to confront the issue of wage rates in an economy which saw manpower demands increase because of war orders, combined with a relative labor shortage due to growth in military manpower needs. To deal with this wage level problem, Congress implemented a wage freeze, and employers could adjust wages only by demonstrating to the War Labor Board, through job evaluation, that wages were out of line (either internally or with respect to the market). In essence, the War Labor Board accepted industry's own criteria for adjusting wages and further institutionalized the job evaluation process by motivating employers to adopt such plans to justify changes in wage rates for their employees.

Today few analysts seriously doubt that job evaluation as a pay setting mechanism will disappear. In 1976, the Bureau of National Affairs, Inc. conducted a survey which revealed that 74 percent of the respondents used a formal job evaluation plan.[13] Almost a decade later, a different researcher found that 86 percent of surveyed organizations used some form of job evaluation plan for one or more employee groups.[14] Despite its inherent problems (to be discussed later), job evaluation will likely remain a popular management tool for the foreseeable future. However, the form of job evaluation systems may change as new criteria are employed (e.g. a movement away from job characteristics, toward employee characteristics such as skill, etc).

Assumptions of Job Evaluation

Although research on job evaluation tends to ignore its underlying assumptions, numerous assumptions do in fact go into every job evaluation plan. First, jobs presumably differ in terms of the required contributions of "skill," "effort," "responsibility," and other criteria. A second assumption is that employees will accept the criteria used to assess job worth. Third, job evaluation plans assume that equity perceptions lie in the eyes of the beholders, the employees. Fourth, since job evaluation plans apparently do not change significantly once established, organizations apparently assume that equity criteria remain stable over time.

The accuracy of these four basic assumptions can vary in actual practice, and may determine the success of a job evaluation plan. The following discussion examines how well each of these assumptions hold up when put into operation.

First, job evaluation assumes that jobs differ in terms of skill, effort, and so on. If jobs are identical, then will employees perceive that pay should be equal across jobs? Anecdotal evidence clearly suggests that equal pay for like work is not universally accepted. For example, universities commonly assign different midpoints and pay ranges for the jobs of assistant, associate, and full Professor. However, a thorough job analysis would suggest that employees in these three jobs do nearly identical work. Elementary and secondary schools also design elaborate wage scales based on employees' levels of experience and advanced credits. But again, these employees all do the same thing: teach children. A private-sector example occurs in the engineering or scientific career ladders within large organizations. A typical career ladder offers such positions as assistant scientist, associate scientist, scientist, and senior scientist and varies pay rates accordingly. Other organizations use "maturity curves" for employees who all work in the same job. Maturity curves express pay level as a function of some criterion such as "years since degree" or the like.

The existence of these wage differentials for identical jobs raises questions about the necessity of assuming differences between jobs. After all, self interest in salary growth might motivate scientists, professors, and teachers to find elaborate rationales for distinctions among jobs. For example, full professors "guide" assistant professors and carry more "administrative responsibility." Likewise, senior scientists "direct research projects" on which research assistants work, and higher levels of experience and education make teachers "better educators." Perhaps humans inherently need to search for distinctions and thus will accept job evaluation even when no large distinctions among jobs exist. Indeed, job evaluation may serve more universally as a tool for rationalizing pay structures.

In this light, an alternative assumption is that employees will perceive even basically equal jobs as unequal and differential pay rates serve to address that perception. Thus a possible goal of job evaluation might be to motivate employee retention through equitable treatment. In a similar fashion, the use of equity criteria may enhance other compelling business goals and strategies. For example, equitable pay for different jobs could become defined as "equal pay" when viewed in the context of larger goals and objectives (e.g. teamwork, cross training) which maximize organizational flexibility.

Second, job evaluation assumes the availability of acceptable criteria for determining job worth. This assumption seems valid, given that job evaluation probably would have disappeared long ago if employees found it unacceptable. Indeed, while empirical research on this subject is lacking, case reports indicate that employees do resist introduction of plans which violate local norms of acceptable pay criteria.

Third, job evaluation assumes that equity resides in the eye of the beholder. This assumption is undoubtedly true, provided that "beholder" is defined as either an individual or a group. Shared perceptions of equity among a group can change the meaning of equity from "different pay for different work" to "an equal day's pay for a day's work." For example, the brewing industry has a tradition of an equal day's pay for an equal day's work. [15] Other situations in which an employer may not want to differentiate between clearly different jobs for pay purposes include projects which depend on team effort. For instance, paying all members of a research team equally may enhance organizational and employee goals of team effort better than differential reward for differential contribution would.

Finally, employers seem to assume that job evaluation criteria remain constant over time. This assumption clearly lacks validity. As employee populations change, new worker values enter an organization, and an organization's goals likewise may change over time.

One manifestation of recent changes in equity criteria is the two-tier wage system. Organizations using such systems have introduced a new compensable factor: whether someone is a new employee or a current employee. Although this strategy may prove useful in the short run for cost containment, some evidence suggests that the ensuing problems with internal equity ultimately undermine two-tier systems. [16] The current debate over comparable worth also reflects a new belief that employers should evaluate predominantly female jobs and predominantly male jobs using the same criteria. Simply put, comparable worth represents a rejection of old criteria and a desire for new criteria. For example, office clerical workers now ask why "responsibility for equipment" does not factor into their job worth, just as it does for shop floor employees who happen to be predominantly male. [17]

Job Evaluation Criteria

The traditional concept of job evaluation is defined here as the process of establishing the relative worth of jobs.[18] To establish relative job worth, and to achieve equity, job evaluation schemes rely upon "compensable factors." An initial question in designing a job evaluation plan concerns which factors to use. In general, this question has two possible answers. First, an organization can use whatever criteria it wishes since ". . . the introduction and use of job evaluation is a management prerogative."[19] However, this answer only determines what criteria decisionmakers' consider to be legitimate. Since equity resides in the eyes of employees, job evaluation plans should also include criteria which employees perceive as legitimate. Unfortunately, as implemented, job evaluation plans often take into account managers' goals and values but do not explicitly take into account employee values.

Organizational Criteria for Internal Equity

Over the years, job evaluation plans have utilized a variety of compensable factors.[20] A partial list of these factors appears in Table 1. Many of these factors date back to the early part of this century and continue in use today. Widespread acceptance of certain job evaluation factors helped to shape provisions of the Equal Pay Act of 1963 which recognize differences in "skill," "effort," "responsibility," and "working conditions" as legitimate standards for wage differences.

However, these traditional factors of job evaluation emerged in industries characterized by relatively stable production and/or work processes as well as relatively stable jobs and job relationships. Such systems may not suit many of today's organizations which have dynamic work environments and/or corporate strategies requiring more dynamic job relationships. For example, some organizations are experimenting with skill-based pay systems which base pay on what an employee is capable of performing and not just the specific job.[21] A skill-based pay strategy would allow greater flexibility in employee assignment and presumably would reduce labor costs if a corresponding reduction in job "jurisdiction" occurred. In a similar fashion, some organizations have abandoned the concept of individual job equity and adopted a concept of team equity. Team equity plans reward all members of a team equally even if members con-

Table 1

Compensable Factors Used in Job Evaluation Plans

Skills

Education
- Education or mental development
- Education or trade knowledge
- Schooling

Experience
- Previous experience

Training
- Training required
- Time required to adapt skill
- Time required to become 80 percent efficient
- Time required to learn trade
- Training time

Job Knowledge
- Knowledge required
- Knowledge of machinery and dexterity with tools
- Knowledge of materials and processes

Job Skill
- Ability to do complex work
- Ability to do detailed work
- Aptitude required
- Attention to detail
- Degree of skill and accuracy
- Difficulty of operation
- Manual accuracy and quickness
- Office machine operation
- Physical skill
- Social skill

Mental Requirements
- Accuracy
- Analytical ability
- Creative ability
- Ingenuity
- Initiative
- Intelligence
- Judgment and initiative
- Mental application
- Mental capability
- Mental skills
- Mentality
- Resourcefulness
- Versatility

Personal Qualities
- Ability to do routine work
- Ability to make decisions
- Capacity for getting along with others
- Capacity for self-expression
- Managerial techniques
- Manual or mental dexterity
- Need for supervision

Effort

Mental
- Attention demand
- Concentration
- Honesty of effort
- Mental application
- Mental demand
- Mental effort
- Mental fatigue
- Mental monotony
- Pressure of work
- Volume of work

Physical
- Eye strain
- Muscular/nerve strain
- Physical application
- Physical demand
- Physical discomfort
- Physical monotony
- Visual demand
- Volume of work

Table 1 continued

Responsibility for

Adjustability	Executive decisions
Accuracy in checking, counting and weighing	Goodwill and public relations
	Market
Commitments, property, money or records	Methods
	Monetary matters
Company cash	Personnel
Company policy	Physical Property
Confidential data	Plant and services
Contact with others	Product
Contact with public, customers, and personnel	Protection of materials
	Quality
Cooperation and personality	Safety of others
Coordination	Spoilage of materials
Cost of errors	Supervision exercised
Dependability	Supervision over others
Details to master	Time span of discretion
Effect on other operations	Work of others
Equipment and machinery	
Equipment and material	
Equipment or process	

Working Conditions

Environmental Hazards
- Danger from machinery or equipment
- Danger from lifting
- Dirtiness of working conditions
- Exposure to accident hazards
- Exposure to health hazards

Job Stresses
- Attendance
- Attention to details
- Difficulty locating work elsewhere
- Disagreeableness
- Monotony
- Out-of-town travel

Source: Adapted from J.L. Otis and R.H. Leukart, *Job Evaluation*, 2nd Ed. Englewood Cliffs, NJ: Prentice-Hall, copyright © 1954, pp. 90–91.

tribute different and unequal inputs.[22] These alternative pay systems imply a need for new wage criteria which transcend a simplistic system of internal wage equity based on differential contributions and rewards.

Employee Criteria for Internal Equity

Employee criteria for determining internally equitable wage rates mirror to some degree organizational standards. After all, thousands of employers across all types of industries, both within the United States and worldwide, have used traditional job evaluation factors for over seven decades without encountering much resistance.[23]

At the same time, traditional factors may omit certain criteria which employees might wish to use. Further, employees' acceptance of equity criteria is a normative judgment and can change over time. For example, employers and employees alike previously had accepted race, gender, and marital status as legitimate criteria for paying different wage rates. Perhaps the greatest failure of job evaluation has been to assume that historical criteria for determining equitable wage rates are valid today. As one observer has noted:[24]

> Lacking any accepted guides, it would appear that issues of equity or inequity in compensation and distribution will plague compensation administration as norms of equitable payment shift with changing social values. The norm of ". . . to each according to need" probably is just as defensible today as the norm of "equal pay for equal work."

Job Evaluation Methods

Over the years numerous job evaluation plans have been developed. Because most compensation texts provide detailed descriptions of various plans, the following discussion will only highlight the most important aspects of job evaluation plans.

Job analysis is a crucial first step in the job evaluation process. Since the goal of job evaluation is to achieve internal equity in pay rates between jobs, employers must know how jobs differ from each other on the compensable factors discussed earlier. Many methods are available to conduct job analyses (see Volume 2 of this series), but the most commonly used methods include the Functional Job Analyses (FJA) developed by the Training and Employment Service of the U.S. Department of Labor, and inventory based approaches, such as the Position Analysis Questionnaire and the Management Position Description Questionnaire.[25]

The job analysis will produce a job description which in turn serves as input into the job evaluation process. While textbook treatments imply that job descriptions are the only input into job evaluation, research indicates that employers actually use other data as well.[26] These other sources of information include discussions

Figure 1
Job Evaluation Dimensions

Comparison Standard	Methodology	
	Nonquantified	Quantified
To other jobs	Job ranking plans	Factor comparison plans
To a predetermined standard	Job classification plans	Point plans

with immediate supervisors (90 percent of the time); a discussion with job incumbents (60 percent of the time); observation of the job (44 percent of the time); and other information sources (26 percent of the time). These findings clearly suggest that while job descriptions are used (99 percent of the time), other sources of information are also important in the job evaluation process.

As Figure 1 illustrates, all job evaluation schemes can be categorized as one of four types, or some combination thereof.[27] First, plans are either quantitative or non-quantitative in nature. Quantitative plans use a numbering scheme to distinguish differing amounts of compensable factors which determine job worth. Nonquantitative methods use no numbering scheme. Second, job evaluation schemes differ as to the type of standard used in establishing relative worth. Some plans establish relative worth by comparing jobs to each other; other plans establish an "a priori" standard and compare jobs to this predetermined standard.

Different job evaluation methods illustrate various combinations of these dimensions. Ranking methods of job evaluation use a job-to-job comparison standard and are nonquantitative. Like ranking methods, job classification methods are nonquantitative, but use a predetermined standard to assess jobs. Classification systems use job grades and grade descriptions; jobs matching the grade description are slotted into that grade. The factor comparison method of job evaluation refines and quantifies the ranking method by assigning monetary values to compensable factors for each job. Point methods of job evaluation seem to be the most prevalent method used in industry. This approach carefully defines compensable factors and degrees within factors, and then allocates set amounts of points to factors and factor degrees. Under the point methods approach, a job evaluation manual explicitly articulates the factors, their definitions, and the points for each factor and degrees within factor. Evaluators then evaluate jobs against the manual's standards and by assigning points for each factor in a job, they end up with a total point value for each job.

Policy Issues in Job Evaluation

Most compensation texts present a "how to" description of the job evaluation process and omit discussion of important policy issues surrounding job evaluation. The following discussion adopts the opposite approach and focuses on the strategic issues involved in job evaluation design.

When to Use Conventional Job Evaluation

A basic but often overlooked issue is whether job evaluation is appropriate for the organization contemplating its usage. Several questions can facilitate this decision. First, does management perceive meaningful differences between jobs? Second, can meaningful criteria for distinguishing among jobs be articulated and operationalized? Third, will job evaluation result in meaningful distinctions in the employee's eyes? Fourth, are jobs stable and will they remain stable in the future? Finally, and most importantly, is traditional job evaluation consistent with the organization's goals and strategies? For example, if the goal is to assure maximum flexibility among job assignments, then a skill-based pay system may be the appropriate strategy. Alternatively, a strategy of work-team reward

---

Table 2

Summary of Policy Issues in Job Evaluation

- Compatibility of conventional job evaluation with organization goals
- Nonequivalency of methods for labor costs
- Plan selection
  1. implementation costs
  2. defensibility (legal, other)
  3. understandability
- Number of factors for face validity
- The appeal of using multiple plans
- The gender bias allegation
- The semblance of science
- PCs make job evaluation available to any firm
- Careful design of the evaluation committee

(implying equal pay for a day's work) may enhance the goal of fostering team effort. For organizations seeking to reduce labor costs, a single-rate plantwide wage system coupled with a plantwide labor cost savings plan (Scanlon Plan) may be the best strategy. These links between business goals and internal equity can create endless variations in pay plans, as the following commentary illustrates:[28]

> Tying compensation programs to organizational strategy will diminish the role of equity. Internal equity will certainly be modified to take into account the differing values of identical jobs in different units in the same organization if the overall contribution of the job to the unit strategy varies. Entirely different methods of valuing jobs may appear in the same unit, with some being paid on potential (skill-based pay), others solely on group output, and others on some basis yet to be developed . . . We are likely to see the development of some compensation programs, or components of programs, that are not based on equity at all, but rather are designed to reach certain limited objectives and may apply only to limited sets of employees . . . Consistent treatment, a key component of equity, is likely to be replaced as well—by planned differential treatment with respect to pay.

Which Methods to Use

Conventional wisdom holds that the particular job evaluation method doesn't matter, and that different methods produce the same results. This conclusion stems from a number of studies that examined various job evaluation methods and found that the plans produced highly similar results.[29] From this correlational viewpoint, job evaluation plans are substitutable for each other.

However, correlational analysis alone is an inadequate test of whether job evaluation plans are equivalent. For plans to have true equivalency, different job evaluation schemes should produce similar classification systems and assign jobs to the same pay grade. One study examined the degree to which six different plans resulted in classification agreement and found that different plans often do assign jobs to different grades.[30] Since different grade assignments create real dollar differences in pay for jobs and in the total wage bill,[31] these discrepancies cast doubt as to the equivalency of plans for achieving internal equity. In short, all job evaluation plans are not equivalent and they should not be treated as the same for compensation purposes.

Criteria for Choosing a Plan

Given different outcomes produced by different job evaluation plans, the next policy issue to consider concerns which plan to use. The answer will vary according to the needs and goals of different employers, but several considerations come into play.

Complexity and Cost

Complexity and cost are two variables to consider in selecting a job evaluation method. Generally speaking, the four job evaluation plans discussed earlier fall on a continuum of simple to complex. Ranking is the simplest method, followed by job classification, then factor comparison, and finally, point plans. This continuum also serves to capture plans in terms of their relative cost. Ranking methods take the least time to design and implement; hence, they generally cost the least. At the other extreme, point plans represent the most time-consuming and costly approaches to job evaluation. Thus, small organizations with few jobs to evaluate and few resources to spend may find a simple ranking approach quite satisfactory. Alternately, very large organizations with hundreds (or even thousands) of jobs and adequate resources may prefer to use the point method.

Legal Conformance

A second criterion for selection concerns the "defensibility" of the method. With recent challenges by employee groups over wage equality and comparable worth, organizations may have to defend their job evaluation plan not only to employees but also to the Equal Employment Opportunity Commission (EEOC) and the federal judiciary. The more rational and systematic the plan is, the more likely it will withstand legal scrutiny. The point method, as the most highly explicit approach, is probably the most readily defensible. However, since the Equal Pay Act recognizes "skill," "effort," "responsibility," and "working conditions" as criteria for wage differences, any plan which uses these compensable factors should, in theory, be defensible.

Understandability

A third criteria for plans is understandability. Understandability simply means that employees and management must understand the system and perceive it as legitimate. While research on this issue is lacking, point methods seem to promote comprehension through the explicit manner in which factors are selected, weighted, and applied. Ranking methods and the factor comparison method appear harder to understand and may appear subjective to employees. Therefore, they may gain less acceptance among a work force. Still, these generalizations are speculative at best; in some situations, employees may accept all types of plans while in other situations, they may reject all types of plans. Perhaps the skill with which an organization implements a job evaluation plan determines the success of the plan more than the method chosen.

Number of Compensable Factors to Use

The number of compensable factors depends in part on the job evaluation method used. The issue is moot in simple ranking; most organizations use the whole job approach, the remainder usually use but one factor. Factor comparison plans typically use about five factors, while job classification plans tend to use five to seven factors.

The issue of how many factors to use largely concerns point plans. While some of the earliest point plans used upwards of twelve to fifteen factors, research indicates that three to five factors usually suffice to capture a desired criterion structure.[32] Additional factors are merely redundant and do not explain unique variation in the job structure. However, job evaluation plans are rationalizations for job relationships and the pay structure and if employees and management believe that additional factors are important, these criteria should be included to provide sufficient "face validity" for the plan. After all, the factors which explain distributional variance in job worth determine the job structure; therefore, redundant factors which have the same distributional variance will not undermine the structure.[33]

Single vs. Multiple Job Evaluation Plans

Most organizations encompass different employee and job groups. A single employment setting may have a manufacturing/production group, an office clerical group, a managerial group, professionals, and so on. This variation provides compelling reasons for developing multiple job evaluation plans—one for each job family. First, it is often difficult to develop compensable factors useful for all of these diverse job groups. For example, the variance in office working conditions differs from that found among production jobs. Second, occupational internal wage structures are typically tied to the market for each separate job/occupational family. Separate plans simply allow for relative ranking within family and avoid the issue of equity between job families.

Recent trends in litigation suggest a third reason for maintaining multiple, but separate, job evaluation plans. In the case of *Briggs v. City of Madison*, the city maintained a job evaluation system which categorized both predominantly male jobs and predominantly female jobs into the same pay grade, and both types of jobs carried the same pay rates.[34] However, the city faced a shortage of employees in the male dominated jobs and was forced to offer a higher wage to attract and retain employees in the male dominated occupation. At trial, the judge found that the predominantly male and female jobs were similar and should be paid the same, but upheld the legitimacy of a market defense for paying higher rates to employees in the predominantly male jobs. The point is that the city might have avoided a suit if it had never attempted to equate the jobs. Legal scholars advise that, "different systems should be used for different job families, so that no direct comparison in the system is possible. . ."[35]

Gender Bias in Job Evaluation

The above discussion raises the issue of whether job evaluation is biased against female occupations. The answer to this question seems to depend on one's point of view, and one's point of departure, on the issue.

Criticisms of Job Evaluation

One view notes that job evaluation plans evolved in predominantly blue-collar settings. Because of this evolution, compensable factors in most existing plans measure job differences for female-dominated jobs in a different manner than they do for male-dominated jobs. A classic example of this difference occurs with the definition of working conditions. In male-dominated jobs, "disagreeableness of working conditions" is measured by "degree of heat," "noise," "hazards," and the like. However, most employers assume that predominantly female office work is pleasant (standardized temperature and the like) and make no attempt to use a "working conditions" factor for office jobs. Critics of traditional job evaluation point out that inclusion of factors like "limitations on mobility" or "concentrated visual fixation on computer terminals" would allow employers to measure the "disagreeableness of office work."[36] In a similar fashion, job evaluation plans usually do not rate female-dominated office jobs on the factor of "responsibility for equipment," even though office workers are responsible for expensive word processing and data entry equipment.

From this perspective, organizations may need to redefine compensable factors so that they more accurately capture jobs in a service economy.[37] Industry has not squarely addressed this challenge to job evaluation fairness, nor does there seem to be a solid defense to rebut challenge. Future developments surely will force industry to face this issue head on. For example, it seems entirely possible that a future lawsuit will argue that application of different compensable factors to different job groups which are gender concentrated constitutes unequal treatment discrimination under Title VII of the Civil Rights Act of 1964.

Rebuttals of Criticisms

Proponents of traditional job evaluation argue that neither the plan nor job pricing is gender biased. This argument points out that organizations make good-faith efforts to use job evaluation plans to establish job heirarchies, and that most employers use more than one plan because of the noncomparability of job characteristics across job families. Since each of these job family heirarchies is then priced against the labor market, this procedure results in a wage structure which captures both internal and external equity.

A closer examination, however, reveals potential problems with this argument. First, as noted above, this system assumes, without concrete proof, that compensable factors cannot be applied across all job families. Second, this argument uses external labor markets to establish the criterion structure for the internal job hierarchy. Yet labor market rates are a function of many things, including historical employment discrimination. Thus, wages in male-dominated labor markets are overinflated, wage rates in female-dominated labor markets are underinflated, and any wage structure which uses market rates as a criterion merely perpetuates this historical employment discrimination.[38]

Proposed solutions to this second criticism concern how the job heirarchy is priced. Specific recommendations include pricing jobs to markets which are either male dominated,[39] or to markets which are gender mixed.[40] However, these proposals rest on the debatable assumption that male-dominated job markets and mixed markets are free of discrimination. In the final analysis, employers still lack a way of identifying bias-free market rates for wages.

Scientific Rigor of Job Evaluation Methods

As the previous discussion points out, job evaluation is not scientific in the sense of determining "unbiased" or "objective" wage rates. All evaluation methods involve some degree of judgment, discretion, negotiations, and rationalization.[41]

However, job evaluation methods, especially the more sophisticated methods, do give an impression of science. The use of advanced statistical techniques, like factor analysis for finding unique and common variance within and between factors and regression to determine pay policy lines, enhance this scientific appearance.[42] Still, statistics in and of themselves do not make a science; they are merely useful tools for analyzing and summarizing massive amounts of information. As a consequence, the real issue is not how scientific a particular method is but its utility as a bureau-cratic, or administrative, mechanism for facilitating wage structure decisions.

Job Evaluation and Computers

Computers can play an important role in designing, imple-menting, and maintaining job evaluation programs. Indeed, computers are almost essential to the more sophisticated job evalua-tion plans, such as point methods. Without a computer, organiza-tions would face the tedious task of manually calculating a regression line to weight the factors statistically, or of statistically calculating a pay policy line using market wage data. Computers have also facili-tated empirical research on job evaluation. Virtually every empirical study cited in this chapter was conducted with the aid of a computer.

For an organization, computers can assist both the design and maintenance of a job evaluation program. For example, computers can weight factors, build pay policy lines, and conduct "what if?" scenarios to determine the impact that alternate policies would have on wage rates and, ultimately, on the wage bill.[43] In the past, only large employers who could afford a large mainframe computer could conduct such analyses. Today, improvements in microchip tech-nology and soft-ware programs allow even small employers to per-form complex statistical analyses on cost-efficient personal comput-ers. The only limitation on performing complex analyses is the knowledge level of an organization's compensation staff.

Affordable software programs for maintaining job evaluation systems, as well as other personnel programs, are also available. Indeed, electronic mail and file systems allow an employer to main-tain information on everything from job descriptions, to pay grades, to the job evaluation manual itself.

Job Evaluation Committees

A job evaluation committee is the group of people who actually design a job evaluation program and conduct the evaluations. While most textbooks talk about such committees, few give any attention to exactly which individuals in an organization make up the commit-tee. In theory, a job evaluation committee should comprise line managers who have jurisdiction over the job(s), staffers from the HR or industrial relations unit, and employee representatives from the pool of jobs being evaluated. Line managers offer working knowl-edge of the jobs in question and undoubtedly have legitimate views about the relative worth of the jobs. Staff specialists bring expertise in the concepts and tools of job evaluation. Employee represen-tatives serve a particularly important function.[44] If employees have not participated in the development of the plan, they are not likely to understand it and they may not agree with management's deci-sions about job worth. As a result, employees may reject the plan, thereby defeating the goal of job evaluation: perceived equity.

However, committee composition is one area of job evaluation where practice diverges greatly from theory. It appears that few organizations include employee representatives on the evaluation committee. In fact, one survey found that only 7.5 percent of the respondents' job evaluation programs involved employee committees.[45]

Part of this reluctance to include employees on job evaluation committees may reflect legitimate concerns about collective bar-gaining issues. In nonunion settings, employee involvement could be interpreted as a willingness on the part of management to meet and bargain collectively over the terms and conditions of employ-ment. In effect, employers would risk creating a de facto labor union and violating the National Labor Relations Act.

To minimize this risk, employers should make it clear that the job evaluation committee is temporary and that management, not co-workers, will select employee representatives to serve on the committee. A conservative approach to this issue would use only first-line supervisors (of the jobs included in the program) to gather employees' perceptions about the fairness of compensable factors and the equity of relationships among jobs. This strategy would remove any hint that employees actually were involved in "negotiat-ing" about the wage structure. However, these precautions only pertain to job evaluation plans which affect individuals protected under the National Labor Relations Act. Job evaluation plans for managerial and supervisory job groups do not fall under the purview of this act and consequently, these concerns do not affect such employee groups.

Communication of a Plan

Communication of a job evaluation plan should commence the very day that the organization makes the decision to implement such a plan. The initial communication should flow from the highest relevant levels (i.e., corporate headquarters, plant manager). This initial communication should inform employees that a new pay plan is imminent, assure employees that the new plan will not adversely affect pay rates, and provide a general time frame for the implementation. This communique should have a "policy" flavor to it and not discuss operational issues. Since employees sometimes overlook written communications, an organization should make multiple attempts to disseminate the information through multiple media. Information in pay envelopes, postings on bulletin boards, verbal communications in staff meetings, and general announcements are appropriate avenues.

Subsequent communications should flow from the job evaluation committee, as necessary, over the appropriate line manager's signature. This strategy will show employees that the program has complete support of the line organization and is not just something devised by the HR department without rhyme or reason.

If employee representatives serve on the job evaluation committee, they probably will informally share information with fellow employees. The chair of the committee should recognize this possibility and advise employee representatives on what not to share. For example, in establishing the specific point level or grade for a given job, committee members may engage in considerable debate. The chair should encourage members to hold such debates as privileged information. On the other hand, employee representatives should be encouraged to promote the belief that the new plan will result in a more equitable and sensible pay structure.

Finally, when the new plan is put in place, each employee should be counseled on the impact that the new plan has on his or her job status, including its effect on his or her pay rate. In this regard, those employees whose wages are "red circled" should know this, and the company's specific policy on dealing with red circle rates should be communicated verbally to each employee.

Rate Adjustment Policy

Implementation of a job evaluation plan implies that wage rates for certain jobs will change, and an organization should have a predetermined policy for handling these rate changes. Jobs with current wage rates that are too low relative to the new policy line are easiest to address: wage rates should immediately rise to the minimum rate of that job's pay range in the new structure. However, rates that are too high relative to the new policy line and pay range for a job pose a different problem. Any attempt at reducing the pay rate for job incumbents will almost surely encounter resistance, but a number of strategies may help minimize the problem.

A "red circle" policy offers one method to avoid resistance.[46] A red circle policy means that all incumbents with rates higher than the new policy line and its attendant pay ranges will have their rates frozen at the current level until, over time, the policy line and ranges move up to capture the red circled incumbent. A second approach is to offer a transfer to overpaid incumbents, when possible, to a job which carries a pay rate consistent with current pay. If an incumbent refuses a transfer, then the organization could reduce pay to the new rate. Of these two approaches, the first approach is probably most desirable in terms of minimizing resistance.

Legal Issues in Job Evaluation

A pay practice will result in a ruling of illegal discrimination only if it is proscribed by law. In the context of job evaluation, the Equal Pay Act of 1963, and Title VII of the Civil Rights Act of 1964 are probably the two most important legal parameters.

Equal Pay Act of 1963

The Equal Pay Act of 1963 (EPA) became the first major piece of federal legislation to deal explicitly with discrimination in wage payments. The EPA prohibits discrimination in wages between men and women in jobs requiring equal "skill," "effort," "responsibility," and which are performed under "similar working conditions." The act also provides for four affirmative defenses:[47]

> Wages may be different if they are paid pursuant to: i) a seniority system, ii) a merit system, iii) a system which measures earnings by quantity or quality of production, or iv) a differential based on any other factor other than sex.

Although the EPA applies only to discrimination on the basis of gender, its standards for determining the presence or absence of illegal wage discrimination have been applied to other protected groups. Therefore, an employer can justify most wage differentials by demonstrating dissimilarity of jobs based on skill, effort, responsibility, and working conditions, or argue for legitimate pay differences within equal jobs on the basis of the four affirmative defenses permitted in the law.[48]

Civil Rights Act of 1964

Title VII of the Civil Rights Act of 1964 prohibits discrimination in the "terms and conditions of employment" on the basis of race, creed, color, sex, and national origin. Since wage payments are a "term or condition of employment," it therefore becomes illegal to discriminate in wage payments on the basis of any of these protected statuses. The act, as amended, is enforced by the Equal Employment Opportunity Commission and applies to state and local governments, employment agencies, labor unions, and private-sector employers with 15 or more employees.

One early issue, which has been resolved, concerned precisely how the EPA and Title VII relate to each other. The issue arose because of the Bennett Amendment to Title VII which basically says that nothing in Title VII should be construed to overturn the standards of the EPA. The case of *Gunther v. County of Washington* brought the issue to the forefront. In this case, the county paid predominantly male guards a higher wage than prison matrons (women), and the wage differential exceeded what the county's job evaluation plan called for.[49] The county's defense argued that since the jobs were not similar in the first place, the matrons had no basis to bring a Title VII suit because the EPA equal job standards applied to Title VII cases. A divided U.S. Supreme Court ruled that while only the four affirmative defenses under EPA applied to Title VII cases, Title VII cases of wage discrimination were not restricted to cases where the jobs were equal. Thus, women wishing to bring a lawsuit in which jobs are not equal could not bring a charge under EPA, but they could bring a charge under Title VII.

State Legislation

Space does not permit a detailed discussion of state anti-discrimination legislation which deals with wage discrimination issues. However, employers should be aware that state standards in their particular jurisdiction may impose restrictions even more stringent than federal standards. For example, the federal age discrimination act prohibits discriminating against persons over 40 years old on the basis of age. However, Iowa state law prohibits basing employment decisions on age for persons 18 and older. Information on state standards can usually be obtained from state departments of industry and commerce and/or state and local human rights commissions.

The Comparable Worth Issue

Like many other aspects of HRM, the comparable worth concept is relatively easy to understand but difficult to operationalize. In concept, the comparable worth issue deals with the question of whether comparable jobs receive comparable wage rates. Underlying the issue is the broader concern of wage equity and the persistent gap between the average wages of men and women. Indeed, the EPA passage in 1963 came about in part as a response to findings that women in the United States on average earn about 60 percent of what men earn.[50] However, 26 years of experience under the Equal Pay Act and Title VII have not reduced this differential.

Comparable worth as a standard for wage equity has been around for the past 40 years.[51] While early drafts of the EPA entertained the language of "comparable work," Congress determined early on that "comparable work" was too vague.[52] As a result, the term "equal work" was written into the final legislation.

Societal level gender-based wage differentials say little about the absence/presence of comparable worth inequities at the firm level. Indeed, substantial wage differentials are known to exist between industries. Further, wage differentials may be due to characteristics of labor supply, such as skill mix, and occupational preference.[53] Given the impact of such variables on the overall wage differential, comparable worth may prove easier to address in terms of organizational policies.

Under a comparable worth philosophy at the firm level, an organization would pay equal wages for jobs that are comparable in terms of their skill, effort, responsibility, and working conditions (or other legitimate compensable factors). Expressing the issue in this manner quickly shows why comparable worth advocates see job evaluation as the remedy for current alleged inequities. Since job evaluation plans are designed in part to establish the relative worth of similar and dissimilar jobs, it seems logical that job evaluation could establish which jobs are comparable, and therefore, should carry similar pay rates. Indeed, one of the ironies of job evaluation plans (especially, although not limited to, job classification plans) is that industry has always, to some degree, been willing to equate non-equal jobs.[54] In this sense, advocates of comparable worth are only asking for internal consistency in policies which industry has utilized for most all of this century.

However, current pressures clearly do go beyond traditional applications of job evaluation plans. Few employers use a single job evaluation plan for all job families (occupational groups) within the firm. As noted earlier, most organizations develop multiple plans because of (1) the difficulty of developing universal compensable factors which apply across diverse job families, and/or (2) a desire to price job families to different labor markets. Proponents of comparable-worth raise serious challenges to both of these traditional aspects of job evaluation. First, at least one report suggests that an employer may be able to use one job evaluation plan.[55] Second, as discussed earlier, a number of analysts have recommended pricing all jobs to either male-dominated (and higher paying) labor markets or mixed-gender labor markets (which are presumably free of gender bias).[56]

Current Status and Likely Trends

Comparable worth is an obvious political issue. In the public sector, both the American Federation of State, County, and Municipal Employees (AFSCME) and the Communications Workers of America are bargaining for job evaluation studies to examine this pay equity issue and attempting to negotiate wage changes based on such studies. One of the most publicized cases has occurred in San Jose, California where AFSCME struck the city over demands for wage rate adjustments for clerical workers to achieve equity with carpenters and technicians.[57] The settlement in the San Jose case included $1.4 million for equity adjustments. The AFL-CIO also has adopted a resolution calling for its affiliates to act on the comparable worth question.[58] Public-sector unions are highly active in the comparable worth arena, and private-sector firms and their unions are not likely far behind.

State Legislation

Comparable worth has generated much political activity at the state level. Fourteen state legislatures have adopted comparable worth as the standard for wage payments.[59] However, these state laws apply only to government, not private-sector, employers and the employee groups which are covered vary from state to state. For example, some state laws cover state employees only (as in Hawaii), while other states cover all state, county, and local jurisdictions (e.g., Minnesota).

These local actions have at least two major implications for private-sector organizations. First, the trend established for state employers could easily lead to efforts to broaden the standards to private employers. Therefore, private-sector employers wishing input into this process should definitely stay in contact with their state representatives. Second, state action may indirectly affect the wages paid by private-sector firms. For instance, a state, county, or local government could implement a comparable-worth wage policy which increases the market wage level for a given occupational group. As a result, private employers who hire in the same labor market could then find themselves competing for a more costly unit of labor.

Court Activity

Proponents of the comparable worth concept have also tried to advance their cause through court action. One of the earliest cases was *Lemons v. City and County of Denver*.[60] In this case, nurses argued that they were underpaid relative to other government employees like tree trimmers. The nurses also argued that Denver's wage policies were illegal because they relied on local wage rates for nurses which were themselves a product of discrimination. The court, however, rejected the comparable worth question and also upheld market rates as a legitimate criterion for setting wage rates.

In *Gunther v. County of Washington*, the U.S. Supreme Court examined whether or not comparable worth discrimination occurred when the county deviated from its own job evaluation plan and paid women matrons less than male guards.[61] According to the county's job evaluation, women prison matrons should have earned about 83 percent of what male prison guards earned. However, the county paid women prison matrons less than the rate indicated by the job evaluation plan. In a narrowly constructed and divided opinion, the court rejected the comparable worth concept as the basis for its decision. However, it ruled in favor of plaintiffs on the grounds that the county had intentionally discriminated on the basis of gender when it ignored its job evaluation plan and knowingly underpaid women prison matrons.

The case of *Briggs v. City of Madison* also touched on the comparable worth issue.[62] In this case, the city had placed a male-dominated job and a female-dominated job in the same pay grade, and then paid the male-dominated job at a higher rate when the lower rate failed to attract and retain employees. The court found that the jobs were substantially equal, but upheld the market defense in light of the city's difficulty in attracting and retaining workers.

AFSCME v. State of Washington is the case receiving the greatest publicity.[63] In that case, the state had, over a number of years, conducted wage equity studies which indicated that female-dominated jobs were systematically under-paid relative to male-dominated jobs. Further, the state had intended, on several occasions, to adjust wages upward for these underpaid jobs; for budgetary reasons, it had never done so. AFSCME sued on the grounds that since the state's own wage equity studies showed wage discrimination, its unwillingness to adjust wages represented an intent to discriminate. Although the trial court agreed with the union's assertion, the appeals court reversed, noting that "what if" studies examining various alternative pay policies do not in and of themselves constitute implementation of the policy, or an intent to discriminate. A similar decision was handed down in the case of *American Nurses Association v. State of Illinois*.[64] In that case, the court ruled that conducting an equity study and then deciding not to act upon the results does not show an intent to discriminate.

Summary of Court Rulings. These cases seem to provide some guidance to employers who might want to do "what if" studies to determine the impact of alternate job evaluation plans on wage rates. It would seem that employers can conduct such studies without fear that failure to act on the results will be interpreted as intentional discrimination. However, the American Society for Personnel Administration (ASPA) recommends labelling job evaluation plans "experimental" until management is satisfied that the plan is workable and makes the decision to implement it.[65]

In light of these and other cases, job evaluation plans resemble seniority systems in that the courts will defer to such systems, providing that they are designed and implemented without an intent to discriminate.[66] Further, an organization should not deviate from its job evaluation plan absent compelling business reasons such as were articulated in the Briggs case. As noted earlier, the easiest defense may be to develop different job evaluation plans for different employee populations and make no effort to equate different types of jobs.[67]

Finally, the legal recommendation of eliminating job evaluation altogether seems to be undesirable. This conservative alternative amounts to "throwing the baby out with the bath water," much as happened with employment tests when the *Griggs v. Duke Power Co.* case was decided 15 years ago.[68] Despite the many inherent limitations of job evaluation, this important administrative mechanism for wage determination has served its purpose well.

Guidelines for Employers

Employers looking to respond to the comparable worth challenge will find few universal guidelines to follow. A given employer's response will depend on the degree of wage differences among male- and female-dominated jobs, the financial health of the organization, and the amount of pressure for change. Inequities in the application of compensable factors to jobs clearly remain; corrective action would be wise if an employer has such a problem. However, a few, relatively sophisticated, employers have quietly conducted equity studies, found disparities, and quietly changed wage levels by slowing the growth rate for wages in male-dominated jobs and accelerating the growth rate for wages in predominantly female jobs. However, this strategy assumes a relatively high ability to pay and probably works only when an employer can eliminate the discrepancies without seriously violating market rate parameters.

Organizations whose ability to pay is severely constrained by product market variables may face the uneasy situation of having wage discrepancies continue because they cannot afford to change. Ironically, these employers might favor legislation which reduces such inequities since such a law will affect all employers, not just one organization. However, the increased wage costs associated with any such legislation will almost assuredly have major impact on product price and therefore, product demand in certain cases. As an example, higher labor costs would greatly damage the textile industry in light of the current pressures to contain costs so as to compete in the world product market.

Against this backdrop, and keeping in mind that no two employers face identical constraints, the following recommendations are offered. First, organizations should aggressively pursue equal opportunity policies. The comparable worth issue arose in the first place largely because historical employment discrimination channeled individuals into particular jobs and occupations, creating genders-dominated employments.[69] (This explanation for gender-dominated occupations obviously presumes that labor suppliers do not have gender-correlated preferences for employment.[70] Aggressive pursuit of equal employment opportunity and affirmative action provides one avenue to reduce the current legal and political pressures for comparable worth.

Second, as noted earlier in the chapter, employees' perceptions of what is "just" or "fair" change over time. Today, female employees think that the equity standards used in traditional job evaluation plans are no longer "fair," "just," or "equitable." Responsible employers must face the issue squarely, examine their job evaluation plans for gender bias, and make a serious effort to correct any problems. Obviously, financial constraints will dictate the degree and pace with which change can occur.

Third, in the short run, employers should probably use multiple job evaluation plans for different occupational groups.[71] Multiple plans, anchored to distinct labor markets and administered consistently, permit an employer to avoid equating unequal jobs, and support a market defense for wage differentials. However, such a strategy works only in the short run and does nothing to address female employees' perceptions of inequity.

Fourth, employers should aim for consistency in job evaluation plan administration. For example, if an employer sets its wage policy line for one job family at the 75th percentile of the market, it should use the same wage policy line for other job families (absent compelling business necessity). In a similar fashion, organizations would do well to establish wage policies based on either labor or product markets, but not both. Employers may even risk challenges if they use national labor market data for a set of highly paid jobs, but local labor market data for a set of lower paid (and female-dominated) jobs. As one observer has noted, "Bias in market wage determinations has received little attention to date, but that may change as compensation specialists contemplate the growing importance of motive in evidence in pay discrimination cases."[72] This observation seems particularly true given the large differences in wage rates both within and between labor and product markets for nearly identical jobs.[73]

Consistency also may become important in the design of multiple job evaluation plans. For example, ramifications could occur if an organization painstakingly develops a point method of job evaluation for (predominantly male) craft workers and then haphazardly uses a ranking method for office/clerical jobs. To be redundant, consistency in job evaluation and job pricing may be critical for defending pay policies.

Auditing the Pay System for Internal Equity

Audits of organizational practice are hardly new to the business community. Accountants regularly audit financial statements for evidence of fraud; production managers audit both raw material and finished goods inventories. While audits often serve as control devices in these other functional areas of the business, many organizations display a curious disinterest in conducting regular audits of HR programs. Herbert Heneman Jr., in his years as a Professor of Industrial Relations in the University of Minnesota's Center of Industrial Relations, was one of the early and vocal supporters of Human Resource audits. Although Professor Heneman probably did not envision the extent to which audits would become central to issues of legal compliance, he was a leader in the subject.

Today, HR audits routinely take place in response to lawsuits. Indeed, the legal concept of "discovery," which commences when a discrimination complaint is filed, is nothing more than an audit by another name. Discovery requires a search of records for evidence to support or refute the allegation of discrimination. Audits need not occur only after a complaint; however, experience indicates that this scenario is the most common impetus. This tendency is unfortunate, since proactive audits could help head off problems in the first place.

Equal Pay Audits

The Equal Pay Act of 1963 provides a starting point for any audit focusing on internal wage equity. As noted earlier, the EPA places constraints on employers, and these strictures may help

---

Table 3

Equal Pay Act Audit Procedures

- Identify and define "the establishment"
- Define the protected groups to be studied
- Identify the jobs to be studied
- Examine wages for incumbents
- Determine if legitimate reasons exist for same/differential treatment
- Use cohort and/or statistical analysis
- Correct inequities if they are present

---

guide a proactive audit of a pay system to thwart charges of unequal treatment discrimination. Table 3 summarizes the following discussion of recommended procedures to use in fashioning such an audit.[74]

First, the EPA requires equal wages be paid to men and women (the Civil Rights Act requires a similar standard for other protected groups) on jobs that require equal skill, effort, and responsibility, and which are performed under similar working conditions within the same establishment. The "same establishment" requirement means that employees of a particular operating unit should receive equal wages. Identifying an "establishment" requires consideration of both a geographic criterion and a personnel policy criterion.[75] The next steps are to determine which groups to compare and which jobs to audit. The groups could include any or all of the protected statuses under the EPA or the CRA. Determining which jobs to include necessitates performing a job analysis. Since jobs must involve equal "skill," "effort," "responsibility," and be performed under "similar working conditions," the job analysis should examine which jobs are similar and dissimilar. Jobs do not have to be identical, only substantially equal.[76]

Next, the organization should collect salary data for these jobs and compare the average wages for members of the protected groups to the average wages of other incumbents. Equal wages between the groups does not eliminate the possibility of wage discrimination problem, since one group may have consistently higher performance than the other group. If wages are, on average, unequal between the groups, there may also be legitimate reasons for this as well. Thus, simple equality of average wages is only the first step of the analysis.

The next step is to determine if different groups have received the same treatment in wage payments. If wage differences exist, employers should determine whether the discrepancies result from one of the four proactive defenses allowed under the EPA: (1) a merit system, (2) a seniority system, (3) a system which measures earnings by quantity or quality of output, or (4) any other factor except sex.

Cohort Analysis

In examining a pay system for EPA compliance, an auditor has several approaches to follow. In the simplest case, a cohort analysis would identify employees who had joined the organization at the same time, had the same performance reviews, and so forth and determine if the individuals in question had received equal treatment. Unfortunately, it is often difficult to conduct cohort analysis since few workers, particularly in smaller organizations, have identical employment histories.

Statistical Analysis

Because of the difficulties of cohort analysis, employers often rely on more sophisticated statistical analyses to determine if employees have received equal treatment. Such analyses usually rely on one or more multiple regression models,[77] and use the legitimate reasons for pay differences (specified in the EPA) as variables to explain differences in pay for members of the various groups. Any unexplained differences presumably reflect discrimination.

Organizations intending to use sophisticated statistical procedures to investigate possible wage inequalities should realize that these models are not perfect and require careful interpretation of the results. Critics have shown that regression procedures result in underprediction and often need further analysis.[78] Other potential problems include restricted samples, missing variables,[79] and/or "tainted" variables (variables such as performance rating, which may be the result of a discriminatory practice).[80] While regression models can assist in making inferences about the presence or absence of discrimination, they are not for the novice.

Correcting Inequities

Regardless of the method of analysis used, an audit ultimately will result in an inference about the presence or absence of inequities. Absence of inequities obviously is the desired outcome and requires no further action. However, the presence of an inequity must receive attention to head off future potential litigation.

On the surface, correcting any inequities in wages which emerge from an audit would seem to be a straightforward matter. For example, suppose that an audit reveals an apparent underpayment to women of $400 per year which cannot be justified using any of the legitimate criteria for pay differentials. A seemingly simple solution would be to adjust women's wages upward by $400. However, this solution poses two problems. First, while women, on average, may be underpaid by $400 per person, this average may not apply to each person. In fact, some women may be overpaid, just as some of the men are. Thus, an average adjustment would be uncalled for. Second, some men are probably underpaid as well relative to the equitable ideal, a possibility often omitted from statistical models. Thus, to adjust inequities only for women could constitute illegal discrimination against a subgroup of men.[81]

Great care obviously must go into equity adjustments to stem further legal liability. Since an employee's total pay is composed of starting pay plus adjustments to pay, the HR unit should also audit pay changes for possible legal liability. This type of audit would involve additional monitoring of performance appraisal data to assure that it is free of bias and error.[82]

Employee Attitude Surveys

Besides auditing for potential legal liability, employers might take other avenues to identify possible inequity in wage payments. One approach is to conduct an employee opinion survey to determine the extent of perceived wage inequity. Employers should probably avoid conducting a survey only on perceived wage equity or inequity since such a questionnaire may simply draw employees' attention to an issue that had gone unnoticed. However, employers often survey employees for their opinions and attitudes on a broad array of topics, and such questionnaires could include a subset of questions dealing with internal pay equity.

Quantitative Indicators of Inequities

Organizations can supplement legal and attitudinal approaches by analyzing other behavioral data that may reflect a problem with inequity. For example, organizations experiencing turnover may wish to examine the reasons for that turnover. Exit interviews, whether structured or unstructured, provide a way to identify the reasons why employees leave.

Another obvious behavioral indicator is grievance of salary amount, or increase. Analyzing the content of such grievances may help determine whether internal wage inequity is the cause. Refusal of promotions, and job bidding patterns, may also indicate problems of internal inequity. For example, in one case, an employer's salary structure has caused severe wage compression between highly paid operatives and their immediate supervisors.[83] In fact, with any overtime payments, the operatives make more than the salaried supervisors. In this plant, operatives refuse promotions to supervisory jobs and new supervisors hired from outside actually request demotions to operative jobs after about six months. While this example is an extreme case of wage compression, it highlights the difficulties which perceived inequitable wage rates create.

Conclusion

This chapter has focused on internal wage equity, but the topic encompasses other components of the compensation package. Indeed, other chapters will examine other equity concerns, such as wage payments among employees within the same job (see Chapter 3.5), employee benefit levels and structures (see Chapter 3.4), and the compensation of special groups (such as executives) (see Chapter 3.7).

At the same time, the types of internally equitable pay relationships discussed here merit serious attention. As noted at the outset of this chapter, the absence of equity will likely arouse employees to exhibit behaviors which are costly to an organization. These undesirable behaviors can range from quitting, to grievances, to lawsuits.

This chapter has focused on job evaluation as the administrative mechanism for achieving internal wage equity between jobs. However, job evaluation does have certain weaknesses. If nothing else, this chapter should have communicated the need to expand current knowledge about job evaluation plans and the way in which they are administered. Areas requiring further research include: a) the job evaluation process, b) what components result in acceptable plans, and c) what leads to the demise of other plans. Further, much work needs to be done to learn how to improve upon job evaluation plans. In the future, organizations may even start to realign their pay systems with different goals and develop entirely different criteria for pay (e.g. skill-based pay). However, the prospects for continued use of job evaluation would seem to be bright. Absent any other mechanism, job evaluation has been and will probably continue to be the only reasonable device for organizations to bring rationality to their internal wage structures.

The discussion on comparable worth should alert HR managers to some of the inherent problems with job evaluation as it is traditionally operationalized. If the viewpoint advanced here is correct, job evaluation contributes to current issues regarding internal equity, in part because the job evaluation plans now in use were conceived and operationalized in an entirely different era. HR managers should not throw out job evaluation, as a result of these problems, but they should assure that their job evaluation criteria reflect the work culture of the 1980s and beyond.

Finally, employers should remember that there is no universally held criteria for "worth." The challenge for HR managers and designers of job evaluation plans is to assure that the scheme used has the endorsement of the employees who work and are paid within its goals and constraints.

♦

Notes

1. Homans.
2. Adams.
3. Hills (1987).
4. Mahoney (1979), p. 202.
5. Adams and Jacobsen; Adams and Rosenbaum.
6. Pritchard, Dunnette and Jorgenson.
7. Hills (1987); Milkovich and Newman; Belcher.
8. Mahoney (1975).
9. Rynes and Milkovich.
10. Zollitsch and Langsner, pp. 152–3.
11. Ibid.
12. Kress.
13. Bureau of National Affairs, Inc. (1976).
14. Lo Bosco.
15. Mahoney (1979).
16. Bernstein.
17. Arvey.
18. Hills (1987).
19. Patten, p. 14.
20. Hills (1987); Milkovich and Newman.
21. Lawler and Ledford.
22. Newman.
23. Elizur; Thomason.
24. Zollitsch and Langsner.
25. Gomez-Mejia, Page and Tornow; McCormick, p. 25; U.S. Department of Labor, Manpower Administration.
26. Schwab and Grams.

3-64   Compensation & Benefits

27. Hills (1987).
28. Fay.
29. Chesler; Peters and McCormick; Robinson, Wahlstrom and Mecham; Rogers; Snelgar.
30. Madigan and Hoover.
31. Madigan and Hills.
32. Lawshe; Lawshe and Wilson; Lawshe, Dudek and Wilson.
33. Schwab.
34. *Briggs v. City of Madison*, 436 F.Supp. 435, W.D. of Wisc., 1982.
35. Schlei and Grossman.
36. Arvey.
37. Treiman and Hartmann, p. 74.
38. Ibid.
39. Thomsen.
40. Madigan and Hills.
41. Hills; Milkovich and Newman.
42. Gomez-Mejia, Page and Tornow; Hills.
43. Gomez-Mejia, Page and Tornow, p. 37.
44. Lawler.
45. Rynes, Rosen and Mahoney.
46. Hills.
47. Equal Pay Act, 29 U.S.C. Sec. 206 (d), 1979.
48. Roberts; Milkovich.
49. *Gunther v. County of Washington*, 451 U.S. 161, U.S. Sup. Ct., 1981.
50. Hills (1987).
51. May.
52. Lorber, Kirk, Samuels and Spellman.
53. Hodson and England; Groshen; Krzystofiak and Newman.
54. Hills (1982).
55. Treiman and Hartman.
56. Thomsen; Madigan and Hills.
57. Farnquist, Armstrong and Strausbaugh.
58. Newman.
59. Cook; Bureau of National Affairs, Inc. (1984).
60. *Lemons v. City and County of Denver*, 620 F.2d 228, 1980.
61. *Gunther v. County of Washington*.
62. *Briggs v. City of Madison*.
63. *AFSCME v. State of Washington*, 678 F.Supp. 846, 33 FEP 808, W.D. Washington, 1983.
64. *American Nurses Association v. State of Illinois*, 606 F.2d, 40 FEP 244 (7th Cir.), 1986.
65. Lorber, Kirk, Samuels and Spellman.
66. Ledvinka.
67. Schlei and Grossman.
68. *Griggs v. Duke Power*, 401 U.S. 424, 3 FEP 175, 1971.
69. Bergmann and Hills (1982).
70. Krzystofiak and Newman.
71. Schlei and Grossman.
72. Ledvinka, p. 58.
73. Rynes and Milkovich.
74. Hills and Bergmann (1987).
75. *Hodgson v. Waynesburg College*, 20 WH 142 (W.D.PA), 1971.
76. *Shultz v. Wheaton Glass*, 421 F.2d 259, 1970.
77. Hills and Bergmann (1982); see also Milkovich for an outline of the general statistical model which is used.
78. Roberts.
79. Bloom and Killingsworth.
80. Finklestein.
81. Birnbaum.
82. Hills, Madigan, Scott and Markham.
83. Bergmann and Hills (1987).

Editor's Note: In addition to the References shown below there are other significant sources of information and ideas on internal pay relationships.

Books

Hay and Associates. 1981. *The Guide Chart Profile of Job Evaluation*. Minneapolis: author.

Jaques, E. 1964. *Time-Span Handbook*. London: Heinemann Educational Books.

McCormick, E.J. et al. 1977. *Position Analysis Questionnaire*. West Lafayette, IN: Purdue University.

U.S. Department of Labor. 1977. *Dictionary of Occupational Titles*, 4th ed. Washington, DC: U.S. Government Printing Office.

Articles

Boshoff, A.B.A. 1969, "A Comparison of Three Methods of Methods for the Evaluation of Managerial Positions." *Psychologia Africana* 12: 212–221.

Charles, A.W. 1971. "Installing Single Factor Job Evaluation." *Compensation Review* (first quarter): 9–17.

Dunnette, M.D. 1979. "Task and Job Taxonomies as a Basis for Identifying Labor Supply Sources and Evaluating Employment Qualifications." *Human Resource Planning, Vol. 2*.

Hay, E.N. and D. Purves. 1984. "A New Method of Job Evaluation." *Personnel* (July).

Madigan, R.M. 1985. "Comparable Worth Judgements: A Measurement Properties Analysis." *Journal of Applied Psychology* 70, 1: 137–147.

Newman, J.M. and F. Krzystofiak, 1977. "Quantified Job Analysis: A Tool for Improving Human Resource Management Decision Making." Paper presented at Academy of Management Meetings, Orlando, FL, August.

Paterson, T.T. and T.M. Husband. 1970. "Decision Making Responsibility: A Yardstick for Job Evaluation." *Compensation Review* (Second quarter): 21–31.

Schwab, D.P. and H.G. Heneman III. 1986. "Assessment of a Consensus-Based Multiple Information Source Job Evaluation System." *Journal of Applied Psychology* 71, 2: 354–356.

Tornow, W. and P. Pinto. 1976. "The Development of a Managerial Job Taxonomy: A System for Describing, Classifying, and Evaluating Executive Office Positions." *Journal of Applied Psychology* 61: 410–418.

Wallace, M.J. 1983. "Methodology, Research Practice and Progress in Personnel and Industrial Relations." *Academy of Management Review* 8, 1: 6–13.

◆

References

Adams, J.S. 1965. "Inequity in Social Exchange." In *Advances in Experimental Social Psychology*, vol. 2, ed. L. Berkowitz. New York: Academic Press.

Adams, J.S. and P.R. Jacobsen. 1964. "Effects of Wage Inequities on Work Equality." *Journal of Abnormal Social Psychology* 69: 19–25.

Adams, J.S. and W.B. Rosenbaum. 1962. "The Relationship of Worker Productivity to Cognitive Dissonance about Wage Inequities." *Journal of Applied Psychology* 46: 161–64.

Arvey, R.D. 1987. "Potential Problems in Job Evaluation Methods and Process." In *New Perspectives on Compensation*, D.B. Balkin and L.R. Gomez-Mejia, (eds). Englewood Cliffs, NJ: Prentice Hall.

Belcher, D.W. 1974. *Compensation Administration.* Englewood Cliffs, NJ: Prentice Hall.

Bergmann, T.J. and F.S. Hills. 1982. "Internal Labor Markets and Indirect Pay Discrimination." *Compensation Review*, (fourth quarter): 41–50.

———. 1987. "A Review of the Causes of and Solution to Pay Compression." In *New Perspective On Compensation*, ed. D.B. Balkin and L.R. Gomez-Mejia. Englewood Cliffs, NJ: Prentice Hall.

Bernstein, A. 1987. "Why Two-Tier Wage Scales Are Starting to Self-Destruct." *Business Week* (March 16): 41.

Birnbaum, M.H. 1987. "Procedures for Detection and Correction of Salary Inequities." In *Salary Equity*, eds. T.R. Pezzulo and B.E. Brittingham. Lexington, MA: Lexington Books, D.C. Heath and Co.

Bloom, D.E. and M.R. Killingsworth. 1982. "Pay Discrimination Research and Litigation: The Use of Regression." *Industrial Relations* 21, 3 (Fall): 318–339.

Bureau of National Affairs, Inc. 1976. *Job Evaluation Policies and Procedures, Personnel Policies Forum, Survey No. 113.* Washington, DC: Bureau of National Affairs, Inc.

———. 1984. *Pay Equity and Comparable Worth*, BNA Special Report. Washington, DC: Bureau of National Affairs, Inc.

Chesler, D.J. 1948. "Reliability and Comparability of Different Job Evaluation Systems." *Journal of Applied Psychology* 32: 465–475.

Cook, A. 1983. "Comparable Worth: Recent Developments in Selected States." Proceedings of the 1983 Spring Meeting of the Industrial Relations Research Association, Honolulu.

Elizur, D. 1980. *Job Evaluation: A Systematic Approach.* Great Britain: Gower Publishing Co Ltd.

Farnquist, R.L., D.R. Armstrong, and R.P. Strausbaugh. 1983. "Pandora's Worth: The San Jose Experience." *Public Personnel Management* (Winter): 358–78.

Fay, C.H. 1987. "Using the Strategic Planning Process to Develop a Compensation Strategy." *Topics in Total Compensation* 2: 127.

Finklestein, M.O. 1980. "The Judicial Reception of Multiple Regression Studies in Race and Sex Discrimination Cases." *Columbia Law Journal* 80: 737–754.

Gomez-Mejia, L.R., R.C. Page, and W.W. Tornow. 1979. "Development and Implementation of a Computerized Job Evaluation System." *Personnel Administrator* (February): 46–54.

Groshen, E.L. 1985. "Sources of Wage Dispersion: How Much Do Employers Matter?" Working paper, Harvard University, Department of Economics, December.

Hills, F.S. 1982. "Comparable Worth: Implications for Compensation Managers." *Compensation Review* (3d Quarter): 33–43.

————. 1987. *Compensation Decision Making*. Hinsdale, IL: The Dryden Press.

Hills, F.S. and T.J. Bergmann. 1982. "Alternate Regression Models in Analyzing Sex Based Pay Discrimination." Paper presented at the National Academy of Management Meetings, August.

————. 1987. "Conducting An Equal Pay For Equal Work Audit." In *New Perspective On Compensation*, eds. D.B. Balkin and L.R. Gomez-Mejia. Englewood Cliffs, NJ: Prentice Hall.

Hills, F.S., R.M. Madigan, K.D. Scott, and S.E. Markham. 1987. "Tracking the Merit of Merit Pay." *Personnel Administrator* 32, 3: 50–57.

Hodson, R., and P. England. 1985. "Industrial Structure and Sex Differences in Earnings." *Industrial Relations* 25, 1 (Winter): 16–32.

Homans, G.C. 1961. *Social Behavior: Its Elementary Forms*. New York: Harcourt, Brace, Janovich.

Kress, A.L. 1939. "How to Rate Jobs and Men." *Factory Management And Maintenance*, vol. IIIC, no. 10.

Krzystofiak, F. and J. Newman. 1982. "Evaluating Employment Outcomes: Availability Models and Measures." *Industrial Relations*, 21, 3 (Fall): 277–292.

Lawler, E.E., III. 1971. *Pay and Organizational Effectiveness: A Psychological View*. New York: McGraw Hill.

Lawler, E.E., III and C.E. Ledford, Jr. 1985. "Skill Based Pay: A Concept That's Catching On." *Personnel* (September): 30–37.

Lawshe, C.H. Jr. 1945. "Studies in Job Evaluation 2. The Adequacy of Abbreviated Point Ratings for Hourly Paid Jobs in Three Industrial Plants." *Journal of Applied Psychology* (June): 177–84.

Lawshe, C.H. Jr. and R.F. Wilson. 1947. "Studies in Job Evaluation 6. The Reliability of Two Point Rating Systems." *Journal of Applied Psychology* (August): 355–65.

Lawshe, C.H. Jr., E.E. Dudek, and R.F. Wilson. 1948. "Studies in Job Evaluation 7. A Factor Analysis of Two Point Rating Methods of Job Evaluation." *Journal of Applied Psychology* (April): 118–29.

Ledvinka, J. 1987. "The Legal States of Comparable Worth." In *New Perspectives On Compensation*, eds. D.B. Balkin and L.R. Gomez-Mejia. Englewood Cliffs, NJ: Prentice Hall.

Lo Bosco, M. 1985. "Job Analysis, Job Evaluation, and Job Classification." *Personnel* (May): 70–74.

Lorber, L.Z., J.R. Kirk, S.L. Samuels, and D.J. Spellman III 1985. *Sex and Salary*. Alexandria, VA: The ASPA Foundation.

Madigan, R.M. and D.J. Hoover. 1986. "Effects of Alternate Job Evaluation Methods on Decisions Involving Pay Equity." *Academy of Management Journal* 29, 1: 84–100.

Madigan, R.M. and F.S. Hills. 1988. "Job Evaluation and Pay Equity." *Public Personnel Management*, 17(3): 323–330.

Mahoney, T.A. 1975. "Justice and Equity: A Recurring Theme." *Personnel* 52: 60.

———. 1979. *Compensation and Reward Perspectives.* Homewood, IL: Irwin.

May, M. 1982. "The Historical Problem of the Family Wage." *Feminist Studies* 8 (Summer): 399–424.

McCormick, E.J. 1976. "Job and Task Analysis." In *Handbook of Industrial and Organizational Psychology,* ed. M.D. Dunnette. Chicago: Rand-McNally.

Milkovich, G.T. 1980. "The Emerging Debate." In *Comparable Worth Issues and Answers,* ed. E.R. Livernash. Washington, DC: EEAC.

Milkovich, G.T. and J.M. Newman. 1984. *Compensation.* Plano, TX: Business Publications.

Newman, J.M. 1987. "Selecting Incentive Plans to Complement Organization Strategy." In *New Perspectives on Compensation,* eds. D.B. Balkin and L.R. Gomez-Mejia. Englewood Cliffs, NJ: Prentice Hall.

Newman, W. 1982. "Pay Equity Emerges as a Top Labor Issue of the 1980s." *Monthly Labor Review* (April): 49–51.

Patten, J.H. Jr. 1987. "How Do You Know If Your Job Evaluation System Is Working?" In *New Perspectives on Compensation,* D.B. Balkin and L.R. Gomez-Mejia (eds). Englewood Cliffs, NJ: Prentice Hall.

Peters, D.L. and E. McCormick. 1966. "Comparative Reliability of Numerically Anchored Versus Job Task Anchored Rating Scales." *Journal of Applied Psychology* 50: 92–96.

Pritchard, R.D., M.D. Dunnette, and D.O. Jorgenson. 1972. "Perceptions of Equity and Inequity On Worker Performance and Satisfaction." *Journal of Applied Psychology* 56, 1: 75–94.

Roberts, H.V. 1980. "Statistical Bias in the Measurement of Employment Discrimination." In *Comparable Worth Issues and Answers,* E.R. Livernash (ed). Washington, DC: EEAC.

Robinson, D.D., O.W. Wahlstrom, and R. Mecham. 1974. "Comparison of Job Evaluation Methods." *Journal of Applied Psychology* 59: 633–637.

Rogers, R.C. 1974. "Analysis of Two Point Rating Job Evaluation Plans." *Journal of Applied Psychology* 30: 579–585.

Rynes, S., B. Rosen, and T. Mahoney. 1983. "Comparable Worth: Summary Report of Survey." American Compensation Association, unpublished manuscript.

Rynes, S.L. and G.T. Milkovich. 1986. "Wage Surveys: Dispelling Some Myths about the "Market Wage." *Personnel Psychology* 19: 71–90.

Schlei, B.L., and P. Grossman. 1983. *Employment Discrimination Law,* 2nd ed. Washington, DC: BNA Books.

Schwab, D.P. 1986. "Job Evaluation and Pay Setting: Concepts and Practices." In *Comparable Worth Issues and Answers,* E.R. Livernash (ed). Washington, DC: EEAC.

Schwab, D.P. and R. Grams. 1983. "A Survey of Job Evaluation Practice Among Compensation Specialists." Scottsdale, AZ: American Compensation Association.

Snelgar, R.J. 1983. "The Comparability of Job Evaluation Methods in Supplying Approximately Similar Classifications in Rating One Job Series." *Personnel Psychology* 36: 371–380.

Thomason, G. 1980. *Job Evaluation: Objectives and Methods*. Great Britain: Institute of Personnel Management, Butler and Tanner Ltd.

Thomsen, D.J. 1978. "Eliminating Pay Discrimination Caused by Job Evaluation." *Personnel* 55: 11–22.

Treiman, D.J., and H.I. Hartmann. 1981. *Women, Work, and Wages: Equal Pay - For Jobs of Equal Value*. Washington, DC: National Academy Press.

U.S. Department of Labor, Manpower Administration. 1972. *Handbook for Analyzing Jobs*. Washington, DC: U.S. Government Printing Office.

Zollitsch, H.G., and A. Langsner, 1970. *Wage and Salary Administration*, 2nd ed. Chicago: South-Western Publishing.

———— ♦ ————

3.3

External Pay Relationships

Charles H. Fay

External equity, as generally defined by compensation professionals, refers to the range of wages and other monetary compensation (such as benefits) paid by employing organizations in some labor market for a similar job. From an employee's perspective, external equity exists if his or her compensation package is equivalent to one offered employees with similar qualifications (e.g., education, experience) who hold the same job but work for a different organization.[1]

The notion of external equity has been central to compensation theory and practice for two reasons. First, jobs have no demonstrable inherent value. This conclusion is true even of jobs, such as sales or production, that have defined value outputs. Knowing the dollar contribution of a job provides only an upper limit on job value. Thus, employers use the range of compensation paid for a job by other employers as a proxy for job value.

Second, a major requirement of any employer is to hire sufficient qualified labor to enable the organization to carry out its business and compensation plays a key role in this process.[2] A compensation package is the only part of a job offer which applicants can readily compare to other offers, primarily because all compensation packages use a common metric, the dollar. A prospective employee can easily choose between a salary of $30,000 and one of $50,000, all other things being equal; choosing with any certainty between two briefly met prospective bosses or two advancement potentials proves much more difficult.

External Equity Strategies of Organizations

Organizations use a variety of strategies to maintain external equity in pay schedules. These strategies generally fall into one of three categories. The first, an internal labor market strategy, insulates an organization's salary structure to some degree from the effects of the market. The second type of strategy uses across-the-board positioning to place an organization's complete salary structure at some set percentage of the market. The third type of strategy involves selectively positioning specific jobs in the market according to the perceived differential importance of the jobs in reaching business goals.

Internal Labor Market Strategies

Under a so-called internal labor market strategy,[3] an organization typically hires individuals only in selected "portal" jobs, which usually form the bottom rung of internal career ladders. Access to other jobs in the organization depends on internal movement. A nearly pure example of an internal labor market strategy is found in the military ranks of the United States Army. The Army offers two portal jobs, recruit and second lieutenant, and movement through the ranks is a function of experience, performance, training, and seniority. (A small number of specialists such as M.D.'s are brought into the organization at other ranks.) Other organizations that tend to follow internal labor market strategies include state and local governments, as well as many large firms, such as IBM, AT&T, and Ford Motor Company, which pride themselves on "taking care" of their employees. However, private-sector firms are much more flexible about labor market strategies.

An internal labor market strategy serves to insulate the majority of jobs from the marketplace. Since most openings are filled internally, only the salaries of portal jobs are subject to direct comparison with competing salaries. In addition, employers may design non-portal jobs so that the market offers no identical jobs for comparison. As an example, including some quality control and inspection tasks in the job of an assembler makes it more difficult to find a similar job in the marketplace.

While the internal labor market strategy focuses employee attention on the internal hierarchy of job values, organizations pursuing this strategy are not necessarily low payers. However, employers who follow an internal labor market strategy do tend to pay less attention to external equity in general, except where turnover in specific jobs or job categories forces concern.

Across-the-Board Positioning Strategy

An organization following an across-the-board positioning strategy adopts what is generally referred to as a competitive pay policy. Such a policy might state that the organization will pay at market, or at 10 percent above market, or even at 75th percentile. Regardless of the competitive position chosen, an employer following this strategy will adopt the same competitive stance for all jobs in the organization. Across-the-board positioning is the most frequently followed compensation strategy in the United States. One recent survey of more than 1400 organizations found that 20 percent have a policy of paying middle management and professionals higher than the competition, 76 percent pay at market, 3 percent pay below market, and 1 percent are uncertain of rates relative to the competition.[4] While an across-the-board strategy does not preclude positioning below market averages (or medians), employers who adopt a below-market stance rarely publicize that policy.

Selective Positioning Strategy

Organizations pursuing a selective positioning strategy have developed overall business strategies and try to use compensation programs as one means of supporting overall strategy.[5] Employers assess jobs in terms of their importance to strategy and position salaries in line with job importance. Thus, in an organizational division with an entrepreneurial strategy, a research engineer might get base pay pegged at the 80th percentile and a production engineer might get base pay pegged at median market rate; in another division of the same organization with an extract profit/rationalize strategy, the reverse might be true.[6] Selective positioning strategies are likely to be less stable than either of the other strategies, since business strategies are likely to change over time and the value of different jobs to the achievement of a new strategy will vary.

Organizations can use selective positioning strategies to serve the traditional "behavioral" goals of compensation programs: to attract, retain, and motivate. For example, the goal of compensation strategies in recruiting is to create a compensation package which will attract "the right kind" of employees for the job.[7] An employer following a selective positioning strategy with respect to recruitment would determine the strategic value of each job in light of current goals of the organization. The market level targeted would likely change as strategies and strategic objectives changed. Marginal revenue product theory provides an economic base for differential values of the same job to an employer depending on individual contributions possible from the new employee which are independent of his or her capabilities.[8]

An employer might also follow a selective positioning strategy with respect to motivation. Traditionally, merit pay systems have provided pay increases (whether lump sum or percentage added to base) as a function of performance (ideally). Seniority or position in the pay range have often been used to modify merit payments. Thus, two engineers in the same pay grade with equivalent performance and seniority (or place in range) would receive the same merit increase, even though the organization's current strategy relies heavily on the one position and not at all on the other. Such reliance may not reflect the individual qualifications of the two engineers; the job is what bears strategic importance and as a result is worth more to the organization. Under a selective positioning strategy, the engineer whose job is more central to strategic goal achievement might start at a higher pay grade and would receive different treatment with regard to merit pay.

Consequences of Violating Norms of External Equity

The costs of violating external equity norms include all expenses associated with the loss of more capable employees and applicants to higher-paying employers and the unnecessary salary expenses associated with overpayment of employees unlikely to find work elsewhere at the same wage rate.[9] Both of these costs are likely to occur regardless of the market level chosen for comparison. An employer who chooses to pay at the 45th percentile of the external market will have higher turnover costs but lower costs associated with overpaying less capable employees. The employer who pays at the 65th percentile of the market will have lower costs associated with employees leaving or applicants turning down offers but higher costs associated with overpayment of less capable employees.

Employers have two options. One option is to match the market level that (a) minimizes costs or (b) optimizes the right mix of employees to meet some set of goals (for example, equal employment opportunity, production, costs, and so on). A second option is to match different jobs to different market levels depending on the importance of the job to the organization. This strategy should minimize costs and yet provide competitiveness in filling important jobs. Consequences of this strategy may also include greater legal costs from "comparable worth" type suits, if selectivity happens to coincide with gender-domination of certain jobs. Regardless of the option chosen, organizations should analyze the economic consequences of the external pay strategy followed.

Employees whose external equity norms have been violated likely will experience pay dissatisfaction. Pay dissatisfaction, in turn, is associated with general dissatisfaction with the job, turnover, and union activity.[10]

Factors Influencing External Pay Levels

Some variation in pay levels will arise for any given job, even in a local labor market, and a single wage level could indicate collusion and wage-fixing.[11] Studies of interorganizational differences in wage levels suggest certain factors which may help to define appropriate jobs to use in external equity comparisons, and to guide the design and interpretation of wage and benefit surveys.[12] Figure 1 summarizes most of these factors, and the following discussion highlights the ones of most interest to compensation analysts: locational, industry, organizational, or job factors.

Locational Factors

Organizations in different locations typically pay different wages for the same job. While this finding may seem self-apparent on an international, or even on a national or regional, basis, it also appears to hold true on a local basis.[13] A variety of explanations have attempted to account for locational wage differentials.[14] Differences in labor supply and demand from area to area is an obvious factor.[15] In local markets that experience a shortage of qualified employees, wage levels will tend to rise. Differences in the cost of living from area to area also impact wage levels even without formal cost-of-living adjustments. Thus, the East and West coasts traditionally have been high wage areas, while the South and Southwest have had lower wage levels. Urban wages typically exceed suburban, and rural wages rank still lower.

Within a local labor market, organizations may have to pay more because of location factors. Desirability of specific work sites, distance from residential areas, and ease of commuting all may affect wage levels. The availability of public services such as education,

Figure 1

Pay Difference Determinants

I. *External* to the Entity
   A. *Market* Factors
      1. Supply and Demand
         a. Learning time
         b. Experience and education
         c. Transferability of skills between industries
         d. Geographic transferability of skills
         e. Employee's perception of the job's desirability
         f. School(s) attended
      2. Union—impact of other entities' settlements
      3. Industry patterns or values
      4. Economic conditions
      5. Historical relationship of jobs
      6. Geographical pay differences
   B. Government Regulations and Laws

II. *Internal* to the Entity
   A. *Entity* Factors
      1. Definition of entity
      2. Union relationship
      3. Ability to pay
      4. Size
      5. Capital or labor intensive
      6. Other pecularities of industry
      7. Philosophies of the Entity
         a. Mix of pay and benefits—total compensation relataionship
         b. Relationship to market
         c. Historical job relationships
         d. Compensation policies, practices and procedures
         e. Part time/full time
         f. Entity's organizational approach
   B. *Job* Factors
      1. *Skill*
         a. Mental requirement
         b. Analytical ability
         c. Complexity of duties
         d. Personal qualifications needed
         e. Ability to make decisions
         f. Managerial techniques
         g. Character of supervision given
         h. Preparation for the job
         i. Essential education, training and/or knowledge
         j. Capacity for getting along with others
         k. Capacity for self expression

Figure 1 continued

      l. Ability to do detailed work
     m. Ability to do routine work
     n. Manual dexterity or motor skill
     o. Creative ability
     p. Judgment
     q. Initiative
     r. Resourcefulness
     s. Versatility/flexibility
     t. Previous experience
     u. Training time
     v. Social skill

2. *Effort*
     a. Physical requirement, effort or demand
     b. Mental effort
     c. Physical or mental fatigue
     d. Attention to details
     e. Pressure of work
     f. Attention span required
     g. Volume of work

3. *Responsibility* (for)
     a. Commitments, property, cash, or records
     b. Decision-making
     c. Supervision of others
     d. Work of others
     e. Financial results
     f. Contact with public, customers and personnel
     g. Dependability and accuracy
     h. Quality
     i. Effect of errors
     k. Material
     l. Equipment
     m. Confidential data
     n. Goodwill and public relations
     o. Work methods
     p. Determining company policy
     q. Contact with others

4. *Working Conditions*
     a. Job conditions
     b. Tangible surroundings
     c. Personal hazard

C. *Other* Factors
  1. Desirability of job—employee's perception
  2. Title
  3. Status
  4. Perquisites
  5. Security of pay
  6. Amount of risk involved

Figure 1 continued

       7. Value added by the employee's work
       8. Group productivity and incentives
       9. Job evaluation system used
      10. Hours of work
      11. Monotony
      12. Out-of-town travel

III. *Individual Employee*
   A. Seniority
   B. Experience
   C. Performance
      1. Productivity
      2. Individual incentives
   D. Potential/Promotability
   E. Personal Preferences

Source: Reprinted with permission from American Compensation Association. *Elements of Sound Base Pay Administration.* Scottsdale, AZ: American Compensation Association, copyright © 1981, p. 22.

---

access to shopping and other service facilities, and perceived level of safety can impact the desirability of a work site. When these factors are negatively perceived in the labor market, employers may have to raise salaries to attract sufficient employees.

Industry Factors

Different industries typically pay jobs at different levels. Dunlop was the first to describe "wage contours" within a local labor market, using as an example the union scale paid to truck drivers in Boston in 1953.[16] Drivers in the scrap iron and metal industry earned the lowest rate, at $1.27 per hour; drivers in the magazine delivery field earned the highest, at $2.49 per hour. Dunlop explained these differences largely as a function of differences in product markets.

Part of the explanation of the influence of product market, or industry, on salary level for a specific job is the association of that job with other jobs. An employee in an industry characterized by highly paid professional and technical employees likely will benefit from that association. Dunlop also maintained that historical accident could account for wage differentials. A new industry that competes with older industries for similar workers typically must pay more, and this differential once established is difficult to remove.

A more convincing explanation is intra-industry competitiveness.[17] If an employer pays substantially more for specific jobs than its competitors, the organization must either obtain higher productivity from its employees, or have some other competitive advantage (for example, patented processes), or be prepared to sacrifice profits. Since few employers meet these demands, pay levels tend to be similar within an industry. Differences in labor costs as a percentage of total costs and differential contributions of specific jobs to organizational outcomes help to explain interindustry differentials.

Organizational Factors

Many organizational factors have been shown to affect wage differentials. The most obvious factor is size, with large organizations tending to pay more for a given job than small organizations.[18] Another organizational factor generally recognized to influence wage level is the degree of union representation, with more heavily unionized employers paying higher wages.[19]

Less obvious organizational factors which impact wage levels may prove more difficult for compensation analysts to track down as they develop wage surveys. Ability to pay clearly serves as a constraint on an organization's choice of wage level. Organizational policies and practices also impact directly on wage levels.[20] Most organizations, for example, adopt a policy stating in which labor markets they will compete and the level of that competition. This level of competition defines both salary levels and benefits levels. Management styles, determinants of individual pay differentials (seniority, performance), and the job evaluation system may affect the level of compensation of any individual job. Even organizational career-ladder policies may affect the wage level of a specific job. For example, a job used as a short-term stepping stone to a more advanced position may receive lower compensation than a job seen as a long-term commitment with little or no chance for advancement.

The benefits offered and the level of those benefits reflect market and employee pressure, as well as the perceived social responsibility of the organization's managers. An organization that is geographically dispersed is more likely to establish a constant benefits package across units than a constant wage level. This tendency arises primarily because employers are more likely to develop and administer benefits centrally and usually view benefits as a membership reward rather than a function of job level or individual characteristics.

Finally, organizational demographics interact with policy and practice to impact wage levels for many jobs. An organization which rewards loyalty and/or seniority and which has an older, predominantly stable work force will probably have higher wage levels than an organization which rewards performance or which has mostly younger workers and a higher turnover rate. On the whole, seniority and performance differences between organizations should influence wage differentials between the two organizations. Demographics also interact with benefit choice and level. Total compensation in an organization offering child care reimbursement is likely to be greater if young females who head single-parent households dominate the employee population.

Job Factors

Job factors are more closely related to internal equity, but also must play a role in external equity estimates. Figure 1 lists nearly 50 specific job skills as pay differentials under the four broad headings of skill, effort, responsibility, and other. The probability of two different organizations having the same levels of each job attribute or requirement may be very small. In fact, most commercial wage and salary surveys recognize the likelihood of differences in job content by asking respondents to note whether the survey's standard job description overstates, understates, or matches the attributes of the respondent's job.

The Dynamics of External Equity Factors

Some aspects of external equity factors, such as wage contours, tend to be relatively stable over time.[21] On the other hand, recent responses to competitive disadvantage, such as two-tiered wage systems, may create permanent changes in wage differentials across industry sectors. More important to the compensation analyst, wage levels for different jobs are likely to change at different rates in different markets in response to differential changes in supply and demand.

These fluctuations impact a compensation program in several ways. If an organization uses a market pricing scheme to set internal wages, its internal wage hierarchy may change substantially from year to year. If only key jobs are priced in the market and used to build salary structures but those key jobs change in market value differently than other jobs, the compensation system may violate both internal and external equity norms. Regardless of the job pricing system in place, instability across jobs in market wage relationships makes it advisable for organizations to audit those relationships carefully and prepare a system allowing for frequent adjustments to wage structures or job placement in the structure.

External Equity and the Market

Economists have traditionally spoken of "wages clearing in the marketplace" as a result of the interaction of supply and demand factors. Textbook explanations of economic wage theory still rely on the monolithic labor market as an explanatory device, even though no single "market" exists. In fact, a whole series of labor markets exist, and while certain jobs may not have a distinct market (for example, the markets for Secretary I and Clerk-Typist I may overlap to some extent), a compensation analyst pricing a set of jobs must be prepared to define and track a whole series of local, regional, national, and even (perhaps) international labor markets.

Market Identification

The definition of relevant labor markets is a two-part effort for a compensation analyst. The first part is to determine which jobs to survey; the second is to decide which market(s) are relevant for each job, given the goals of the surveying organization. Since an organization will not always try to get market rates for every job, the survey should sample representative jobs and representative markets in which the organization competes for labor. Thus, if an organization competes primarily in local labor markets, its compensation analyst may oversample the few regional or national labor market jobs, or cut some local market jobs from the survey process.

Which Jobs to Survey

The jobs typically chosen for a survey will include most of the more important jobs in an organization. Incumbents will collectively make up a significant proportion of total employees. These jobs will vary in characteristics, especially in the job specifications used as compensable factors in a job evaluation system. Most jobs selected for a survey will have relatively stable tasks and specifications. However, an analyst will probably want to include any jobs that have high turnover or that prove difficult to fill, which may lead to the inclusion of jobs in transition. At one time, most compensation analysts concentrated their attention on 25 to 35 so-called "key" jobs. With the proliferation of survey data available at relatively low cost and the increasing numbers of organizations taking a market pricing approach to wage-setting, more analysts seem to be getting market information on all the jobs they can.

Which Markets to Use

Defining relevant markets has traditionally been done on the basis of geography. That is, an analyst considers the geographic area in which an organization will recruit, and the geographic area to which departing (and valuable) employees go. These geographic areas are likely to be the same, but not necessarily. An organization might, for example, hire MBAs only within a regional market but find that better ones leave through a national market.

The geographic splits traditionally used to define labor markets are local, regional, national, and international. For most jobs, and especially non-exempt jobs, the local labor market has been the most relevant one for comparison purposes. Some technical and professional job markets are regional; others are national. As the economy becomes increasingly globalized, international labor markets have begun to form for some international operations-related jobs.

Certain jobs may have "tiered" markets. For example, the labor market for MBAs is generally regional, but a national market exists for most MBAs from a few top schools and for a few MBAs from a slightly larger number of better schools. Business school faculty tend to classify schools as first-, second-, or third-tier; these classifications tend to parallel the market tiers for graduates fairly closely.

Not all organizations choose to define relevant markets in terms of geography. As noted earlier, one strategic approach to compensation practice defines "relevance" in terms of product market competitors. While an organization may adopt this approach across the board, a more likely approach would blend geographic and product-competitor definitions of relevance. Such an approach would start with product competitors as the initial market and then adjust downwards as the geographic market allowed. Only in exceptional circumstances (such as, inability to fill positions) would an organization match geographic rates which were higher.

Other market definitions might prove useful to organizations as well. Any of the factors explaining wage differentials discussed earlier might serve as a starting point in defining the relevant labor markets. In fact, most compensation analysts rely on these factors to identify good matches among other organizations and use the wage, salary, and benefit levels in those organizations as benchmarks for comparison purposes. While a consistent approach is aesthetically appealing (and may avoid litigation), research might indicate that different approaches with different jobs (or job families) would serve compensation goals better, and at lower cost.

Definition of Market Rates

The definition of market rates was, until recently, a relatively simple matter. Employees (other than those in sales and in upper management) got a fixed benefit package and a fixed base salary (or hourly wage). This situation is clearly no longer the case, and this change complicates the task for the compensation analyst trying to develop cost estimates for a total compensation package.

Comparison of benefit packages has always been difficult, but these comparisons have become nearly impossible given the widespread adoption of flexible benefit plans, the increase in defined contribution (as opposed to defined benefit) pension plans, the inclusion of co-payment and/or co-insurance costs, and the proliferation of various stock ownership and savings plans. In addition, the interaction between employee demographics and benefit plan details can make comparison data irrelevant. For example, day-care facilities will have more perceived value in an organization with many young single parents than in an organization with older employees, while the reverse would hold true for the relative value of nursing home insurance.

A final issue in the definition of a market rate is the appropriate statistic to use. Salary information typically is developed through a survey that takes into account the types of benefits available in respondent organizations but fails to attach benefit dollar values to salary figures. A compensation analyst must collect data on benefit dollar values separately and blend the two sources to determine total compensation for a job in some market.

Because rate distributions exist for both salary and benefit values, an analyst must select a statistic representing the most appropriate "point estimate," usually the arithmetic mean or the median of a distribution. Given the positive skew observed in most salary distributions associated with a single job, the average salary will almost always be higher than the median. That is, extremely high salaries in the distribution pull the average up but do not affect the middle value. Because those upper-end values are thought to be anomalies (due to the incumbent receiving extra pay for non-job reasons such as being related to the boss), many compensation analysts choose the median as the best point estimate of market value. The choice of median or arithmetic average does not impact the usefulness of the measure; that is, either may be used in multiple regression market pricing models or other salary determination processes. Consistent use of one or the other is important and analysts should note the measure used in documentation of salary determination methods.

Competitive Pay Strategies and Market Rates

After defining appropriate markets and appropriate market rates, employers still must determine the market level at which they choose to compete. In practice, competitive pay policies are probably less determined by organizational strategies than they ought to be. However, few empirical studies have investigated the impact of competitive pay policies on HR or organizational outcomes.[22]

It does seem clear that paying all jobs in an organization at the same rough market level is inappropriate. Such a policy implies that no one functional area of an organization has greater strategic importance than any other. If marketing "drives" a company and is the basis for organizational success, then management might well choose to follow a very competitive pay policy for all jobs in the marketing group, including secretarial and clerical employees, and to do so without resorting to title proliferation, special "series," or other subterfuges. In this example, an organization might compensate all marketing jobs at the 80th percentile of market distributions, even though compensation for similar jobs in other departments might match much lower market levels. In extreme cases, strategies might dictate that an organization use a multiplicity of market comparison levels both across and within jobs, departments, and organizational levels.

Figure 2

Lead, Lag, and Lead/Lag Policies

Lead Policy: Structure matches competitive pay at *end* of plan year.

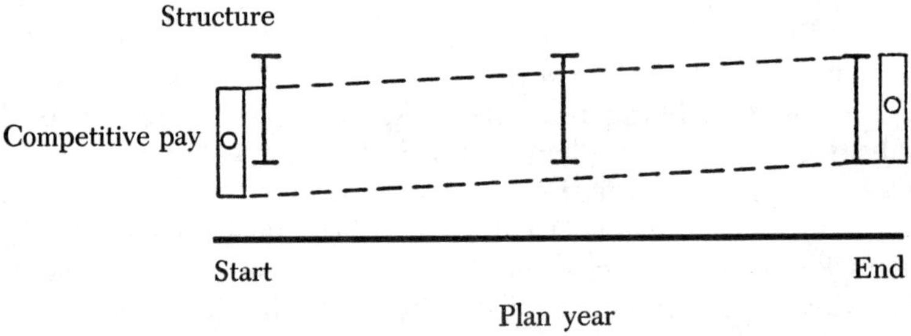

Lag Policy: Structure matches competitive pay at *start* of year

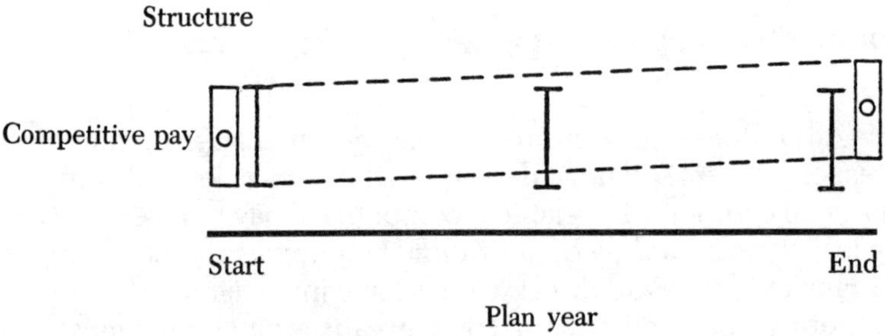

Lead/Lag Policy: Structure matches competitive pay at *middle* of plan year

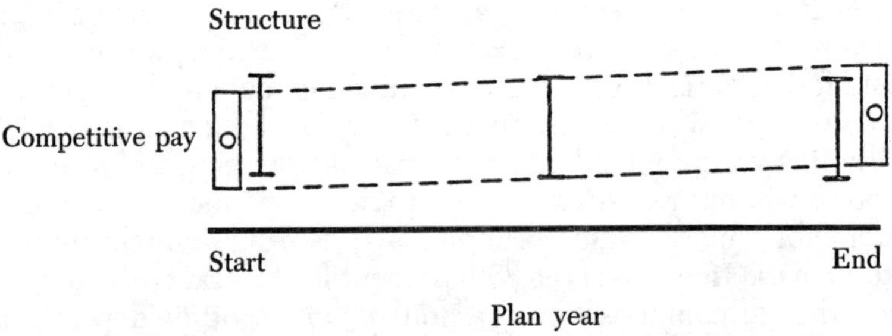

Source: Reprinted with permission from *Quantitative Analysis for Compensation Decision Making.* Scottsdale, AZ: American Compensation Association, copyright © 1989, pp. 4.7–4.9.

Lead, Lag, and Lead-Lag Strategies

Terminology in the matter of competitive pay policy is confused. Some compensation specialists refer to "leading" or "lagging" the market when talking about competitive pay policy. The American Compensation Association reserves these terms for a "time match" structural policy.[23] That is, market prices for labor are dynamic and move constantly throughout the year. In contrast, a wage and salary structure is static during the budget year. As a result, an organization must choose a single point in time at which its salary structure will match the market.

When an organization chooses to have its salary structure match the market at the beginning of the year, the structure will "lag" the market. That is, except for the first day of the year, the midpoints of the salary structure will fall below the midpoint of the market distribution. If a salary structure matches forecast market levels at the end of the year, a company has adopted a "lead" policy. By the end of the year the average market rate will catch up to the midpoints of the structure if market forecasts are accurate. Most organizations adopt a "lead-lag" policy; that is, they set structural midpoints to match the forecasted market levels at midyear.

A competitive pay policy relates to market level of actual salaries paid rather than the structure used to administer those salaries. For example, an organization may choose to pay its average employee higher than 65 percent of equivalent employees in relevant markets, or at the 65th percentile of the market. This practice is possible whether an organization operates within a lead, lag, or lead-lag structural policy.

The relationship of actual salary and structure is controlled through the competitive "compa-ratio." This index relates desired market position arising from an organization's competitive pay policy to its salary structure, and takes into account its structural policy (lead, lag, lead/lag). Figure 2 shows examples of competitive pay policies that match the market under lead, lag, and lead-lag structural policies.

Linkages to Business and HR Strategies

Organizations might be expected to tailor their competitive pay policy to match business strategies, or at least HR strategies. As noted previously, there is little real-life evidence of such practices or of the effect of such practices. Given that organizations tend to apply a competitive pay policy across the board (i.e., all jobs are paid at the 50th percentile of the market), strategic pay positioning seems to receive little attention. Otherwise, competitive pay policies would vary across jobs, with those jobs considered most important to achievement of organizational strategy pegged at higher market levels than other jobs. Strategy might even dictate differences in competitive pay policy within jobs across different departments of an organization.

The HR strategies which seem most closely linked to competitive pay policies are those related to attraction and retention. Job groups which present recruitment difficulties or which experience excessive voluntary turnover rates might be pegged at higher market rates than other job groups.

Business strategies most closely linked to competitive pay strategies are product market positioning strategies and related product pricing strategies. Jobs closely related to products with higher profit margin might be pegged at higher market rates. This competitive pay policy presumably might allow the attraction and retention of employees who can or will more readily maintain product quality or otherwise sustain the organization's competitive edge.

Wage and Salary Surveys

When organizations set wages for their employees, they typically make use of wage surveys. A 1986 survey by the Bureau of National Affairs, Inc. found that 93 percent of the respondents made use of wage and salary surveys in administering compensation programs, and 55 percent of survey users found them essential or absolutely necessary.[24] An additional 30 percent found surveys very helpful in administering a compensation program.

Organizations that use wage and salary surveys recognize the importance of the market in establishing competitive pay programs which can attract and retain employees. At one time, wage and salary surveys were conducted somewhat haphazardly (and many company-sponsored ones still are), but survey results were used casually. In contrast, many current uses of wage survey data, such as market-pricing models relying on multiple regression techniques, assume rigor in data collection and analysis, and a knowledge of survey methods and techniques has become necessary to interpret and apply survey findings.

The federal government uses market wages in a variety of restrictive legislation, and more recently concepts arising from antitrust legislation have been applied to wage survey methods. It has thus become important to understand the external equity concepts underlying the use of market surveys, and the relationship between external equity and internal and individual equity issues.

There are a large number of surveys available at a relatively low cost; unfortunately, the data reported for similar jobs varies greatly. While elaborate survey technology has been developed by marketing researchers, political scientists, sociologists, and other researchers who depend on getting valid and reliable estimates of economic, demographic, behavioral, and attitudinal characteristics of particular populations, most analysts doing salary surveys neglect this technology. One exception is the Bureau of Labor Statistics: it adheres to rigorous sampling and survey methods and publishes those methods along with the surveys so that the "goodness" of BLS data can be determined.[25]

Convenience and Judgment Samples

The most obvious shortcoming of most salary surveys is the absence of any rigorous sampling procedure. Sampling procedures for most wage and salary surveys can be characterized as convenience samples or judgment samples. A convenience sample is just that; a compensation analyst makes a few telephone calls to colleagues in other organizations and gets the going rate. Many commercial survey groups conduct a more elaborate form of the convenience sample by purchasing mailing lists known to include people or units with compensation responsibilities and using those lists as a sample.

Judgment samples are likewise appropriately named: A compensation analyst chooses a specific set of organizations thought to match to the surveying organization and those organizations form the sample. Many private and association surveys are based on judgment samples. If a compensation analyst surveyed only those employers who had successfully outbid the surveying organization for desirable job applicants, or who formed the major destination of voluntary quits, or who served as a major source of job applicants, that survey would constitute a judgment sampling strategy.

Flaws Affecting Survey Data

The problem with convenience and judgment sampling strategies is that analysts have little or no idea of how well sample statistics represent population parameters. Depending on the use made of survey results, this problem may not matter that much, particularly if a judgment sample is used and the judgment of the analyst is good. Unfortunately, only after the consequences of decisions made on the basis of survey results begin to appear will the representativeness of survey results become clear.

Most salary surveys have other problems beyond sampling. A number of problems with surveys in general also apply to salary surveys.[26] Typical concerns include whether survey questions are explicit and capable of being answered by respondents, use clear terminology, provide exhaustive but non-overlapping categories, and allow sufficient space for answering. These issues probably flaw more benefits surveys than salary surveys.

Wage surveys do have some unique problems. The most serious issue concerns assurance of accurate job match. Almost all wage survey forms include short job descriptions for sampled jobs. More sophisticated surveys request respondents to note whether their salary data for a job is a direct match, or somewhat higher or lower than the one described (and therefore deserving of more/less compensation).

A second problem peculiar to salary surveys has resulted from the explosion of "at risk" forms of pay, some based on individual performance and some based on organizational profitability.[27] Base pay is becoming a smaller part of the total compensation package for an increasingly broader range of employees, making it unclear what incumbents in a job actually make. It is certainly more difficult to make comparisons across very different pay systems. When "at risk" pay may take the form of lump sum bonuses, payments into employee stock ownership or savings plans, or additional time off with pay, comparison of salary figures which may include only base pay or direct cash payouts becomes misleading.

A third problem concerns the use of survey data rather than its collection. Survey data typically is collected three to six months before a new salary structure based on the data goes into effect. Thus, the surveying organization must estimate market movements during the intervening period and then "age" the survey data to take this movement into account. The organization must make further adjustments to the structure if it adopts a lead or lead/lag structural policy. The data thus accurately reflect market prices only to the extent that estimates of market movement in the two periods are accurate.

Assets of Using Surveys

Despite the obvious drawbacks of salary surveys, the alternatives to current practice may be less desirable. Few organizations could routinely bear the cost of "pure" sampling and survey techniques. It is also unclear whether greater precision is necessary. The purported purpose of a survey is to make sure that wages offered to current and prospective employees will match wages in relevant markets. Since neither prospective nor current employees will have a good sample of market wages for comparison, employers may need only an approximation of market levels for salary setting purposes.[28]

In addition, most organizations (which do not follow a pure market pricing strategy) adjust survey data to create the salary structure. A compensation analyst may average market medians for five different jobs obtained from three different surveys to create a midpoint of a salary range. Differences between midpoints may then be adjusted to "smooth" midpoint progression. To quibble about the purity of the data used as the starting point of such a process is akin to arguing about the freshness of the egg in the cake you let burn.

Standard Surveys

A description of even the major surveys is beyond the scope of this chapter. Descriptions with sample pages from many of the major wage and salary, and benefit surveys can be found in the standard compensation textbooks.[29] In addition, the major looseleaf services (for example, Bureau of National Affairs, Commerce Clearing House, Prentice Hall) carry comprehensive listings of surveys available in their volumes on compensation. These services also usually report highlights of findings from major surveys.

There are three major external sources of survey data. The U.S. government conducts wage surveys as part of its responsibilities in enforcing Davis-Bacon and other federal contractor pay regulation statutes. These surveys are probably the best available in terms of survey technique, but job coverage and time lapse between data collection and publication limit their use. In fact, Bureau of Labor Statistics Surveys were the least frequently used of any type of wage survey reported in a recent study.[30]

The most frequently used surveys reported in the same study are ones conducted by industry or professional associations, or by associations of employers in a geographic area. The quality of these surveys varies greatly, but all are more likely to give users a closer match in the type of jobs and the market cut desired (for example, production wages in the chemical industry or clerical wages in downtown Pittsburgh).

The third major source of wage data is the commercially available surveys conducted by consultants and survey companies. Organizations reporting survey usage in the study mentioned earlier relied almost as much on commercial surveys as on association surveys. The quality of these surveys varies somewhat, but most are competently conducted and provide useful data.

Linkages Between Market Data and Internal Pay Relationships

After collecting market information, a compensation analyst must relate these findings to the internal job value hierarchy and build a salary structure. Techniques used for this task vary primarily in the relative emphasis paid to internal and external equity issues. Pure market pricing systems pay little attention to internal pay relationships; other pay structure approaches use market data only to price a structure based on internal value relationships.

Market Pricing

In a pure market pricing system, each job is paid at market rate (or some consistent level such as 65th percentile). This approach requires an organization to collect market data on all jobs possible and then use a model to estimate market rates for positions which lack an actual market. Employers typically regress actual market wage data on job analysis information (e.g., education required, number of employees supervised) to develop a multiple regression model. This model is then used to provide best estimates of market wages for other jobs in the organization. This approach creates a salary program which ignores any separate consideration of internal pay relationships.

Pay Policy Lines

Organizations that adopt a pay policy line approach use a regression model similar to the model of the market pricing approach. However, instead of paying market rates for those jobs which have actual market prices, an organization pays all jobs based on the regression model. (Exceptions are made for jobs seriously underpriced by the model.) This approach recognizes internal equity issues in two ways. First, an organization is more likely to use job scores from traditional job evaluation scales as independent variables in the regression model. This practice contrasts with market pricing models, which are likely to consider a wider set of variables. In addition, use of this model to price all jobs assures that job attributes are consistently weighted across jobs.

Pay Grades Approach

A pay grade strategy usually places more emphasis on job evaluation processes and internal equity considerations than on market rates.[31] This approach first divides an organization's total range of job evaluation scores either into arbitrary sets to provide the desired number of job grades, or into sets determined by natural clustering of job evaluation scores. Next, market data for sets of jobs in each range are averaged to produce midpoints for the grades. These initial midpoints are usually adjusted to provide an even progression of midpoints. Finally, all jobs with job evaluation scores in the same grade are priced at the same level. This series of averaging and clustering operations tends to produce a salary structure that emphasizes similarity in job evaluation scores rather than similarity in market rates.

Microcomputers and Job Pricing

The introduction of microcomputers has brought significant changes in organizational practice. Access to microcomputers has increased the amount of analysis done on survey data and has emphasized collection of specialized market data that more narrowly mirrors an organization's characteristics. Until regression packages became available, market pricing and policy line approaches proved difficult to implement, especially in large organizations. Out of necessity, most organizations used pay grade approaches that treated jobs consistently with respect to market levels, since calculating pay ranges for each job based on different pay level policies was an overpowering task.

The commercial software packages now available allow sophisticated modeling of market data for different jobs.[32] Analysts can play "what if" scenarios, estimating the impact of various pay policies, market movements, and organizational shifts on total salary costs. The next logical development would be a major on-line data base of wage, salary, and benefit survey data. Analysts tapping into such a data base could get best estimates of market data for specific jobs, taking into account all the organizational, employee demographic, industry, and locational factors described earlier. Organizations also could adjust data and forecast figures for future time periods based on past experience, economic forecasts, and other factors.

Regulation of Organizational Market Policies and Practices

Federal and state legislation regulating wages has the important effect of constraining market levels for wages. Legislation which affects organizational market policies and practices falls in three areas. The first area, embodied in the Fair Labor Standards Act, defines minimum standards for all employers with respect to wage bargaining. The second thrust of legislation sets special standards for employers who receive income derived from federal (or in some states, other public) funds. The third thrust, based on interpretations of antitrust legislation, regulates the process by which employers "discover" market rates and assures that the method used to collect market information does not become a conspiracy to fix wages.

Fair Labor Standards Act

The Fair Labor Standards Act, passed in 1938, contains provisions addressing minimum wage, overtime pay, gender discrimination in pay, child labor laws, and recordkeeping requirements for support of the Act. The two provisions relevant to external pay relationships deal with minimum wage and overtime.

Minimum Wage

The minimum wage provisions of the Fair Labor Standards Act set the lower limits of wages that can be paid to most workers.

While some workers are exempt from these provisions (for example, students working for schools or colleges, apprentices), most workers at the lowest wage levels are "nonexempts" who must be paid minimum wage.

The federal minimum wage has been set at $3.35 since 1981, but recent proposals could impact minimum wage laws significantly. One revision under debate would raise the minimum wage level, possibly to $4.85, to be achieved in several steps. A second proposal would exempt certain employees from the minimum wage provisions in an effort to reduce the level of youth unemployment.

In addition to the federal law, states also have minimum wage laws. Some states have passed a higher minimum wage, while others have set the minimum wage at the federal level, or lower, but have extended coverage to workers not covered by federal law.[33]

Overtime

Overtime provisions of the Fair Labor Standards Act regulate the wage effort bargain for covered employees. Overtime provisions require covered employers to pay time and one half to nonexempt employees for all hours worked in excess of 40 hours per week. The act provides some exceptions; for example, hospitals may operate on the basis of 80 hours over 14 consecutive days. Some states also have passed legislation regulating overtime. State regulations primarily differ from federal law in that some require overtime pay for hours worked in excess of 8 per day.[34]

Prevailing Wage Legislation

A number of federal and state laws requires organizations that receive income from public funds to pay their workers at prevailing market rates. The following sections highlight important aspects of three such laws: the Davis-Bacon Act, the Walsh-Healey Public Contracts Act, and the McNamara-O'Hara Service Contract Act.

Davis-Bacon Act and Similar State Laws

The Davis-Bacon Act of 1931 is one of three federal statutes (along with Walsh-Healey and the Service Contract acts) requiring that employers who work for the U.S. government (whether directly or indirectly) pay "prevailing wages" to employees. The difficulty of separating wages related to government business from other wages, along with the perceived inequity of doing so, means that most employers covered by prevailing wage legislation pay all employees the prevailing wage. Organizations following a market-oriented strategy, however, might choose to make such distinctions.

The Davis-Bacon Act applies to all laborers and mechanics employed on federal or federally assisted contracts worth in excess of $2000 for construction, alteration, repair, painting, or decorating of public buildings or public works. The act requires employers to provide the wage rates and fringe benefits found by the Secretary of Labor to prevail in an area. Since 1985, "prevailing wages" have been defined as the rate paid to at least 50 percent of individuals in a designated class of workers.[35] The major determinant of a prevailing wage appears to be the union rate in the locality.[36] The Congressional Budget Office has estimated that average wages on Davis-Bacon projects are about 5.3 percent higher for building construction and about 5.4 percent higher for residential construction projects.[37] The Grace Commission estimated that total excess costs on federally funded construction projects attributable to Davis-Bacon regulations range between $1 and $2 billion annually.[38]

Thirty-four states and the District of Columbia also have prevailing wage laws. These laws generally apply Davis-Bacon precepts to projects funded with state money.[39]

Walsh-Healey Act

The Walsh-Healey Public Contracts Act of 1936 applies to federal contractors holding contracts for the manufacture or provision of materials, supplies, or equipment in excess of $10,000. Walsh-Healey requires federal contractors to pay covered employees the "minimum prevailing rate" for "persons employed on similar work or in the particular or similar industries or groups of industries" rather than the prevailing rate. Thus, the act really impacts only the lowest paid workers.[40]

Service Contract Act

The McNamara-O'Hara Service Contract Act of 1965 extends Davis-Bacon concepts to the services sector of government contracting. For contractors doing business in excess of $2500, employees must be paid not less than the wage rates and fringe benefits found by the Secretary of Labor to prevail in the area, or those contained in the previous contractor's collective bargaining agreement. The impact of the Service Contract Act is estimated to cost on the order of $500 million a year.[41]

Antitrust Legislation

The Sherman Act and the Clayton Act prohibit any activities which restrain trade. The laws apply to buyers as well as sellers; thus employers who act in concert to fix wages violate the acts. Employers who participate in wage surveys also could be charged with wage fixing.[42] This possibility becomes particularly acute if participating employers restrict the survey to a single industry, provide individual employee rates, and discuss future intentions with respect to wage increases, even though no collusion may take place. An informal local meeting in which representatives from major employers in a market discuss wages in specific job categories is probably inadvisable. However, participation in the types of surveys (discussed earlier in this chapter) is unlikely to present any cause for concern.

Auditing and Evaluating External Equity Processes

Organizations should audit and evaluate their compensation programs to make sure that the programs achieve their intended ends at a reasonable cost. As more organizations start thinking in terms of compensation strategy, auditing becomes both more feasible and more necessary.

Auditing Approaches

The specific criteria for an audit will depend on the goals of the compensation strategy. External equity audits generally examine whether salaries do in fact match the competitive levels suggested by the pay policy, and whether the markets covered by wage and salary or benefit surveys are appropriate for the organization's comparison purposes. If organizations adopt policies favoring differential compensation levels for different jobs based on a position's strategic value, the audit also investigates the impact of such policies on protected groups.

A continuing analysis of individual surveys can prove as worthwhile as an audit. Do different surveys purporting to cover the same markets provide similar kinds of data? Do the salary increases forecasted one year match the actual increases reported the following year? Both cross-sectional and longitudinal comparisons of this sort will help an analyst identify the most useful surveys.

Compensation managers should probably become more familiar with sampling and survey methods and ask for information on those methods from vendors. They should also use better methods when they run their own surveys.

Evaluation Approaches

Most evaluation approaches that address external equity issues are related to staffing success and cost. Information on refusal of employment offers by job type may indicate faulty data due to improper market definition or poor survey methods. This information may also suggest a faulty competitive pay policy for that job. While many causes can create refusal of job offers, a cluster of refusals suggests that pay may be an issue. Follow-up interviews with applicants rejecting (and accepting) offers can provide insight into perceived and actual market rates.

Organizations should also evaluate voluntary turnover due to noncompetitive salaries. If valued employees leave for other employers, exit interview data should be analyzed to determine the cause. As before, when voluntary turnover clusters around specific jobs, faulty pay policy may be a cause. In addition, voluntary turnover rates of other employees should receive scrutiny. If few poor performers leave, salary rates may be too high.

When evaluating compensation costs, employers should investigate the probable effects of changes in competitive pay policy, installation of differential pay policies for different jobs, and the degree to which compensation is tied to the market. Such an evaluation would compare the actual and opportunity costs of several different combinations to find the set which maximizes organizational goal achievement.

Organizations which use compensation as a strategic tool clearly need to audit and evaluate the success of their program in achieving strategic goals. First, if an employer uses market positioning policies to communicate internally the differential importance of jobs, then employees should recognize such differences and see them as equitable, given organizational strategy. A second strategic issue to examine is whether the compensation program serves to attract and retain capable and motivated employees at the level of capability and motivation required by jobs. Differential positioning strategies should produce optimal mixes of employees who perform well at the lowest cost. However, achievement of organizational goals can not be attributed solely to an appropriate strategic compensation program, and particularly not to external market relationships. To the extent possible, organizations should attempt to determine what portion of strategic success is attributable to market positioning.

Summary

Organizations have always based compensation programs in large part on labor market information. As more detailed market information has become available, this reliance has increased. The increase in strategy-based compensation programs has required refinements and changes in market definitions and facilitated differential positioning of jobs in the market. At the same time, the advent of microcomputers has made possible the development and administration of compensation programs of such increased complexity.

◆

Notes

1. Wallace and Fay, p. 20.
2. Rynes, Schwab, and Heneman III.
3. Doeringer and Piore; Robinson.
4. Risher and Fay.
5. Milkovich; Fay (1987).
6. Schuler.
7. Rynes.
8. Wallace and Fay.
9. Mahoney, pp. 367–381.
10. Ibid.
11. C. Kerr, cited in Robinson.
12. See, for example, Douty; Fay, Wallace, and Crandall.
13. Rees and Schultz.
14. Cropper and Arriaga-Salina.
15. Johnson and Ash.
16. Dunlop.
17. Reynolds.
18. Lester.
19. Mitchell.
20. Lester.
21. Dunlop.
22. Milkovich; Ehrenberg and Milkovich.
23. Fay (1989).
24. Bureau of National Affairs, Inc. (1986).
25. U.S. Department of Labor.
26. Fay and Wallace.
27. O'Dell.
28. Granovetter.
29. Milkovich and Newman; Wallace and Fay.
30. Risher and Fay.

31. Schwab, p. 68, notes that "as practiced, job evaluation chooses and weights factors to conform to a wage distribution which is assumed to be appropriate, i.e., reflects the market."
32. For a directory of commercial software for compensation, see Frantzreb.
33. For detailed information on state minimum wage law, see Bureau of National Affairs, Inc. (1987).
34. For detailed information on state overtime legislation, see Bureau of National Affairs, Inc. (1985).
35. Thiebolt, p. 14.
36. Ibid, p. 69.
37. Ibid, p. 96.
38. Berg and Erickson.
39. Thiebolt, pp. 137–205.
40. Ibid, p. 212.
41. Ibid, p. 265.
42. Fisher.

◆

References

Berg, J.T., and R.C. Erickson. 1985. "An Evaluation of the Impact of the Davis-Bacon Act." *Government Union Review* 6, 3 (Summer): 1–32.

Bureau of National Affairs, Inc. 1981. Personnel Policy Forum Survey No. 131, "Wage and Salary Administration." (July).

———. 1987. "Comparison Chart—State Minimum Wage." In *Compensation*, BNA Policy and Practice Series.

Cropper, M.L. and A.S. Arriaga-Salinas. 1980. "Inter-City Wage Differentials and the Value of Air Quality." *Journal of Urban Economics* 8: 236–254.

Doeringer, P. and M. Piore. 1975. *Internal Labor Markets and Manpower Analysis.* Lexington, MA: Heath.

Dunlop, J.T. 1957. "The Task of Contemporary Wage Theory." In *New Concepts in Wage Determination*, ed. G.W. Taylor and F.C. Pierson. New York: McGraw-Hill.

Douty, H.M. 1961. "Sources of Occupational Wage and Salary Dispersion Within Labor Markets." *Industrial and Labor Relations Review* 15: 67–74.

Ehrenberg, R.G. and G.T. Milkovich. *Compensation and Firm Performance.* Working Paper No. 2145. Washington, DC: National Bureau of Economic Research.

Fay, C.H. 1987. "Developing a Compensation Strategy." *Topics in Total Compensation: Compensation Strategies for Achieving Organizational Objectives* 2, 20: 117–128.

———. ed. 1989. *Glossary of Compensation Terms.* 2nd ed. Scottsdale, AZ: American Compensation Association.

Fay, C.H., and M.J. Wallace Jr. 1987. *Research-Based Decisions.* New York: 1987.

Fay, C.H., M.J. Wallace Jr., and N.F. Crandall. 1980. "Internal and External Determinants of Salaries in a Local Labor Market." Paper delivered at the 42nd Annual Meeting of the Academy of Management, August.

Fisher, G.D. 1985. "Salary Surveys—An Antitrust Perspective." *Personnel Administrator* 30, 4 (April): 87 ff.

Frantzreb, R.B. 1987. "Microcomputer Software: What's New in HRM." *Personnel Administrator* 32, 7 (July): 67–100.

Granovetter, M. 1981. "Toward a Sociological Theory of Income Differences." In *Sociological Perspectives on Labor Markets*, ed. I. Berg. New York: Academic Press.

Johnson, N.B. and R.A. Ash. 1986. "Integrating the Labor Market with Job Evaluation: Clearing the Cobwebs." Paper delivered at the 1st Annual Conference of the Society for Industrial and Organizational Psychology, Inc., Chicago, April 10.

Lester, R.A. 1952. "A Range of Theory of Wage Differentials." *Industrial and Labor Relations Review* 5: 483–500.

Mahoney, T.A. 1979. "Toward an Integrated Theory of Compensation." In *Compensation and Reward Perspectives*, ed. T.A. Mahoney. Homewood, IL: Richard D. Irwin, Inc.

Milkovich, G.T. In press. "A Strategic Perspective to Compensation Management." In *Research in Human Resource Management*, ed. K. Rowland and G. Ferris. Greenwich, CT: JAI Press.

Milkovich, G.T. and J. Newman. 1987. *Compensation*, 2nd ed. Plano, TX: Business Publications Inc.

Mitchell, D.J.B. 1980. *Unions, Wages and Inflation*. Washington, DC: Brookings Institution.

O'Dell, C. 1987. *People, Performance and Pay*. Houston: American Productivity Center.

Rees, A. and G.P. Schultz. 1970. *Workers and Wages in an Urban Labor Market*. Chicago: University of Chicago Press.

Reynolds, L.G. 1967. "Pay Differentials by Size of Establishmnent." *Industrial Relations* 7: 57–67.

Risher, H.W. and C.H. Fay. 1987. "Salary Management Practices in the Private Sector; a Survey Conducted for the U.S. Advisory Committee on Federal Pay." Philadelphia: The Wyatt Company.

Robinson, D. 1870. "External and Internal Labor Markets." In *Local Labour Markets and Wage Structures*. London: Gower Press.

Rynes, S.L. 1987. "Compensation Strategies for Recruiting." *Topics in Total Compensation: Compensation Strategies for Achieving Organizational Objectives* 2, 2: 185–196.

Rynes, S.L., D.P. Schwab, and H.G. Heneman III. 1983. "The Role of Pay and Market Pay Variability in Job Application Decisions." *Organizational Behavior and Human Performance* 31: 353–364.

Schuler, R.S. 1987. "Personnel and Human Resource Management Choices and Organizational Strategy." *Human Resources Planning* 10, 1: 1–17.

3-100   Compensation & Benefits

Scwab, D.P. 1980. "Job Evaluation and Pay Setting: Concepts and Practices. In *Comparable Worth: Issues and Alternatives*, ed. E.R. Livernash. Washington, DC: Equal Employment Advisory Council.

Thiebolt, A.J. Jr. 1986. *Prevailing Wage Legislation: The Davis-Bacon Act, State "Little Davis-Bacon" Acts, The Walsh-Healy Act, and the Service Contract Act.* Philadelphia: University of Pennsylvania.

U.S. Department of Labor, Bureau of Labor Statistics. 1986. *BLS Measures of Compensation*, Bulletin No. 2239. Washington, DC: U.S. Government Printing Office.

Wallace, M.J. Jr., ed. 1984. *Glossary of Compensation Terms.* Scottsdale, AZ: American Compensation Association.

Wallace, M.J. Jr. and C.H. Fay. 1987. *Compensation Theory and Practice.* Boston: Kent Publishing Company.

———— ◆ ————

3.4

Employee Benefits and Services

Robert M. McCaffery

Over the past 50 years, employee benefits have advanced from serving as minor enhancements on the "fringe" of wages to become an essential collection of services, allowances, pay supplements, and income protections representing a substantial portion of employer payroll expense. For 1987, the U.S. Chamber of Commerce estimated the total cost of employee benefits in the United States at $814 billion, about 36 percent of wage and salary payments.[1] A number of forces account for this growth, and the following discussion summarizes the most noteworthy influences.

Employer initiatives and innovations. With the assistance, and sometimes prodding, of a burgeoning consulting industry, employers have progressively expanded their benefits packages to include an assortment of plans designed to satisfy employee needs and wants while supporting organization objectives.

Favorable federal tax policies. Subject to some limitations, employers can deduct their current expenditures, and employees have received benefits on a tax-free or tax-deferred basis.

Imitation of Western Europe. Although European employers rely more on government leadership than U.S. employers do, our Social Security, workers' compensation, and unemployment insurance programs tend to follow many of the public policy directions taken earlier by Great Britain, Germany, and France. European-based companies' vacation and holiday policies also have influenced paid time-off benefits in the United States.

Labor union efforts. Buoyed by federal labor laws that make virtually all benefits mandatory subjects for collective bargaining, unions have successfully extended employer-sponsored coverages to large numbers of workers through national pattern-setting contracts. Lobbying by major international unions also has greatly influenced the statutory benefit programs and workers' rights in private plans.

Increasing employee awareness. As employees became familiar with the advantages of basic benefits, perceptions of the special values and tax-efficiencies of benefits grew. As coverages became more diverse, the concept of trade-offs between pay and benefits gained popularity. This phenomenon became evident during the 1980s with the rapid growth of 401(k) plans and flexible or cafeteria compensation arrangements.

By the late 1970s, the need for unified direction in employee benefits activity had become evident. Up to that time, management of various benefit plans tended to be diffuse and HR departments commonly took a subordinate role to finance and insurance departments. In fact, for many years the American Management Association grouped its employee benefits education courses in the insurance division.

But today most employers realize that because benefits form a key ingredient in a complex system of rewards and compensation, an HR department must have primary management responsibility for the benefit function to succeed. As a result, HR managers are gradually acquiring the requisite expertise to meet that responsibility through a combination of professional education and experiential learning.

Strategic Issues in Benefits Planning

In small companies, personnel administrators are generalists who manage employee benefits along with a myriad of other activities. The number and diversity of duties facing HR managers in small companies can impede their ability to handle broad strategies. In larger firms, top HRM executives rarely handle day-to-day benefits minutia but, as a result, they may lose touch with current developments. Irrespective of organization size, top HR managers must find a way to play an active role in the overall planning for employee benefits. Key considerations to address in benefits planning include organizational objectives, work-force characteristics, legal requirements, benefits' cost and competitiveness, and total compensation strategy.

Organizational Objectives

For a benefits plan to succeed, it must match an organization's overall business directions and internal culture. In particular, HR managers should examine an organization's strategic business plan and its HRM philosophy before selecting a benefits program.

Strategic Business Plan

A strategic plan outlines the basic directions in which an organization is expected to head over the next three to five years. Strategic issues that could influence benefit plan decisions include employment growth, downsizing, geographic redeployment, acquisitions, centralization/de-centralization, and changes in profitability.

HRM Philosophy

An organization's fundamental assumptions about employees and about the nature of the employer-employee relationship form its HRM philosophy. It may be partially expressed in a written document, but it is more subtly demonstrated by management actions and attitudes. The balance between egalitarianism and executive privileges, the sense of social obligation to employees and retirees, and the importance of seniority in individual reward systems are philosophical issues that have implications for employee benefit plans.

Work-Force Characteristics

The design of a benefits package should suit its primary users— employees. Benefits planners should pay particular attention to employees' needs and to the status of unions within the organization.

Employee Needs

Heightened awareness of benefits and recognition of the value of various trade-offs have made employees increasingly unwilling to accept inflexible benefits programs. Yet most managements now avoid committing funds to plans unless some evidence shows that employees will perceive the benefits as relevant and useful.

Unions

When some employees are covered by collective bargaining agreements, an organization's labor relations goals and objectives must factor into benefit planning. Relevant issues to weigh include the timing of plan changes relative to contract re-negotiations; whether to offer identical, parallel, or unrelated coverages for non-represented employees; and the extent to which bargaining unit members should participate in companywide plans initiated prior to union recognition.

In a non-union setting, an organization's posture regarding continuation of a union-free status will affect the nature of employee benefits. The types and levels of benefits secured by unions in the same industry and/or area are important standards of comparison in a union avoidance strategy.

Tax and Social Legislation

While federal tax law has largely favored employee benefits, the Internal Revenue Code has undergone numerous shifts in policy and changes in specific provisions over the years. Since the mid-1980s Congress has progressively imposed limits on plan features that discriminate in favor of highly compensated employees. A notable example of this is IRC section 89 which was created by the Tax Reform Act of 1986. In addition, two types of social legislation have had major implications for employee benefits management. The first type concerns laws covering such programs as Social Security, workers' compensation, and unemployment compensation. These regulations mandate employer contributions and provide a foundation of benefit protections for employees and their dependents. The second group of laws include the Employee Retirement Income Security Act of 1974 (ERISA), the Retirement Equity Act of 1984 (REA), and the Consolidated Omnibus Budget Reconciliation Act of 1985 (COBRA). These laws secure employee benefits and rights in pension and welfare plans sponsored by employers.

Effective benefits planning requires a thorough grasp of both current provisions and scheduled changes in the various laws dealing with taxation and social issues. Benefits planners also must be alert to pending legislation and regulations as well as to emerging issues. HRM executives can usually obtain much useful assistance in this area from the staffs of professional, trade, and industry associations.

Program Competitiveness and Cost

The issue of benefits program competitiveness is much more complicated than the question of salary level competitiveness. In assessing the latter, both employees and management focus on the same item: salary. For an employee, salary represents a benefit received; for management, it is a discrete expenditure.

In determining benefits competitiveness, senior management tends to focus mainly on cost, while employees are more interested in value. HRM strategists may discover that satisfying employee perceptions of competitive program values can lead to excessive costs in the eyes of top management, while achieving cost competitiveness provides no assurance that employees will perceive the program positively.

Some firms have begun to solve this predicament by introducing cafeteria-type plans. These plans allow exchanges of cash and benefits that effectively separate the cost of benefit plans from their form. This concept will be discussed more fully later in this chapter.

Another consideration related to competitiveness concerns the cost of a benefit program. Although cost issues are inescapable, HR managers should keep these concerns in a balanced perspective. Detailed cost analyses of benefits proposals ideally should follow identification and evaluation of employee wants and needs. Then, with the involvement of financial, tax, and insurance specialists, HR planners can collect and analyze cost data on a variety of alternative approaches for satisfying organizational objectives.

Total Compensation Strategy

In order to make a budgetary allocation covering all employee compensation, each organization should prospectively establish an optimum mix of pay and benefits. This determination requires a full understanding of all the foregoing issues concerning employee compensation and must integrate salary and benefits in a package that will best achieve organizational goals and objectives. Responsibility for establishing this balance now almost always lies within the HRM function.

Types of Benefit Plans

A widely accepted concept posits that direct forms of employee compensation, such as salary and wage payments, create an employee's basic standard of living, whereas indirect compensation or benefits serve to protect a standard of living. This viewpoint can prove very helpful in understanding the core elements of group benefit programs and the coverages that employees tend to value most.

The five principal types of income protection offered by group benefit plans are medical expense benefits, disability income replacement, retirement income replacement, income continuation following involuntary termination, and payments for survivors. The following discussion examines each of these sources of income protection, along with three other benefit categories: time off with pay, miscellaneous benefits, and flexible benefit plans.

Medical Expense Benefits

Many employees perceive a plan providing medical coverage as *the* benefits package, and the meaning of the word "benefits" often seems synonymous with coverage for hospital, physician and laboratory charges. This perception became heightened through legislation enacted in 1986 which allowed employees and dependents to continue group health benefits, at their own expense, for a limited period following such events as an employee's death or other termination of employment.

The United States remains unique among major nations in not having a universal social insurance system ensuring a basic level of medical care for all of its citizens. The enactment of Medicare took a step in that direction, and Congress began to seriously consider minimum health benefits legislation in 1988. However, employers continue to bear the prime responsibility for providing this protection to employees and their families, and organizations have a great deal of latitude in plan design and financing arrangements.

The early group plans tended to provide only hospital and surgical expense benefits, but coverage has expanded progressively, largely due to the influence of major labor unions. Today, medical benefit plans commonly recognize expenses for alcoholism and drug abuse treatment, health care while at home or in an extended care facility, and dental care. Because of widened coverage and escalating costs of services, group health benefits have become a burdensome expense for many employers. According to a Johnson & Higgins study of some 1,600 companies, the average cost of health benefits per employee was $2,354 in 1988, an increase of 18.7 percent over the previous year.[2]

To cope with the continuing challenge of cost pressures, organizations now pursue a variety of strategies, including creation of health plan cost management staff positions. The most notable effects of employer cost containment efforts during this decade include the following.

Increased Cost Sharing

In addition to added payroll deductions for premium costs, cost sharing has resulted in higher deductible levels and employee copayment requirements for eligible expenses. An Administrative Management Society survey of 2,512 North American companies revealed that 44 percent of the companies footed the full cost of medical expense coverage in 1987 compared with 52 percent in 1985.[3]

Plan Design Changes

The structure of benefit plans has undergone a striking shift away from a two-tier design to a comprehensive plan. Two-tier consists of a base plan, with no deductible or copayments, plus a superimposed major medical plan with a deductible and copayments. Use of these plans declined from 62 to 27 percent between 1982 and 1986 according to a national survey of 263 employers.[4] The same survey found that use of comprehensive plans, which feature an initial deductible of $100 or more and employee copayments thereafter, rose from 37 to 72 percent during that period. In addition to shifting costs to employees, comprehensive benefit plans feature a more rational construction which makes a plan easier to administer and explain. (See Figure 1.)

Financing and Funding Alternatives

Employers no longer rely entirely on commercial insurors or Blue Cross-Blue Shield associations to deliver group health benefits. Two factors have altered that pattern in this decade. Alternative delivery systems, such as health maintenance organizations (HMOs)

Figure 1

Alternative Medical Plan Designs

1. *Basic Plan plus Supplemental Major Medical Coverage*
   (Early Model)

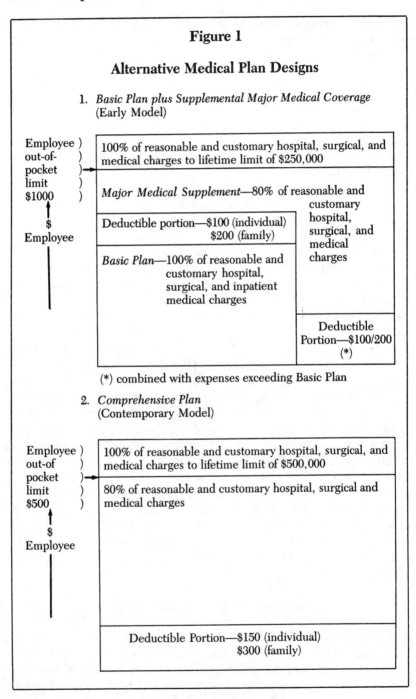

(*) combined with expenses exceeding Basic Plan

2. *Comprehensive Plan*
   (Contemporary Model)

and preferred provider organizations (PPOs), have emerged to become significant factors in the health care market. In addition, the use of self-funding mechanisms, primarily by large and medium firms, has become extensive. The resulting price competition among delivery sources has greatly expanded the ways in which group health plans are now financed and funded.

Despite initial reservations regarding the dual choice alternative mandated by the Health Maintenance Act of 1973, many employers now find this prepaid system of health care to be cost effective because of its emphasis on preventive measures. The HMO Act Amendments of 1988 also provided greater flexibility in determining employer contributions to HMOs in which their employees enroll and repealed the mandatory dual choice provision effective October 24, 1995.

A PPO is a network of providers who negotiate and contract with employers and insurors to provide health care services at discounted rates. They are not covered by any of the special regulatory requirements currently applicable to HMOs. Group plan participants can opt not to utilize PPO services, but they are offered economic incentives to use the PPO. For example, to encourage use of its PPO network in Toledo, Ohio, Owens-Corning Fiberglass Corporation offered to reduce deductible amounts by 50 percent and to lower employee copayment percentages from 15 percent and 20 percent to 5 percent.

According to a 1986 Health Care Financing Administration study, 80 percent of firms with 5,000 or more employees self-insured their health benefits, compared with about 10 percent of organizations with less than 100 employees.[6] This disparity reflects employers' belief that the degree of accuracy needed for predicting unfunded health care expenses requires a significantly large and diversified risk pool.

By self-funding all—or a substantial part—of health benefits, an employer saves on insurance company charges and premium taxes, and gains improved cash flow and investment flexibility. (See Table 1.) An insurance company may still handle claims processing and other services under an administrative services only contract; alternatively, a third-party administrator may be utilized.

Wellness Programs and Incentives

Many employers now encourage smoking cessation, regular exercise, diet and weight control, health screening, and other ini-

Table 1

Health care financing: insured vs. self-funded plans.

	Insured	Self-Funded
Beginning reserves	$ 800,000	$ 600,000
Income (premiums or deposits)	3,000,000	2,700,000
Paid claims	2,500,000	2,500,000
Operating costs		
Premium tax	60,000	—
Risk and contingency	30,000	—
Administration	200,000	150,000
Interest on reserves	(40,000)	(60,000)
Total	250,000	90,000
Addition to reserves	250,000	110,000
Total reserves	$1,050,000	$ 710,000

Source: Reprinted with permission from Robert M. McCaffery, *Managing the Employee Benefits Program,* New York: AMACOM copyright © 1989, author.

tiatives that they believe will improve employees health and well-being. In addition, group medical plans are increasingly extending financial incentives to those who participate in these programs or otherwise demonstrate good health habits. For example, one prototype of a group insurance plan specifies premium discounts of 10 percent for nonsmokers, 5 percent for those who always wear seatbelts, and similar adjustments for participants who exercise regularly, maintain appropriate weight and blood pressure levels, and restrict alcohol consumption.

A variety of data suggests that wellness programs and incentives are cost effective. New York Bell claims that it spent $2.8 million on wellness and saved $5.5 million. Control Data has documented a 36 percent decrease in costs for employees enrolled in its wellness program, and Campbell's Soup says that it has prevented three of four strokes in employees age 55 to 65 through their program.[7]

Restrictions and Conditions

In order to qualify for full benefits in most current plans, employees must comply with a variety of relatively new requirements. The most common specifications concern second surgical

opinions, preadmission testing, outpatient surgery, precertifica-
tion, and concurrent review of hospitalization. Employers have
found it necessary to stress to employees the medical efficacy of
these various restrictions. Unless workers perceive these conditions
as reasonable and appropriate, they quickly become dissatisfied
since benefit reductions are generally imposed for non-compliance.

Employee Choice

At a minimum, most employers now offer employees the
opportunity to join an HMO as an alternative to the standard group
health plan. And many companies now provide other options as part
of a flexible benefits program. By allowing employees to choose from
a "menu" of options, sponsors satisfy diverse individual needs while
containing costs by eliminating excessive and duplicative benefits
for some. Table 2 illustrates typical choices available to salaried
employees and their dependents in a contemporary program of this
type.

Disability Income Replacement

A sound benefits program should include provisions to replace
income during periods of disability. While employees should consider the level of disability benefits to be adequate and equitable,
the program must not create disincentives for employees to return
to work. Achieving these dual goals requires effective coordination
with mandatory coverages, notably Social Security and workers'
compensation disability benefits. For planning and design purposes, employers should consider these mandatory programs as
employees' primary source of income replacement and view
employer-sponsored plans as a secondary or supplemental source.
In this way, HR managers can design a group program according to
specific total objectives and factor in benefits provided through
mandatory programs so that excessive payments do not occur.

In developing an overall strategy for an organization's disability
income replacement program, a benefits manager must consider
and evaluate the following issues.

Tax Treatment of Benefits

Since benefits funded by employee contributions and most
payments from mandatory programs are not considered taxable

Table 2

MediChoice Options

	Medical Plan/Basic Option	Preferred Provider Option	HMO Option
Employee contributions (monthly)	None	$8.00 (employee only) $16.00 (employee + 1) $24.00 (employee + 2)	None
Deductibles (annual)	$300 (individual) $500 (family)	$100 (individual) $200 (family)	None
Employee annual out-of-pocket expense limit (after deductible)	$2500 (individual) $5000 (family)	$1000 (individual) $2000 (family)	N/A
Lifetime Maximum	$500,000	$1,000,000	N/A
COVERAGE: Preadmission Tests Second Surgical Opinions Outpatient/Ambulatory Surgery Home Health Care Hospice Care		Expenses covered at 100% of reasonable and customary charge levels subject to deductibles.	Covered in full
Hospital room & board Inpatient hospital services Surgical fees (inpatient) Diagnostic tests Physician visits (when medically necessary) Inpatient substance abuse treatment	Expenses covered at 80% of reasonable and customary charge levels after deductible	Expenses covered at 90% of reasonable and customary charge levels after deductible	Covered in full except for $3.00 physician visit copayment

Table 2 continued

Psychiatric Care Chiropractic Care Outpatient substance abuse treatment	Expenses covered at 50% of reasonable and customary charge levels subject to deductibles	Covered in full except for $8.00 copayment for outpatient drug abuse treatment
Routine Physical Exams Well Baby Care Immunizations	Not covered	Covered in full
Special Conditions	Specified reductions in benefits for non-compliance with pre-certification and concurrent review requirements and second-surgical opinion provisions. No coverage for non-emergency weekend hospital admissions.	Coverage is coordinated through a specific group of doctors, hospitals and medical services associated with the HMO.

compensation, overall replacement earnings should target a level that will not give employees higher net income while disabled than when working. Reflecting that objective, the most common replacement ratio in long-term disability plans equals 60 percent of pay.

Frequency/Severity of Risk

Based on its business and its work-force demographics, an organization can make certain assumptions about the probable frequency and severity of disabilities for various classifications of employees. These assumptions will influence group insurance rates and other plan costs. They will also provide insights into the likely degree of employees' concerns and expectations regarding income protection. While an employer's goals may be at odds with workers' expectations, a benefits planner should seek an optimum balance with respect to coverage and cost sharing.

Scope of Benefits

Most organizations offer either a sick pay (salary continuation) plan, a short-term disability plan, or a combination of the two to protect employee income during the first three to six months of disability. In addition, many employers offer a long-term disability plan and, in the case of permanent disabilities, a pension plan that provides group benefits at a later date, usually when an employee reaches age 65. With all of these plans coordinated in various ways with mandatory coverages, communication with employees can become very difficult. Figure 2 shows a graphic explanation of disability benefits excerpted from the employee handbook of a large multi-national company.

Attendance Incentives

Some firms offer cash and other rewards to employees for unused sick days at year end. Such arrangements presumably discourage abuses of short-term paid absence allowances, thereby improving attendance and productivity. However, some organizations have rejected this concept as needlessly costly and philosophically objectionable in creating additional compensation for regular work time.

Figure 2

Benefits While Disabled

The following graph shows disability benefits payable to a disabled employee whose monthly earnings at the time of disability were $1,600.

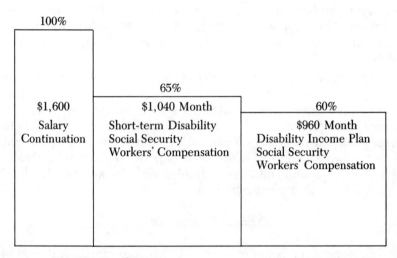

| First Six Months | | Later |

Duration of Disability Benefits. Disability Income Plan benefits would be payable until one of the following happens: you recover, your pension payments under the Retirement Income Plan commence (see "Pension" section), you die, or you engage in work for compensation or profit.

Other Benefits

Although potential loss of income tends to be employees' chief concern related to disability, a disability program should also address employees' worries about job loss, discontinuation or additional charges for group life and medical benefits, and loss of pension or capital accumulation plan accruals. Most employers make some accommodations for disabled workers who also receive some protection under federal and state laws.

Retirement Income

Workers in the United States receive support during their retirement years through a three-legged stool of income protections. Each of the legs depends at least in part on employer contributions and actions. The first component, Social Security, is funded by payroll taxes shared equally by employers and employees. Pension plans, the second source of support, are primarily financed by employers, and the third leg, individual effort, has been encouraged and assisted by company-sponsored, tax-favored savings and investment plans and by the creation of alternative work options for older workers.

The 1974 enactment of ERISA and subsequent federal tax reform and employee protections acts have subjected pension plans to pervasive government restrictions and controls. As a result, benefit managers have lost considerable flexibility in their ability to shape plans to meet organizational objectives. However, benefit planners may still choose which form of pension plans to use, a key decision that should undergo careful review by and receive final approval from senior management.

Defined Benefit Plans

Pension plans come in several forms, the most traditional of which is a defined benefit plan. In a defined benefit plan, the more traditional type of pension plan, a participant is assured of a determinable income starting at the time of retirement. The plan insulates an employee from adverse market fluctuations since the company bears the risks of pension fund investments. A plan can credit an employee's pre-plan service and/or weight benefits more closely to the final years of earnings. Defined benefit plans offer employers a consistent long-term funding method to provide retirement income for employees and integrate company benefits with Social Security benefits.

Defined Contribution Plans

Defined contribution plans, which include profit sharing, money purchase plans, savings arrangements, and employee stock ownership plans, utilize a concept of capital accumulation. Sponsors make regular specified contributions to individual participant accounts, and some plans also include participant contributions.

Benefits become whatever the amounts accumulated produce. The rewards are quickly visible and employees have a great deal of flexibility with respect to their own contributions, investment options, loan provisions, and disbursement alternatives. However, since company contributions and investment returns may vary, employees may have difficulty planning retirement income. For employers, defined contribution plans generally cost less than defined benefit plans. Defined contribution plans also are easier to implement and administer since employers do not face past service funding requirements or mandatory payments of pension plan insurance premiums to the federal Pension Benefit Guaranty Corporation (PBGC).

Defined contribution plans may also serve to supplement a defined benefit plan. In this system, a defined benefit plan is the primary vehicle for producing retirement income and a defined contribution plan can form either part of the third leg of the retirement income stool, or a source of capital that employees can use for shorter-term goals, or both. As indicated in Table 3, combinations of plans typify retirement programs in large firms.

Smaller and newer organizations more commonly use defined contribution plans as the exclusive form of pension plan. This choice reflects the desire of such companies to avoid the fixed obligations of a defined benefit plan and to emphasize earlier benefits for partici-

---

Table 3

Prevalence of Pension and Capital Accumulation Plans in 1988

Type of Plan	Percent of Employers/*
Defined Benefit Pension	87
Savings/Thrift	81
Deferred Profit Sharing	16
Money Purchase	4
Subsidized Stock Purchase	8
Employee Stock Ownership	4

(other than payroll-based tax credit plans. Tax credits for these plans expired at the end of 1986)

*/N = 822 employers

Source: Reprinted with permission from "Salaried Employee Benefits Provided by Major U.S. Employers in 1988," copyright © 1989, Hewitt Associates.

pants without creating long-term cost commitments. Characteristic defined contribution plans for achieving these goals include cash or deferred arrangement (CODA) or 401(k) plans. These plans began to evolve during the early 1980s and are now widespread among small as well as large organizations.

Guaranteed Account Balance Plans

A recent development in the pension field is a hybrid form called a guaranteed account balance plan. Some benefits authorities have described this new model as a defined benefit plan that looks like a defined contribution plan. Under a guaranteed account balance plan, also known as a cash balance plan, benefits accrue in individual accounts as if specific contributions were being made each year. For example, a participant's annual benefit accrual could equal 5 percent of pay. In addition, each account grows at a predetermined rate of interest. Benefits become payable at retirement or separation as either an annuity or a lump sum.

For employees, this plan is similar to a money purchase type of defined contribution plan except that the account balance is always guaranteed and the participant bears no investment risk. However, since these plans are classified as the defined benefit type under ERISA and the Internal Revenue Code, a sponsor's annual costs can be limited to amounts actuarially calculated to satisfy minimum funding standards. This funding method is not allowed under defined contribution plan rules and allows employers to amortize investment gains and losses and to anticipate turnover in making annual plan contributions. In addition, guaranteed account balance plans provide more predictable projections of future costs than most defined benefit plans since benefits are based on each year's pay, not final average earnings.

The first significant plan of this type was introduced by Bank of America in 1985 and the approach, while not universally applicable, will likely influence pension planning in the 1990s.

Benefits Following Involuntary Termination

During the past two decades, American workers have experienced job displacements due to automation, plant relocations, transfer of work to foreign installations, and industry consolidation. Although the national rate of unemployment has generally remained below 7 percent during this period (compared with an estimated 25 percent in 1933), some geographic areas and age and race groups have experienced much higher incidence. Given uncertain job security and the ability to quickly find suitable new employment, workers expect employers to provide some economic bridge of protection. But they no longer view as sufficient the traditional practice of granting two weeks pay in lieu of notice coupled with the mandatory financing of state unemployment compensation insurance (UCI).

Severance Pay

Since severance pay plans and policies are classified as welfare plans under ERISA, many employers prefer to administer these benefits, which may take the form of lump sum allowances or continuing payments, on a more informal or ad hoc basis. In addition, Department of Labor data indicates that more than three-fifths of white-collar employees are eligible for severance pay, about twice the proportion of blue-collar workers covered by severance plans.[8]

Supplemental Unemployment Pay

Supplemental unemployment benefit plans are a standard feature in a few industries, notably automobile and steel. These plans are pre-funded through employer contributions in accordance with union contract requirements, and are designed to produce adequate levels of replacement income in coordination with state UCI benefits. Supplemental unemployment benefits initially served to protect employees during seasonal layoffs, but the plans have taken on broader significance as particular industries have become increasingly affected by permanent layoffs.

Other Plans

Many employers now favor a strategy that combines a limited period of pay and benefits continuation with professional outplacement assistance. Besides helping an individual to adjust and relocate, and probably enhancing employee and public relations, this approach can conserve the amount of severance pay required and should reduce UCI claims. The duration of economic assistance usually varies according to such factors as service, organizational level, and age, but in all cases, support ends when a person starts a new job. Outplacement assistance can take place on either an individual or group basis depending largely on the above-mentioned factors.

Managerial and professional employees tend to receive more generous severance allowances because they usually need more time to find comparable positions. A few key executives also may have "golden parachute" contracts that specify compensation continuation for two or three years after involuntary termination (except for cause) or resignation following a hostile takeover.

Payments for Survivors

The principal mandatory sources of income maintenance for survivors of deceased employees are workers' compensation insurance and Social Security. These mandatory benefits address issues of need and social responsibility. Eligibility for these benefits depends on such factors as age, marital status, parental responsibility, and dependency status of the survivors. Workers' compensation benefits are financed entirely by employers, while Social Security receives half of its funding from employer taxes.

In contrast to these mandatory benefits, employer-sponsored death benefit programs often resemble a random collection of unconnected plans. Death benefits generally vary as a multiple of pay, thereby favoring survivors of highly paid employees. Most plans will make payments to any designated beneficiary, irrespective of relationship, but they produce income replacement levels that differ enormously in relation to the cause of death. For example, employer-financed benefits payable on behalf of someone killed while traveling on company business could be ten times greater than payment on behalf of a colleague who earned the same salary but died from an illness, regardless of the number and dependency status of survivors in each situation.

Motivated by tax code changes, rising costs, and employee dissatisfaction, benefits managers have begun to redesign group death benefit packages so as to incorporate many choice elements related to flexible compensation. Table 4, a composite of programs sponsored by several large firms, illustrates the more rational design that is now evolving.

By setting a maximum of $50,000 on the company-paid term life coverage, this program recognizes two tax code provisions. The Internal Revenue Code specifies that the cost of coverage in excess

Table 4

Death Benefits

Employer-paid death benefits

Term life insurance	1 times salary (maximum—$50,000)
Accidental death & dismemberment insurance	Same
Business travel accident insurance	3 times salary (maximum—$150,000)

Employee-paid death benefits (optional)

Term life insurance	Up to 3 times salary in units of $10,000 (maximum—$150,000)
Group universal life program	Same
Accidental death & dismemberment insurance	Same
Dependent life insurance	$5,000 for spouse $2,000 for each dependent child

of $50,000 must count as an employee's taxable income. In addition, most employees who earn more than $50,000 a year now fall within the tax code's definition of "highly compensated" for plan discrimination testing purposes. Other employer-provided coverages are non-taxable benefits, fairly inexpensive, and in line with reasonable employee expectations of special protection in the event of a sudden death or for taking added risks.

The optional segment of the program illustrated in Table 3 gives employees a wide range of flexibility for satisfying their personal needs. For example, while younger single persons may find the employer-paid portion entirely adequate, married employees with dependent spouses and children tend to elect all the additional coverage they can afford. The inclusion of a group universal life program option probably will prove particularly attractive to individuals starting a plan for their retirement when employer-paid insurance coverage either ends or drops sharply. This relatively new form of life insurance combines insurance protection and a portable investment element.

A number of organizations, particularly larger firms, have begun to use age-related premium rates, rather than composite average rates, to determine employee contributions for optional life insurance. Employees usually view this system as equitable since the composite method unfairly penalizes younger workers. When optional coverages form part of a comprehensive flexible benefits program, employees frequently can be paid for these options with "flexi-credits" or "benefit dollars." These credits are amounts generated by some combination of employer subsidies and/or employee agreements to forego other benefits or to earn less salary.

Time Off With Pay

As a component of employee compensation and benefits, paid time off represents an enigma for managers of HR programs. The cost of this benefit consistently ranks as one of the highest expense elements in the annual benefit surveys of the U.S. Chamber of Commerce. Yet employees never see the cost of the benefit since it is part of regular pay. Moreover, both the amount of time off granted and the timing of observances have major operational implications, but coordination among the heads of employee benefits, employee or labor relations, personnel policy administration, and major operating units is often lacking.

A total resolution of this dilemma clearly goes beyond employee benefits management, but this function can certainly contribute to cost containment. One significant strategy in this area involves flexible compensation since employees tend to show high interest in trading options for their paid time-off allowances. For example, some employees will take a shorter vacation in order to pay for a more expensive medical insurance option; others will pass up extra life insurance coverage in order to gain additional vacation days. Regardless of employees' choices, an employer's costs remain the same. Interchangeable benefits also makes employees more aware of the costs of time-off allowances, traditionally called "the hidden payroll."

Whether an organization uses a traditional or a flexible benefits program, it should communicate the cost and values of paid time-off benefits to current and prospective employees. Although ERISA does not require reporting and disclosure of these benefits, employers should include appropriate information in employee handbooks and annual benefit reports, as well as in recruitment brochures and employment advertisements.

Other Benefits and Services

The three categories of employer-provided benefits (mandatory coverages, protection programs, and paid time off) discussed to this point account for about 95 to 99 percent of benefit costs in most organizations.[9] The remaining costs result from a great variety of plans and allowances, some of which are unique to particular industries while others are fairly standard or emerging on a widespread basis. Industry-specific benefits include travel privileges for airline industry employees and their families, and tuition remission for college and university staff members and dependents. More prevalent provisions offer relocation assistance, subsidized food service, employee assistance programs (EAPs), service recognition awards, and educational expense reimbursement. Among the emerging, or leading edge, benefits are vision care, hearing care, dependent care assistance, adoption benefits, long-term care, and group legal service.

In addition to the above-mentioned benefits and services, most of which are either inherently inexpensive or not widely utilized by employees, employers usually extend other cost-free considerations. Such nonfinancial rewards include flextime, or flexible work hours, credit unions, and certain product and service discounts. Although none of these programs can be included in benefit cost reports for management, HR managers should never overlook that *employees* perceive these as benefits. Management should therefore recognize specific nonfinancial rewards as *de facto* employee benefits in all summaries and communications of total compensation.

Flexible Benefits and Cafeteria Plans

Flexible benefit plans offer participants an opportunity to choose levels of benefit coverage from a package of employer-designated options. When the choices include two or more benefits consisting of cash and nontaxable benefits, the plan must satisfy nondiscrimination requirements of the Internal Revenue Code relating to cafeteria plans (IRC §125).

Although these nondiscrimination requirements date back to 1978, cafeteria plans did not catch on until proposed regulations were issued in 1984. Data maintained by Hewitt Associates, a compensation and benefit consulting group, shows that at the end of 1983, only 88 organizations offered such programs, but by the end of 1988, more than 800 programs were scheduled to be operational.[10]

Early interest in flexible plans stemmed mainly from their compatibility with an increasingly heterogeneous work force and from employee dissatisfaction with rigid programs. These factors continue to be influential, but employers now realize that cafeteria plans can also maximize the tax effectiveness of benefits and help to contain costs.

Tax Effectiveness

A relatively simple form of a cafeteria plan allows employees to opt for salary reductions in order to obtain benefit coverages on a pre-tax basis. Table 5 illustrates such a plan. Each year employees have an opportunity to designate a portion of their pre-tax earnings for use in paying group health plan premiums and/or for deposit in separate reimbursement accounts for medical expenses and dependent care. In this example, a plan participant could increase take-home pay by $1,232 and an employer would save $326 in Social Security taxes. In communicating this type of plan, employers should emphasize that allocations not utilized for designated purposes during the plan year become forfeited. Participants should

---

Table 5

Illustration of a Cafeteria Plan with a Premium Payment Option, Dependent Care and Medical Reimbursement Accounts*

	Without Cafeteria Plan	Using Cafeteria Plan
Salary	$25,000	$25,000
Flexible Plan		
Premium Payments	—	(300)
Dependent Care Account	—	(3,600)
Medical Expense Account	—	(600)
Federal taxes	(3,294)	(2,378)
Social Security (FICA) taxes	(1,878)	(1,562)
After-tax pay	$19,828	$16,560
Contributory premiums	(300)	—
Dependent Care expenses	(3,600)	—
Medical expenses	(600)	—
Take-home pay	$15,328	$16,560
Increase in Take-home pay	—	$ 1,232

*Assumes a single taxpayer with no other income using the standard deduction and based on 1988 tax rates and I.R.C. Section 125 provisions.

also realize that the plan's salary reductions could cause small decreases in future Social Security benefits for some employees.

Cost Containment

A key attribute of cafeteria plans is the separation of an employer's funding decision from the pricing of employee benefits. This feature contrasts strikingly with traditional programs in which employers' financing costs increase automatically whenever insurance companies and other providers raise their rates. In those instances, an employer can contain costs only by eliminating or reducing existing coverages or by increasing employee contributions. Neither alternative is apt to please employees, especially if these choices are the only ones available.

In a cafeteria plan, an employer prospectively determines the level of contribution for benefits and then allocates an amount of flexible "dollars" that each employee will receive. As shown in Figure 3, employees can voluntarily supplement this allocation through salary transfer (reduction) and, under some circumstances, vacation "selling." At the beginning of the year, employees choose from the various benefit options and plans, and those who find the employer contributions more than adequate can select a cash option.

In planning for the following year, employers should determine the amount of the flexible dollar subsidy independently in much the same way as salary expense, rather than react primarily to price increases. For example, rising costs may suggest a need to increase the prices of benefit options by an average of 10 percent, but an increase of 6 percent in employer contributions for flexible dollars might suffice based on an analysis of total compensation costs. In effect, this strategy contains an employer's benefits cost increase to 6 percent, while allowing employees to increase their flexible dollars by transferring salary, selling vacation, and/or changing some of their benefit choices.

Management of Employee Benefits

Management of employee benefits essentially consists of planning, developing, and implementing new and improved pension and welfare plans; administering and communicating established

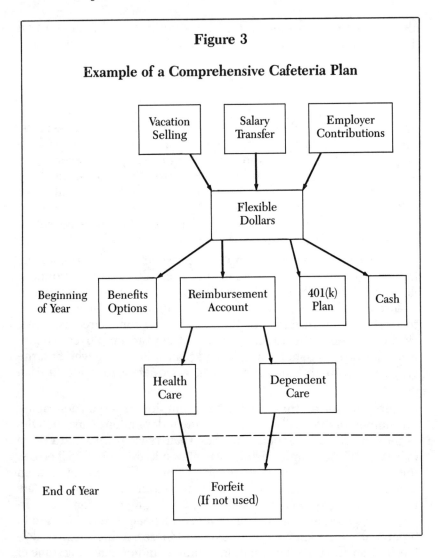

Figure 3

Example of a Comprehensive Cafeteria Plan

plans; and assuring compliance with ERISA and other legal requirements.

Organizations with fewer than 500 employees rarely have a discrete employee benefits unit. As a result, all of the responsibilities for employee benefits fall within a personnel director's immediate sphere of activity with much reliance on outside resources. In contrast, large corporations usually have several levels of benefits professionals directed by a head of compensation and benefits reporting to a top HRM executive. Figure 4 depicts the

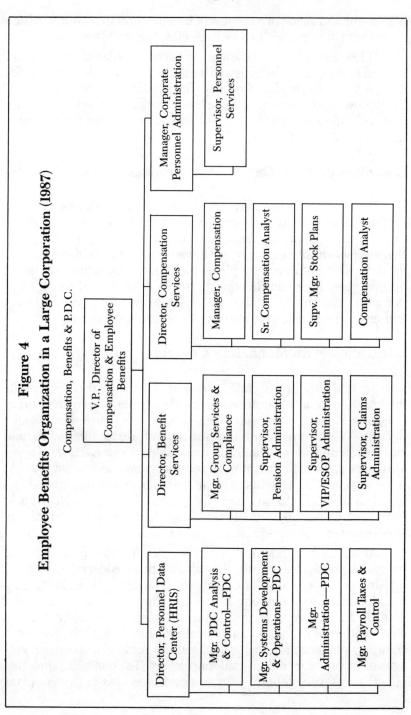

Figure 4

Employee Benefits Organization in a Large Corporation (1987)

Compensation, Benefits & P.D.C.

placement and scope of a corporate benefits unit in a multi-division manufacturing firm with more than 60,000 employees.

While a strong correlation exists between organization size and staffing for employee benefits, this relationship also depends on the degree of emphasis placed on benefits in the total rewards system. The following discussion summarizes some of the specific activities that will influence staffing, depending on the amount of attention they receive.

Coordination With Direct Compensation

In any organization, the person in charge of benefits needs to establish operational coordination with the head of direct compensation. Salary adjustments create roll-up costs for many benefit plans that are pay-sensitive, and salary increase projections affect funding for defined benefit pension plans, particularly those that are based on final pay. Poor coordination between benefits and direct compensation can thwart attainment of total compensation objectives and create needlessly excessive costs within both areas.

Integration With Mandatory Coverages

Several federal and state programs provide or specify benefits for employees and require contributions from employers and/or employees. The most pervasive program is the federal Social Security system which provides retirement, disability, health, and survivor benefits for virtually all working persons. Each state operates its own unemployment insurance program and mandates workers' compensation benefits to protect employees who incur occupational disabilities. In addition, five states (California, New York, New Jersey, Hawaii, and Rhode Island) have temporary disability laws covering non-occupational illnesses.

Although benefits available to employees under these public programs are set by statute, they should be considered as a partial fulfillment of private plan objectives. Mandatory benefits form a foundation upon which employers can then construct customized plans to fill in coverage gaps and avoid duplicative benefits. For a combination of economic and social reasons, benefit levels under statutory plans are rather low and tend to replace smaller percentages of income for higher-paid employees. To counterbalance that effect, employers generally try to design features in private plans that favor the more highly paid. This process of plan integration is subject to numerous Internal Revenue Service rules regarding non-discrimination and requires knowledgeable tax counsel. However, coordination with mandatory coverage is a critical factor in initial design and ongoing administration of an employee benefits program.

Design of Private Plans

Some fundamental questions that need to be raised at the outset of the design process include the following.

- What is required? Most pension plans must conform to ERISA standards regarding participation, vesting, and benefit accrual minimums, as well as to IRS integration rules. Insured welfare plans are subject to state insurance laws which may mandate certain coverages (such as, mental health benefits) and specify minimum benefit levels.

- What benefits will be included in the employer-sponsored program? Which ones will be implemented now and which later? Employers should make some measurement of employees' perceived needs and preferences before making these determinations.

- To what extent will employer-sponsored plans cover full-time employees? Part-time employees? Spouses? Other dependents? Retirees?

- What degree of participant choice will be allowed within the various plans and/or between plans? A wide range of choices tends to increase employee satisfaction, but also adds complexity and administrative burdens.

Plan Financing and Funding

One of the first issues to resolve is whether to require employee contributions and if a contributory plan is selected, what level of employee contributions to require. The outcome of these considerations will impact heavily on benefits management. Companies with contributory plans gain the advantages of employee cost sharing and heightened awareness of benefit plans. But they also incur the added administrative burdens of plan enrollments, payroll deductions, and extra recordkeeping, as well as the potential of employee dissatisfaction. In terms of equity, many employers now offer non-contributory group health plans for employee coverage and allow dependent coverage on a contributory basis.

Another key decision involves selecting a funding mechanism and delivery system for group welfare plans. Employers traditionally made insurance companies or Blue Cross-Blue Shield Associations fully responsible for these functions. This system proved highly convenient and protected employers against unpredictable risks, but it also was very expensive. For example, insurance carrier retention charges (the portion of the premium not directly allocated to paying claims) often account for 10 percent or more of a company's premium for group medical insurance. In recent years, practically all large employers, and many small and medium-size firms, have shifted to some form of self-funding in an effort to contain costs. A typical program will utilize an insurance firm for protection against extraordinary claims experience, but for a much lower premium. In addition, health maintenance organizations (HMOs) and preferred provider organizations (PPOs) (discussed earlier in this chapter) have become significant alternatives to traditional group health plans.

Managers of pension plans must separate plan funds from company assets in order to obtain IRS tax qualification. As an alternative, most employers either have pension monies trusteed by a bank or similar financial institution, or fund the plan through insurance contracts. The pros and cons of each approach need to be carefully evaluated and once a decision is made, the trustees' performance should undergo regular reviews. Managers of benefit plans need not have expertise in investment strategy, but they can clearly benefit from selecting and retaining outstanding managers of pension fund assets. For defined benefit plans, high rates of return on assets means lower annual additions for an employer, and in defined contribution plans, investment fund performance can affect employee satisfaction—positively or negatively. This negative impact became very evident in organizations with 401(k) and similar plans following the stock market crash of October 19, 1987.

Administration of Benefit Plans

For employees, the accuracy and timeliness of benefit claims and entitlement payments often serves as the principal measure of a total program's effectiveness. Processing errors which result in underpayments and unexplained delays in issuing checks can become major sources of employee dissatisfaction if these problems occur frequently. Many employers assign these administrative functions to outside parties, such as insurance carriers, third-party administrators, and financial institutions, for reasons of cost. Because of the routine and repetitive nature of administrative tasks, these large organizations with specialized staffs generally prove more economical than in-house processing. However, employees continue to view the plans as company benefits and hold the employer responsible for administrative failures. Here again, effectiveness in benefits management depends on success in selecting and controlling outside resources.

Communication With Employees

ERISA prescribes basic reporting and disclosure requirements for private-sector sponsors of pension and welfare plans. These requirements represent the core of a benefits communication program. The most notable ERISA provisions mandate that each plan participant is entitled to receive automatically:

- a summary plan description (SPD) containing information on what the plan provides and how it operates, and

- a summary annual report (SAR) that contains financial information about the plan.

However, simply meeting these requirements probably will not fully satisfy employees' needs. A recent article dealing with workers' knowledge of retirement plan features cited these findings from the 1983 Survey of Consumer Finances (SCF):[11]

Most [defined benefit pension] plans permit early retirement if certain age and service criteria are met, but almost one-fifth of the respondents are unable to provide any answer to the eligibility question. Among the subset of workers who believe they will eventually be eligible for early retirement, almost 40 percent cannot answer the question at all. Those who do respond estimate early eligibility requirements accurately only about one-third of the time.

The late Dr. Hideya Kumata, a former professor of communications at Michigan State University, offered this caution and counsel concerning printed communication:[12]

Knowing that reading is a high effort phenomenon in our society, and recognizing the difficulty in raising audience interest for fairly routine benefit messages, perhaps we ought to be practical about the real effectiveness of our written messages. Maybe they will never go beyond being simply an awareness device. We need to integrate printed communication with face-to-face messages and keep studying the situation, looking for feedback.

Face-to-face communication is time-consuming and ultimately expensive. But as benefit plans progressively become more complex and offer increased flexibility and choices for employees, this approach has become essential and is destined to expand.

To enhance communication aimed at building employee understanding of and appreciation for benefits, many companies now make extensive use of audiovisual media, including videos, audio tapes, and interactive PCs. Since senior management inevitably questions the costs for such features, the following observation by a benefits communication authority may prove useful:[13]

> The size of the (communication) budget should reflect the overall costs for the entire benefits package. A good rule of thumb is to budget at least one percent of the total costs for benefits communications less the cost of payroll for staff.

Government Reporting

To comply with ERISA requirements, benefit plan sponsors and administrators must file numerous annual and special reports with the IRS, the Department of Labor, the Securities and Exchange Commission, and the Pension Benefit Guaranty Corporation. Willful violations of federal reporting requirements can result in both criminal and civil actions against responsible individuals, and prescribed penalties include fines of up to $100,000 and imprisonment of up to one year.

Because of these personal liabilities and the potential for public embarrassment, plan reporting to government agencies is an aspect of benefits management that merits careful attention and good organization. In some organizations, administrative responsibility for this activity belongs to the law or tax department.

Conclusion

Three factors that became more dominant during the 1980s will clearly shape employee benefit programs in the future. These influences are government regulation and taxation, employee choicemaking, and recognition of benefits as a part of total compensation.

Government Involvement

Many authorities believe that the enactment of a mandatory health insurance law in Massachusetts in 1988 will serve to stimulate a similar federal law within several years. Since the passage of ERISA in 1974, the federal government has steadily expanded the scope of legal requirements and restrictions affecting benefit plans. This trend can be expected to continue since advocacy groups for older workers and working women will lobby aggressively for benefit protections favorable to these constituencies. At the same time, Congress, in its constant quest for deficit reduction measures, will probably continue to look for ways in which private benefit plans can eliminate or lower government expenditures.

These influences suggest that organizations will face higher costs for mandatory coverages and stricter qualification standards regarding benefit plan tax preferences for employees and employers. In particular, stronger limitations on features that seem to favor highly compensated executives are apt to emerge.

Employee Choicemaking

Given the availability of cafeteria plans, flexible benefits, or participant option arrangements, employees will expect to have a significant degree of choice in the selection of their benefit coverages. This expectation will become particularly apparent among the so-called "Third Wave" workers who value independence and individualism.[14] Employers who have already implemented flexible-type plans strongly believe that such programs produce competitive advantages in recruiting, motivating, and retaining workers with these characteristics. This finding suggests that other employers will inevitably imitate the types of plans that appear successful in achieving common objectives.

Benefits as Compensation

Adoption of the flexible concept ultimately could lead to a complete recharacterization of employee compensation. The traditional boundaries between pay and benefits will disappear and the total compensation package might eventually delineate three categories of pay. The first category, restricted pay, would encompass contributions to mandatory programs and employer-required coverages. A second category, earmarked pay, would set aside funds which employees could use to pay for options from a designated group of basic benefits. Finally, payments designated as unrestricted pay could be used for any purpose, including current income, deferred compensation, or the purchase of supplemental group benefits.

While this new concept of compensation is evolving, employers must continue to sponsor an array of benefit plans that is adequate and appropriate for an organization and its employees. Benefit planning managers will still need to cope with competitive pressures, administrative burdens, and frequent changes in legislation and regulations. These changes will have greatest impact on employees, who will assume more responsibility for choices and financing of benefit plans. As long as employees perceive their total compensation as equitable and consider benefit options to be fairly priced, the new style of compensation should have broad appeal. At the same time, flexible programs will relieve management of many benefits decisions that are best handled by individuals who use the plans—the employees.

♦

Notes

1. U.S. Chamber of Commerce, p. 27.
2. A. Foster Higgins & Co., p. 11.
3. Prentice-Hall Information Services.
4. Wyatt Company, p. 13.
5. Sears and Berlacher.
6. McDonnell et al.
7. *Employee Benefits Plan Review.*
8. U.S. Department of Labor, Bureau of Labor Statistics, p. 81.
9. Author's extrapolation from U.S. Chamber of Commerce data.
10. Hewitt Associates.
11. Mitchell, p. 14.
12. Kumata, p. 90.
13. Mara, pp. 6–27.
14. Toffler, pp. 400–403.

Editor's Note: In addition to the References shown below, there are other sources of information and ideas on employee benefits and services.

Books

Beam, Jr., B.T. and J.J. McFadden. 1988. *Employee Benefits*, 2nd ed. Homewood, IL: Richard D. Irwin.

Employee Benefit Research Institute. 1987. *America in Transition: Benefits for the Future.* Washington, DC: EBRI.

———. 1987. *Fundamentals of Employee Benefit Programs*, 3rd ed. Washington, DC: EBRI.

Griffes, E.J.E. 1983. *Employee Benefits Programs: Management Planning and Control.* Homewood, IL: Dow Jones-Irwin.

McCaffery, R.M. 1988. *Employee Benefits: A Total Compensation Perspective.* Boston: PWS-Kent.

J.S. Rosenbloom and G.V. Hallman. 1986. *Employee Benefit Planning* 2nd ed. Englewood Cliffs, NJ: Prentice-Hall.

Salisbury, D.L., ed. 1984. *Why Tax Employee Benefits?* Washington, DC: EBRI.

Schultz, L. 1987. "An Unhealthy Forecast." *CFO* (June): 27.

◆

References

A. Foster Higgins & Co. 1988. *Health Care Benefits Survey 1988.* Princeton, NJ: Foster Higgins.

Employee Benefits Plan Review. 1987. "Adapt Wellness Programs Aimed at Cost Reductions," 41, 7 (January).

Hewitt Associates. 1986. "On Flexible Compensation." Lincolnshire, IL: Hewitt Associates.

Kumata, H. 1978. *Communication Dynamics for Employee Benefit Plans.* Brookfield, WI: International Foundation of Employee Benefit Plans.

Mara, R.N. 1987. "Communication of Benefits." In *Employee Benefits Handbook* (revised edition), ed. J.D. Mamorsky. Boston: Warren, Gorham & Lamont.

McDonnell, P. et al. 1986. *Health Care Financing Review* (Winter):

Mitchell, O.S. 1988. "Planning for Retirement: What Do Workers Know?" *ILR Report* 24, 2 (Spring): 14.

Prentice-Hall Information Services. 1988. *Personnel Management Compensation,* Bulletin 4 (April 13).

Sears, R.W., and P.D. Berlacher. 1986. "—And So Owens-Corning Created a PPO." *Topics in Total Compensation* 1, 2.

Toffler, A. 1980. *The Third Wave.* New York: William Morrow.

U.S. Chamber of Commerce. 1988. *Employee Benefits 1987.* Washington, DC: U.S. Chamber of Commerce.

U.S. Department of Labor, Bureau of Labor Statistics. 1986. *Employee Benefits in Medium and Large Firms, 1985.* Washington, DC: U.S. Department of Labor.

Wyatt Company. 1986. *1986 Group Benefits Survey.* Washington, DC: The Wyatt Company.

────── ◆ ──────

3.5

Pay for Performance: A Strategic Analysis

Edward E. Lawler III

The idea of paying for performance is so widely accepted that almost every organization says it has performance-based pay. Confirmation of this is provided by a survey of 557 large U.S. corporations which found that 80 percent rate pay for performance as a very important compensation objective.[1] Even the U.S. government calls its pay system a merit system and legislation passed in the 1970s (the Civil Service Reform Act) called for increasing the system's linkage between pay and performance.

The popularity of paying for performance rests on the belief that such a system can motivate job performance and increase organizational effectiveness. Indeed, psychological research evidence clearly demonstrates that pay can act as a particularly powerful incentive.[2] Studies show that productivity increases of between 15 and 35 percent occur when employers install pay for performance systems.[3]

Although pay for performance is often treated as a single approach, it is, in fact, many different approaches. Because different pay for performance plans have very different consequences, they need separate treatment. Performance-based compensation plans can be best classified based upon the level of performance targeted: individual, organizational subunit, or total organization. Within each of these general approaches, literally hundreds of different approaches to relating pay to performance exist.

This chapter will focus on the strategic choices involved in designing pay for performance systems and their relationship to organizational effectiveness. The details of pay system technology and management will not be covered since a number of sound books provide information on this topic.[4]

In choosing an approach to pay for performance, organizations need to consider, first, whether they want to pay for performance, and then they need to choose the approach which best fits them. The plan selected should vary depending on what an organization wants the pay for performance system to accomplish. Just as different objectives call for different systems, organizational structure, culture, and management style also come into play. Some approaches to performance pay fit more participative management styles, while others fit a more traditional control-oriented approach.[5] In a similar fashion, some approaches fit work performed by individuals, while others fit work performed by teams or groups.[6] Thus, decisions about pay for performance require consideration of both the objectives of the pay system and the nature of the organization.

Objectives of Pay Systems

Any discussion of pay for performance systems should focus first on what impacts reward systems can have. The research on reward systems suggests that compensation systems can potentially influence six factors which in turn impact organizational effectiveness.

Attraction and Retention

Research on job choice, career choice, and turnover clearly shows that the kind and level of rewards offered by an organization influences who is attracted to work there and who will continue to work there.[7] Overall, organizations which give the most rewards tend to attract and retain the most people. This outcome seems to occur because high reward levels lead to high job satisfaction, which in turn leads to lower employee turnover. Individuals who are presently satisfied with their jobs expect this satisfaction to continue and, as a result, want to stay with the same organization.

The relationship between turnover and organizational effectiveness is not a simple one. Because turnover is expensive, lower turnover rates should increase organizational effectiveness. Indeed, studies have computed the cost of turnover and found that replacing an employee can cost an organization five or more times that employee's monthly salary.[8] However, not all turnover is harmful. Organizations certainly can afford to lose some individuals and may even profit from losing them if the employees are either poor performers or easy to replace. In addition, if replacement costs are low, as may happen with unskilled jobs, an employer may find it more cost effective to keep wages low and suffer with high turnover. Thus, the impact of turnover depends on turnover rate, who turns over, and replacement costs.

The ideal reward system should be very effective at retaining the most valuable employees. To achieve this objective, a compensation system must distribute rewards so that the more valuable employees feel satisfied when they compare their rewards with those received by individuals performing similar jobs in other organizations. One way to accomplish this goal is to reward everyone at a level that exceeds the reward levels in other organizations. However, this strategy has two drawbacks. First, it is very costly. Second, it can cause feelings of intraorganizational inequity because the better performers may feel unfairly treated if they are rewarded at the same level as poor performers. Faced with this situation, better performers may not quit, but they may feel dissatisfied, complain, look for internal transfers, and mistrust the organization.

What then is the best solution? The answer often lies in having competitive reward levels and basing rewards on performance. This strategy satisfies better performers and causes them to stay with an organization. It also serves to attract achievement-oriented individuals since the organization will reward their performance. However, better performers must receive not only *more* rewards but *significantly more* rewards than poor performers. Just rewarding better performers slightly more may do little other than make better and poorer performers *equally* dissatisfied.

In summary, managing turnover means managing anticipated employee satisfaction, and success depends on effectively relating rewards to performance. When this differentiation is impossible, an organization can only try to reward all employees at an above-average level. When turnover is costly, this strategy should prove cost effective, even if it involves giving out costly rewards.

Motivation to Perform

Under certain conditions, reward systems serve to motivate performance.[9] A requisite condition is that employees must perceive a close and timely linkage between important rewards and effective performance. Organizations get the kind of behavior that leads to the rewards valued by employees. This occurs because people have needs and mental maps of what the world is like. They use these maps to choose those behaviors that lead to outcomes that satisfy their needs. People possess no inherent incentive or disincentive to perform effectively; performance motivation depends on the situation, how employees perceive it, and the individual needs of employees.

The approach that best explains how people develop and act on their perceptions is called expectancy theory.[10] While the theory appears complex, it in fact involves a series of fairly straightforward observations about behavior. The three concepts discussed below serve as the key building blocks of expectancy theory.

Performance-Outcome Expectancy

Every behavior has associated with it, in an individual's mind, certain outcomes (rewards or punishments). In other words, individuals believe that if they behave in a certain way, they will get certain things. For example, individuals may expect that if they produce 10 units, they will receive their normal hourly pay rate, while if they produce 15 units, they will receive their hourly pay rate plus a bonus. Individuals also may believe that certain levels of performance will lead to approval or disapproval from members of their work group or from their supervisor. Each performance level usually involves a number of different expected outcomes.

Attractiveness

Each outcome has an associated level of attractiveness which differs for different individuals. Outcome values vary because they result from individual needs and perceptions, which differ depending on the factors in an individual's life. For example, some individuals may value an opportunity for promotion or advancement because of their needs for achievement or power; others may not want to be promoted and leave their current work group because of needs for affiliation with others. Similarly, a fringe benefit, such as a pension plan, may have great value for older workers but little for young employees.

Effort-Performance Expectancy

Each behavior also creates an associated expectancy or probability of success. This expectancy represents an individual's perception of how hard it will be to achieve such behavior and his or her probability of successfully achieving that behavior. For example, employees may have a strong expectancy that if they put forth the effort, they can produce 10 units an hour, but see only a fifty-fifty chance of producing 15 units an hour even if they try.

Putting these concepts together, an individual's motivation to attempt to behave in a certain way is greatest when:

- The individual believes that the behavior will lead to outcomes (performance-outcome expectancy).

- The individual feels that these outcomes are attractive.

- The individual believes performance at the target level is possible (effort-performance expectancy).

Given alternative levels of behavior (10, 15, or 20 units of production per hour, for example), an individual will choose the performance level which has the greatest motivational association, as indicated by a combination of relevant expectancies, outcomes, and values. In other words, when faced with choices about behavior, an individual considers questions such as: "Can I perform at that level if I try?" "If I perform at that level, what will happen?" and "How do I feel about those things that will happen?" The individual then decides to behave in a way that seems to have the best chance of producing positive, desired outcomes.

Expectancy Model of Employee Behavior

The expectancy concepts, form the basis for a general model of behavior in organizational settings as shown in Figure 1. Working from left to right in the model, motivation serves as the force leading to a level of effort by an individual. Effort alone, however, is not enough. Performance results from a combination of individual effort and that individual's level of ability. Ability reflects an individual's skills, training, information, and talents.

Effort thus combines with ability to produce a given level of performance. As a result of performance, an individual attains certain outcomes. The model indicates this relationship using a dotted line to reflect that sometimes people perform but do not get outcomes. As this performance-reward process occurs time after time, actual events provide further information that influences an individual's perceptions (particularly expectancies) and this affects

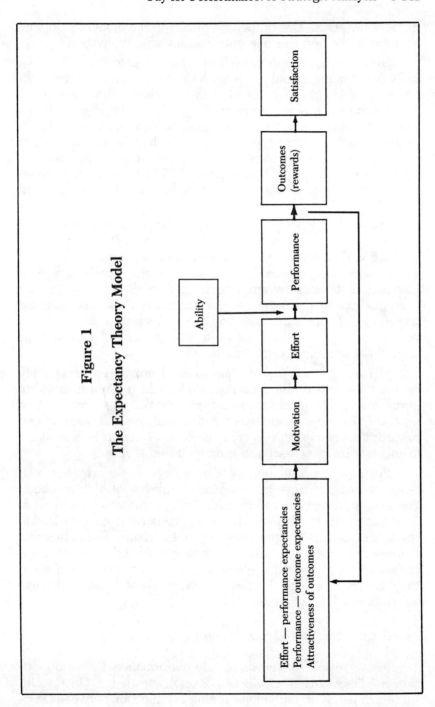

Figure 1

The Expectancy Theory Model

future motivation. This influence appears in the model by the line connecting the performance-outcome link with motivation.

Outcomes, or rewards, fall into two major categories. First, an individual can obtain outcomes from the environment. When individuals perform at a given level, they can receive positive or negative outcomes from supervisors, co-workers, the organization's reward system, or other sources. A second type of outcome occurs purely from the performance of the task itself (for example, feelings of accomplishment, personal worth, achievement, and so on). In a sense, individuals control these rewards: The environment cannot directly give or take away these rewards; it can only make them possible.

The model also suggests that satisfaction is best characterized as a result of performance rather than as a cause of it. Strictly speaking, satisfaction does influence motivation in some ways. For instance, when employees view satisfaction as a result of performance, it increases motivation by strengthening people's beliefs about the consequences of performance. Satisfaction can also decrease the importance of outcomes (a satisfied need is not a motivator), and as a result, lower motivation for performances linked to whatever reward has become less important.

In many ways, the expectancy model provides a deceptively simple statement of the conditions under which rewards motivate performance. The model appears to suggest that all an organization must do to motivate employees is to relate pay and other valued rewards to obtainable levels of performance. Not only is this linkage insufficient on its own, it also is difficult to establish.

For employees to believe that a pay for performance relationship exists, an organization must establish a visible connection between performance and rewards, and generate trust and credibility among its work force. The belief that performance will lead to rewards is essentially a prediction about the future. For individuals to make this kind of prediction, they have to trust the system that is promising them rewards. When they trust the system and when they see clear linkages between the rewards and their behavior, motivation will be present.

Motivation for Self-Development

Just as reward systems motivate performance, they can motivate employees to learn skills and develop knowledge. Once again, success depends on individuals seeing a connection between learning skills and a valued pay reward. Effective pay for performance systems motivate learning and development because individuals perceive that they must develop their skills in order to perform effectively. Of course if individuals feel they already have the requisite skills, then a pay for performance system may not have this impact.

Sometimes pay for performance systems may discourage individuals from learning new skills. This outcome can happen when skills are not directly related to present performance. As a result, acquiring those skills is not likely to lead to a reward and indeed may detract from a performance-based reward. In order to establish a clear relationship between skill development and pay some organizations use skill-based pay. This approach is particularly effective at motivating individuals to add new skills and to develop a broader understanding of how the business operates.[11]

Definition of Organizational Structure

An organization's reward system can reinforce and define its structure.[12] Compensation managers often overlook this feature in the design of reward systems. As a result, the impact of a reward system on organizational structure frequently is unintentional. This tendency does not mean, however, that a reward system has minimal impact on structure. Indeed, a reward system can help determine the status hierarchy, the degree of cooperation between and within departments, and the decision structure.

A pay for performance system can have a particularly strong impact on the degree to which emloyees feel they share a common fate. As a result, performance-based pay strongly influences the degree and kind of cooperation which exists within an organization. Implementation of a pay for performance system is an important structural decision that both integrates and differentiates individuals and parts of organizations.[13] Performance-based pay systems differentiates affected workers from others, creating a kind of structural boundary that reduces cooperation and sharing with individuals and groups outside the pay for performance system. If the system pays affected workers the same based on their collective performance, it can integrate them and cause them to cooperate and to work as a team. On the other hand, if the reward system asks individuals to compete among themselves for a fixed amount of raise or bonus money, it can cause competition among individuals within the system.

Contribution to Culture

Reward systems are one feature of organizations that contributes to their overall culture or climate. Depending upon how reward systems are developed, administered, and managed, they can cause the culture of an organization to vary quite widely. For example, a reward system can influence the degree to which employees see an organization's culture as HR-oriented, entrepreneurial, innovative, competence-based, hierarchical, political, or participative.

The utility of reward systems in shaping culture reflects their important influence on motivation, satisfaction, and membership. The behaviors generated by compensation plans become the dominant patterns of behavior in the organization and lead to perceptions and beliefs about what an organization stands for, believes in, and values. Perhaps the most obvious tie between pay system practice and culture concerns performance-based pay. The absence or presence of this policy can have a dramatic impact on organizational culture because it so clearly communicates to employees what performance norms operate.

Many other features of a reward system also influence culture. For example, relatively high pay levels can produce a culture in which people feel they are an elite group working for a top-flight company. Introducing such cutting-edge pay practices as skill-based pay can produce a culture of innovativeness. Finally, involving employees in pay decisions can produce a participative culture in which employees influence business decisions and as a result are committed to the organization and its success.

Cost Level

Reward systems are often a significant cost factor in organizations. Indeed, a pay system alone may represent over 50 percent of an organization's operating cost. Thus, two issues to address in strategically designing a reward system concern at what level to set compensation costs and how to vary these costs as a function of the organization's ability to pay. For example, a reasonable outcome of a well-designed pay system might allow increased cost when the organization has the money to spend and decreased cost when the organization does not have the money. An additional objective might be to have lower overall reward system costs than business competitors.

Relationship to Strategic Planning

Figure 2 presents a way of viewing the relationship between strategic planning, organization design, and reward systems. It suggests that once a strategic plan is developed, an organization needs to identify the kind of organizational design and management style that will make the strategic plan effective. The next step is to design a pay for performance system which will motivate the right kind of performance, attract the right kind of people, and create a supportive culture and structure.

The remainder of this chapter will look first at pay for performance approaches which reward individuals, such as incentive and merit pay plans. The next section will consider approaches which focus on groups of individuals and total organizations, such as gainsharing, profit sharing, and ownership plans.

The discussion of different approaches to paying for performance will focus on their impact on organizational effectiveness. Pay for performance systems do not stand alone; to be effective, they need to fit the organizational context in which they operate. Thus, as different approaches to pay for performance are reviewed, attention will also be given to how the plans fit with different management styles and organizational designs.

Pay for Individual Performance

Incentive pay and merit pay are two common approaches to paying for individual performance. While the popularity of incentive pay has been declining for decades, merit salary increases remain very popular. Both approaches measure and reward individual performance, but differ in how they measure performance and adjust an individual's pay according to performance. Table 1 summarizes the characteristics of the two approaches.

Incentive Pay

Incentive plans pay employees bonuses based on the number of units produced. They are perhaps the most direct way to relate pay to performance. A great deal of evidence suggests that incentive pay can motivate individual behavior; indeed, much of this research

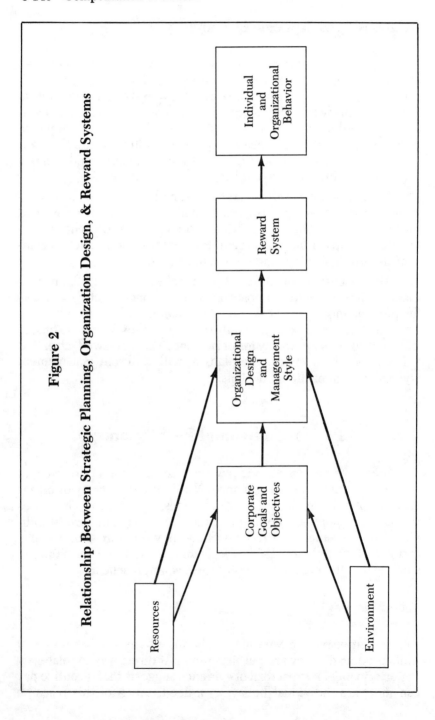

Figure 2

Relationship Between Strategic Planning, Organization Design, & Reward Systems

Table 1

Pay for Performance Individual Approaches

Plan Characteristics	Incentive Pay	Merit Pay
Payment method	Bonus	Changes in base pay
Frequency of payout	Weekly	Annually
Performance Measures	Output, productivity, sales	Supervisor's appraisal
Coverage	Direct labor	All employees

dates back decades.[14] It also appears that incentive pay can attract and selectively retain good performers since these individuals end up receiving higher pay.

Pitfalls

The literature on pay incentive plans provides vivid descriptions of the counterproductive behaviors which piece-rate incentive plans produce.[15] Most of the earlier accounts concern manufacturing organizations, but the same issues arise when salespersons and other service personnel are put on incentive pay. In many respects, these behaviors result not so much from the concept of incentive pay, but from the way it has been managed. Nevertheless, it is difficult to separate the practical problems with particular plans from the general idea of incentive pay. The following sections briefly review the major problems with incentive plans.

Beating the System. Numerous studies have shown that piece rate plans can create an adversarial relationship between system designers and employees.[16] Employees engage in numerous behaviors in order to get rates set so that they can maximize their financial gains relative to their productivity. They work at slow rates in order to mislead the time study expert when he or she comes to study their job. They hide new work methods or new procedures from the time study person so the job will not be restudied. In addition, informal norms develop about productivity. Workers set limits on their production, and anyone who goes beyond this limit is socially ostracized and even physically punished. Unfortunately for the organization, this limit often falls far below what people are capable of producing.

Other forms of gaming include producing at extremely low levels or filing grievances when the rates are set at levels that the employees consider too difficult to reach. Another version of gaming involves doing only what is measured. Production workers may refuse to perform clean-up chores and material-handling work, while salespersons may avoid customer service activities or tie up customers so that other salespersons can not get the sale.

Finally, employees may organize unions so that they can gain leverage in negotiating piece rates. When unions do exist, they often manage to negotiate plans which allow workers to work off standard, while retaining a pay rate which represents a previously high level of performance. Thus organizations end up with the combination of high pay and low performance.

In summary, incentive plans often set up an adversarial relationship between workers on the plan and managers who design and administer the plan. As a result, both sides often engage in practices designed to win the war at the cost of organizational effectiveness.

Divided Work Force. Since many support jobs and nonproduction jobs do not lend themselves to piece-rate pay, most organizations that use incentive pay have part of the work force on it and part of the work force on some other plan. This system often leads to a we/they split in the work force that can prove counterproductive and lead to noncooperative work relationships. This split, interestingly enough, is not a management–worker split, but a worker–worker split that horizontally differentiates units of an organization. In its most severe form, this division can lead to people on incentive plans complaining about materials-handling people, maintenance people, and others on whom they depend for support. This split also can lead to some dysfunctional career paths. Individuals often will bid for and stay on incentive jobs, even though the work does not fit their skills and interests, simply to obtain higher pay. In addition, the higher pay of incentive jobs may cause individuals to resist any temporary change in jobs and any new technology which calls for a rate change.

Maintenance Costs. Because incentive plans are relatively complicated and need constant updating, maintenance of the plan requires a significant number of people. The problem of maintaining incentive systems is further complicated by the adversarial relationship between employees and management. Since employees try to hide new work methods and avoid rate changes (unless, of course, the change is to their advantage), management must exercise extreme vigilance in determining when new rates are needed. In addition, every technological change or introduction of a new product requires readjusting rates.

Organizational Culture. The work-force divisions created by using different pay plans and the adversarial process of rate setting can create a hostile, differentiated organizational culture. In particular, use of incentive pay for one group of workers can produce a culture of low trust, lack of information sharing, conflict between groups, poor support for joint problem solving, and inflexibility. Overall, incentive pay works against creating a climate of openness, trust, joint problem solving, and commitment to organizational objectives.

Small-Group Incentive Plans

Closely related to individual incentive plans are small-group incentive plans. These plans differ from individual ones since pay rates depend upon the performance of groups. They tend to fit situations where group performance is more easily measured than individual performance because group products form the desired output. They are usually somewhat less effective in motivating performance than individual incentive plans are because the lines of influence and sight are less clear. However, group plans can be quite effective if the size of the group is kept small. They are particularly good at encouraging cooperation and teamwork among those employees who are in the same group. In general, small-group plans suffer from all the same problems of the individual incentive plans since they too feature a top-down installation process, engineered standards, and adversarial relationships.

Summary

Installation of incentive pay is, at best, a mixed blessing. Although incentive pay may improve productivity, the counterproductive behaviors, the maintenance costs, the division of the work force, and the poor culture associated with incentive pay may make it a poor investment. Many organizations have dropped incentive pay or decided not to put plans in simply because the negative effects and maintenance costs appear to outweigh the increases in productivity it typically produces.

Incentive pay clearly fits some organizational situations better than others. It best fits situations where the work is designed for individuals or, in some cases, small groups. It best suits work that is simple, repetitive, and easy to measure comprehensively. More than any other system, it differentiates a work force to create isolated individuals or small groups who often feel they are competing with each other. Thus, an organization should use incentive pay only for jobs that require little integration or where other mechanisms can produce integration.

Incentive pay tends to work best for jobs that are stable and can be carefully studied. Finally, incentive pay clearly fits the control approach to management. However, even control oriented managements who use incentive pay must establish a sense of fairness and due process; otherwise, the situation may deteriorate into all-out confrontation, mistrust, and deceit.

Merit Salary Systems

Merit pay has become so widely accepted that almost every organization says that it has a merit pay system. Merit pay systems typically give salary increases to individuals based upon a supervisor's appraisal of their performance. The purpose of merit pay is to affect motivation and to retain the best performers by establishing a clear performance–reward relationship.

Pitfalls

Despite the widespread adoption of merit pay, considerable evidence shows that in most organizations, merit pay systems fail to create a close relationship between pay and performance.[17] As a result, they also fail to produce the positive motivational effects which are expected of merit systems. In addition, organizations may find it more difficult in the future to have effective merit pay programs. But before examining what the future holds and what can be done to make merit pay systems effective, readers need to understand the reasons why merit pay systems often do not produce the perception that pay and performance are related.

Poor Performance Measures. Credible, comprehensive measures of performance are fundamental to an effective merit pay system. Without these measures, it is impossible to relate pay to performance in a way that motivates employees. A great deal of evidence suggests that most organizations handle performance appraisals poorly. As a result, some observers have concluded that, while some good measures of plant or group performance exist, good measures of individual performance typically do not exist.[18] In the absence of good objective measures of individual performance, most organizations rely on the judgments of managers. These judgments are often seen by subordinates as invalid, unfair, and discriminatory. Because employees do not trust the performance measures, pay systems based on these measures do little to create the perception that pay reflects performance.[19] Indeed, in the eyes of many employees, merit pay is a fiction, a myth that managers try to perpetuate.

Poor Communication. The salaries of most individuals in organizations are kept secret, and some organizations do the same with many of their pay practices. For example, organizations typically keep secret such things as the amount given out in salary increases and the highest and lowest raises awarded. Given such secrecy, a typical employee lacks the facts to determine if pay and performance are related and must accept on faith that some linkage does exist.

In situations of high trust, employees may accept the organization's statement that merit pay exists. However, trust depends on the open exchange of information; thus, secrecy often produces skepticism among many individuals. A significant number of organizations exacerbate mistrust by failing to explain the pay system adequately and by communicating in ways that lead people to doubt the system. For example, organizations often state that all pay increases are based on merit, even though virtually everyone gets an increase because of inflation and changes in the labor market. As a result, individuals often question how much merit had to do with their "merit increase."

Poor Delivery Systems. The actual policies and procedures which make up a merit pay system often lead to actions which do little to relate pay to performance. In addition, policies and procedures often are so complex that they do more to obfuscate than to clarify the relationship between pay and performance. The typical merit salary increase is particularly poor at relating pay and performance, because it allows for only small changes in total pay to occur in one year. All too often only a few percentage points separate the raises given good performers from those given poor performers. This situation is particularly likely to occur in times of low inflation when salary increase budgets are usually low.

Salary increase systems further compound the problem of relating present pay levels to present performance by making past "merit payments" part of an individual's base salary. In this situation, the merit payment becomes an annuity and allows a formerly productive individual to slack off for several years and still earn high pay. A new employee who is a good performer, on the other hand, has to perform well for a number of years in order to achieve a relatively high pay level. This situation can have disastrous effects as far as retaining outstanding performers. Because good performers lack the ability to increase their pay quickly, they often find it best to look for a job elsewhere.

The annuity feature leads to one other problem: topping out. After a long period in a job, individuals often reach the top of the pay range for their job. As a result, pay no longer serves as a motivator because it cannot go up as a result of performance.

Poor Managerial Behavior. Managers may do a number of things that adversely affect the perceived and actual connection between pay and performance. Perhaps the most serious shortcoming is the failure to recommend widely different pay increases for subordinates when large performance differences exist. Some managers avoid recommending very large and very small pay changes, even when warranted, so as to escape the unpleasant task of explaining why someone got a low raise.

The difficulty of explaining low raises often leads to a second destructive behavior on the part of managers: disowning the pay decision. Even when supervisors recommend a small raise and believe it is appropriate, they sometimes deny or discount their role in determining their subordinates' pay. They may, for example, say that they fought hard for the subordinate to get a good raise but lost out. This disavowal clearly communicates to subordinates that pay increases are beyond their control and thus are not based on performance.

Individual Merit Pay and Organizational Performance

The existence of any one of the common problems which plague merit pay programs can destroy employees' belief that pay is related to performance, and as a result, merit pay loses its motivational impact. In reality, the merit pay systems of most organizations suffer from all or most of these typical problems and fail to achieve intended objectives.

The problems with merit pay do not mean, however, that employers should write it off entirely. An organization can solve most of the problems if it makes a strong commitment to doing so and if merit pay fits the organization's structure and needs. Like incentive pay, merit pay focuses on individuals and does little to integrate members of a work force. Indeed, the typical approach of allocating a budget to be divided into raises for a small group of employees clearly sets up competition among workers for the larger raises. This competition can create serious problems if an organization needs employees to cooperate in order to achieve its goals.

One approach to fostering team work is to appraise teams and distribute merit increases on a team basis. This practice can support cooperation and overcome the dysfunctions of pitting team members against each other for merit increases. However, merit pay systems seem to work best when the job design allows individuals to work independently of others.

Some observers question whether basing pay on appraisal can work in a pure top-down organization. Since appraisals involve judgment, merit pay systems necessitate an atmosphere of trust for subordinates to believe that they will be paid fairly based upon their performance. Trust is difficult to build in the absence of openness and at least a minimal degree of mutual influence. These factors seem to call for using merit pay only in work places that practice at least a minimal level of participative management.

Effective Merit Increase Delivery Systems

The annuity problems, discussed earlier, forms the main problem in merit salary delivery programs. The only solution is to eliminate the annuity feature; otherwise the system will never put enough pay at risk to motivate performance and differentiate the total compensation of good performers from that of lesser performers. The most straightforward solution is to establish a bonus plan that links bonuses to individual performance appraisal results. For example, an organization could pay a flat job rate to everyone who holds a particular job and then establish a merit bonus range and pool of money to use to raise some individuals substantially above the job rate. Each year, the system should require new appraisals and open the total bonus range to each individual so that past performance gives no assurance of present total pay or bonus. Since someone new to a job who performs well can quickly become quite highly paid, the system can retain the best performers even if they have just entered the organization or the job. In this type of system, market movement can change the job rate but these annual adjustments should clearly differ from the merit bonuses or, as they are sometimes called, the lump sum increases.

Finally, the amount of the bonus pool can vary according to organizational performance, or it can simply reflect a budgeted amount of salary costs. Basing the bonus pool on organizational performance can reduce the internal competitive dynamic since part of an individual's reward depends on collective performance. It can also help tie salary costs to an organization's ability to pay.

Pay-Performance Linkages

Linking the performance appraisal system to pay can produce positive and negative impacts on performance appraisal. On the positive side, recent research suggests that when pay is discussed during performance appraisals, supervisors and subordinates tend to take appraisals more seriously and exchange better information about performance expectations and performance results.[20] The same research also suggests that individuals approve of linking pay and performance and discussing both factors at the same time so that employees will understand how the performance appraisal system affects their pay.

On the negative side, evidence indicates that when pay and performance are discussed, career development issues and future performance concerns tend to get overlooked. Instead, the conversation focuses on past performance and on the impact of performance on pay. A subordinate also may withhold negative information about his jor her job performance in order to look good during the performance appraisal. This tendency can cloud the validity of the performance discussion and, if employee feedback is used for planning purposes, it can cause poor planning.

In addition, when individuals feel that their performance appraisal results determine their pay, they often set lower goals and make more conservative estimates of what they can accomplish.[21] This tendency can have a negative effect on motivation,[22] and mislead the planning process.

When pay is tied to performance appraisal ratings, it can greatly influence the behavior of appraisers. Supervisors feel pressure to give high ratings so that their subordinates will get a "good" raise or bonus. Indeed, ratings may reflect the efforts of a supervisor to get a particular pay action rather than a person's performance. The result can produce false and very inflated ratings of performance.

To summarize the discussion so far, a pay system puts certain stresses on a performance appraisal system when the two are connected. These stresses are not all negative, but organizations do need to take them into account in the design of any performance appraisal system.

Effective Performance Appraisals

Unless performance appraisal can be done well, an organization is foolish to tie performance appraisals to its pay system. The advantages of relating performance to pay will disappear under the negatives of tying pay to a poorly done performance appraisal. This point highlights the need to consider what conditions promote effective performance appraisals.

A large number of factors can determine the effectiveness of a performance appraisal system.[23] The following discussion first examines those factors that are situational in nature and separate from the appraisal system. Next, the analysis will address issues concerning the design and structure of performance appraisal forms and procedures.

Job Design. Job design is probably the single most crucial determinant of whether performance appraisal should be used in a pay for performance system. Unless job design allows measurement of individual performance, conducting effective performance appraisals becomes extremely difficult. Many of the job design characteristics which lead to effective performance appraisal also are associated with effective individual job enrichment. As research on individual job enrichment has shown, when jobs are designed so that people can do a whole piece of work, have responsibility for performing that task, and get feedback on their task performance, intrinsic motivation is high.[24] The same characteristics also permit effective performance appraisals of individuals. Indeed, the individual feedback which generates intrinsic motivation is the same kind of information needed to appraise performance. Without clear-cut individual responsibility for a whole piece of work, both individuals and supervisors will have difficulty judging performance.

Communication. Effective performance appraisal also depends on open, effective communication between superiors and subordinates. Supervisors usually need to gather information from subordinates in order to find out how well an individual has performed, and individuals need to gather information from supervisors in order to understand what performance is expected of them and how their performance will be and is judged. Without good superior/subordinate relationships and effective communication, a performance appraisal system may reach invalid conclusions about performance.

Organizational Culture. Appraising performance is a time-consuming and often difficult task. It requires skills that many supervisors lack and behavior that supervisors often find difficult to demonstrate. Because of these difficulties, effective performance appraisals require an organizational culture that strongly supports the appraisal system. The culture needs to reward efforts at doing performance appraisal well, provide positive role models of effective performance appraisal behavior, and demonstrate that the top levels of the organization take performance apparisals seriously. Lacking these positive cultural conditions, conducting effective performance appraisal becomes extremely difficult. Thus, any discussion of linking pay to performance appraisals must consider the type of organizational culture concerning performance measurement and the degree to which top management will support and encourage effective appraisals.

Summary. No formula exists which will allow highly programmed decisions about the design and use of a performance appraisal system. The complexity of the situation requires tough judgment calls on the part of system designers. System designers have a natural inclination to favor relating pay to performance appraisals because of the important positive results which can come about. However, making a hasty decision to implement such a system often creates significant problems.

As was stressed earlier, tying pay to performance poses great risks that can far outweigh any positives. Even with effective performance appraisals, tying pay to appraisal results may lead to less open communication and more conservative goal setting. Organizations should tie pay to appraisal results only when most of the favorable conditions exist and when no adequate substitutes exist. Without a strongly supportive culture, good job designs, and adequate superior–subordinate relationships, organizations should not relate pay to appraisal results. To do so without the right conditions will render the pay system ineffective and may cause the appraisal system itself to collapse under the stress of trying to support an inappropriate pay system.

All the favorable conditions do not necessarily have to exist prior to starting performance appraisals; they can come about after an appraisal system is put in place. Thus, system designers should first decide whether the organization can create such conditions. Creating these conditions may involve organizational change of a magnitude that makes it uncertain whether an organization can adapt. Sometimes installation of an appraisal system can help move an organization in a positive direction, but it is a high risk strategy to assume this will happen.

The warning is clear: Managers should not be seduced by the potential advantage of tying pay to performance appraisal results. Positive results require favorable organizational conditions. Compensation planners need to assess the situation realistically to determine whether favorable conditions exist or can be created. A combination of attitude surveys, observations, and interviews can assist this assessment. Most design processes omit this consideration, a mistake equivalent to entering unexplored territory without a map.

Appraisal System Design

Designers of performance appraisal systems must consider a number of design issues that impact on a system's success. The following discussion examines several key considerations.

Appraisal Cycle. The design of an appraisal system for driving pay should first identify the appropriate time period for conducting performance appraisals. Picking too short a time period runs the risk of measuring performance before an individual has had a chance to demonstrate the desired behavior. Picking too long a time period may cause individuals to lose sight of the connection between pay and performance, thus, diminishing the motivational impact of appraisals. Organizations typically pick an annual appraisal cycle in which everyone gets appraised once a year. At the lower levels of an organization, an annual cycle is probably too infrequent since the performance of people in these jobs typically becomes evident within a much shorter term. Indeed, at this level, individuals may have left the job or the organization before the appraisal takes place. At the top level, an annual cycle often fails to provide sufficient time for individuals to demostrate their performance effectiveness. At the top levels, an appraisal cycle of two years or more might prove appropriate.

A sometimes desirable option is to vary the frequency of appraisals as a function of performance. Poor performers might benefit from having more frequent reviews, yet some organizations do just the opposite. Managers should use reviews of poor performance to work on employee development and to give positive feedback and rewards if performance has improved.

Sequence of Events. An organization must determine the sequence of events during the performance period. Table 2 illustrates the best sequence of events for most performance appraisal situations. At the beginning of the performance period, supervisors and subordinates should agree upon specific goals and measures as well as on the impact of these goals on pay. In short, this discussion forms a type of performance contract that identifies measures of performance, levels of performance, and pay results. This discussion should be a two-way one in which both supervisors and subordinates feel that they have impacted upon the ultimate contract. If a subordinate at this point does not see the goals as achievable and does not understand the relationship to pay, the system will have no motivational impact.

Not shown in Table 2, but potentially important, are midcourse reviews of the goals, objectives, and individual performance. Situational change often makes initial goals unrealistic. This case requires resetting and adjusting goals to fit current conditions and to

---

Table 2

Sequence of Events in Relating Pay to Appraisals

Prior to Performance Period	*Following Performance Period*	*After Pay Action*
1. Agree on performance desired	1. Employee gives input to appraisal	1. Communicate final pay action
2. Agree on performance measures	2. Supervisor reacts to input and gives own views	2. Explain how pay action fits pay system and give information on how others were treated
3. Agree on how results will affect pay	3. Agree on final performance judgement and if possible at this time, agree to pay action	

maintain motivational impact. In addition, ongoing feedback can sometimes help individuals correct their performance problems.

The schedule shown in Table 2 calls for two discussions at the end of the performance. The first provides an individual with the opportunity to self-evaluate his or her performance during the time period. Research shows that this important step can determine whether an individual perceives the performance appraisal process as fair and reasonable.[25] Organizations often omit this step, leading individuals to feel that they lacked adequate input into the appraisal process and that their supervisors did not have the correct information upon which to base the appraisals. As a result, employees view appraisals as invalid and fail to perceive the connection between pay and performance.

The final meeting should evaluate the overall performance of the individual and specify the pay action. While Table 2 does not show this final step, the actual pay action should follow quickly. This step serves the important function of establishing a clear connection between pay and performance. It makes no sense to separate the pay action from the appraisal action as some organizations do. This separation often occurs, for example, when an employer conducts appraisals throughout the year, but saves pay actions for year end.

One other timing issue deserves attention. This issue concerns the practice of varying the frequency of pay actions according to the favorableness of appraisal ratings. In some organizations, low-rated individuals are "stretched out" so they go longer between pay changes and appraisals. While this approach attempts to relate pay to performance, it produces some undesirable effects. From a motivational point of view, the long separation between performance and any changes in pay eliminates the immediate incentive to improve. This practice also creates a problem with respect to the timing of the next appraisal. As noted earlier, an appraisal cycle should support a pay action and, if anything, the cycle should be shorter for poor performers. Rather than give a small increase with a long period before the next increase, organizations should give no increase to a poor performer, but promise an early pay review if performance improves.

Rating Methods. The discussion so far has not mentioned the type of form used. Any appraisal form should do three things. First, it should focus as much as possible on observable behavior and results. Second, it should give some quantitative score that can be translated into a pay action. Third, it should encourage appraisers to avoid inflating ratings and to report differences in performance only where defensible.

Organizations often force raters to come up with a particular distribution of ratings in order to avoid inflation and similar ratings for all employees. Methods commonly used for this purpose include ranking and forced distribution appraisal. Ranking is particularly bad because it creates indefensible differences and ignores the absolute level of performance. The forced distribution approach is better if designed well and applied to a large enough group of individuals. However, it also has problems. The key issue in a forced distribution approach concerns what type of distribution is used. A typical approach assumes a normal distribution and then asks raters to put individuals in different parts of a normal or bell-shaped curve. Raters then break the distribution of individuals into something like the following four categories: top 15 percent, next 35 percent, next 35 percent, bottom 15 percent.

This approach creates two very important problems. First, the assumption of a normal distribution probably is incorrect. Normal distributions assume randomness, yet performance in organizations is deliberately influenced by selection, training, and other activities. Further, this distribution asks raters to split individuals in the middle of the performance distribution into good performers and poor performers. Breaking up a performance distribution in the middle is almost always impossible to defend. Falling above or below average is a very emotional issue and supervisors find it hard to specify and communicate what separates someone who is just over the line from someone who is just short of it. Many people are, in fact, around the middle of the distribution, but of course, they all tend to see themselves as above average. Thus, trying to draw a line down the middle of a performance distribution will cause a lot of individuals to feel poorly treated.

A preferable alternative is to identify only the extreme cases, such as the top and bottom 5 to 10 percent. These groups often are the easiest to identify and by putting a large number of individuals in the middle, organizations avoid the dissatisfaction caused by telling many individuals they are below average. While using only extreme categories prevents fine-tuning pay actions, this disadvantage seems preferable to basing pay actions on indefensible ratings.

In any forced distribution, employers should avoid applying the distribution to a group of less than fifty individuals. Otherwise inequities will inevitably occur because one small group has many good performers while another one has mainly poor performers. Forcing a distribution on small groups can also introduce undesirable competition because individuals realize that in order to get a high rating, they must "beat out" other members of their work group.

One complexity occurs when forced distributions are used for multiple work groups. This system involves multiple raters and necessitates developing some procedure or process to assure consistency in the standards used to rate individuals from different groups. The best approach usually involves holding mandatory meetings in which raters reach mutual agreement on how to evaluate all individuals. These meetings are difficult and time consuming but usually produce better results than arbitrarily forcing raters to fit a particular distribution. Such conferences also can provide a good check-and-balance system that prevents rating inflation and can motivate raters to do their homework with respect to appraisal documentation. Indeed, in some organizations, these meetings have become so effective in fighting ratings inflation they have made forced distributions unnecessary.

One last interesting way to address the form issue is to allow each supervisor and subordinate pair to pick a form that they feel fits their situation. In this approach, an organization's main responsibility involves providing acceptable forms and, if needed, helping a supervisor and subordinate to pick the best one. This choice process can prove quite effective since it commits both parties to the appraisal process and enhances the perceived validity of the form selected.

The suggested sequence of performance appraisal and pay actions in Table 2 includes no discussion of career development. This intentional omission reflects the need to handle career development in a separate session and on a somewhat different cycle. Research evidence shows that without this separation, the discussion of past performance and pay tends to drive out consideration of career issues.[26]

Conclusion: Paying for Individual Performance

The potential positive effects of tying pay changes to an appraisal system are as great as the downside effects of doing it poorly. Table 3 highlights the advantages, disadvantages, and

Table 3

Pay for Individual Performance

Organizational Impact/Fit	Incentive Pay	Merit Pay
Performance motivation	Clear performance reward connection	Little relationship between pay and performance
Attraction	Pays higher performers more	Over time pays better performers more
Culture	Divides work force, adversarial	Competition within work groups
Organization structure	Many independent jobs	Helped by measurable jobs and work units
Management style	Control	Some participation desirable
Type of work	Stable, individual easily measurable	Individual unless group appraisals done
Costs	Maintenance high	Requires well developed performance appraisal system

design issues involved in deciding whether to implement a pay for individual performance system. System designers need to gather data, analyze the risks, and ultimately decide whether the advantages of such a system outweigh the disadvantages. The decision should depend not only on systematic data collection but also on input from potential administrators of the system and those individuals whose pay will be affected. Without the commitment of these people to a pay system driven by performance appraisals, the system will never operate effectively.

Organizations should approach implementation of individual incentive systems with a great deal of caution. As shown in Table 3, these systems can serve as a positive motivator but they don't fit most situations. Thus, use of such systems seems likely to decline in the future and ultimately may be limited to individual sales positions, low-level clerical posts, and simple repetitive manufacturing jobs.

Pay for Organizational Performance

Bonus payments based on organizational performance are an old and potentially quite effective way to enhance business performances. Proponents argue that these types of bonuses can improve motivation, build employees' commitment to and concern about an organization's effectiveness, and finally, adjust labor costs to an organization's ability to pay.[27] Indeed, some organizations have achieved precisely these outcomes as a result of paying bonuses based on organizational performance.[28]

When it comes to designing an effective plan, organizations can select from literally thousands of approaches to paying for organizational performance. Designers must address many complex organizational issues to assure the plan's success. The good news is that decades of research have pointed out a number of things that must be done if plans are to be successful.

Over the years, two major approaches have been used to pay for organizational performance. The oldest approach pays bonuses based on the profitability of an organization. This method is undoubtedly the most widely accepted around the world. It has important advantages and disadvantages that will be discussed later. Stock ownership plans give individuals complete or partial ownership of the organizations for which they work. Both stock ownership and profit sharing plans use existing measures of performance, and treat employees like investors, rewarding them when the organization does well and reducing their wealth when the organization does poorly.

A third less well-known but increasingly popular approach is gainsharing. Gainsharing differs from profit sharing and stock ownership in two respects. First, it always involves a participative approach to management, and secondly, it typically measures controllable costs or units of output, not profits or stock price in its approach to calculating a bonus.

Table 4 gives an overview of the characteristics of the three major types of pay for organizational performance systems. The following discussion will first consider what is known about gainsharing, and then consider profit sharing and stock ownership plans.

Table 4

Approaches to Paying for Organizational Performance

Plan Characteristics	Gainsharing	Profit Sharing	Ownership
Payment method	Bonus	Bonus	Equity changes
Frequency of payout	Monthly or quarterly	Semi-annually or annually	When stock sold
Measures	Production or controllable costs	Profit	Stock value
Coverage	Production or service unit	Total organization	Total organization

---

Finally, the analysis will examine issues that organizations should consider in selecting among these different approaches.

Gainsharing

Hundreds of organizations have successfully used gainsharing during the past 40 years.[29] Employees and companies have profited from gainsharing: companies have realized reduced costs and employees have garnered bonus payments and improved job satisfaction. The original and best-known gainsharing plan is the Scanlon Plan; other gainsharing plans include Improshare and the Rucker Plan. In addition to these plans, many companies have customized gainsharing plans.

The typical gainsharing plan uses a formula to calculate financial gains in organizational performance. Most formulas measure only controllable costs and compare these costs against performance during a historical base period. Unless a major organizational change takes place, the historical base stays the same during the entire history of the plan; thus, performance is always compared to the time period prior to the start of the gainsharing plan. When performance improves relative to the base period, a bonus pool is funded. When performance falls short, no bonus pool is created. In a typical plan, employees receive at least half of the bonus pool, while the company keeps the rest. A typical bonus schedule provides monthly payments, with all employees in the unit getting equal percentage amounts.

No one has an accurate estimate of how many organizations in the United States and Europe utilize gainsharing plans. At least a thousand plans probably are in operation and there seems to be little doubt that their popularity has increased tremendously in the last 10 years. One recent survey in the United States indicated that about 13 percent of all firms have gainsharing plans and more than 70 percent of these plans were started in the last five years.[30] The White House Conference on Productivity, the U.S. General Accounting Office, and the President's Task Force on Industrial Competitiveness have all recently endorsed gainsharing.

Until 10 years ago, gainsharing was used primarily in small manufacturing organizations. Companies cited as successful users of gainsharing include Herman Miller, Lincoln Electric, and Donnelly Mirrors.[31] All three of these companies have plans that date back more than 30 years. During the 1970s, an interesting and important trend developed. Large companies like General Electric, Motorola, Rockwell, TRW, Dana, and Firestone began installing gainsharing plans in some of their manufacturing plants. The trend of large corporations creating separate gainsharing plans for organizational units is continuing and has led to the adoption of many more gainsharing plans. Dana and Motorola, for example, now cover virtually all of their employees with gainsharing.

The increased popularity of gainsharing relates to an important feature of most gainsharing plans. Gainsharing is more than just a pay incentive plan; it is a management style and technology for organizational development. In particular, gainsharing requires a participative approach to management and organizations often use these plans as a way to install participative management.

Need for Participative Management

Joe Scanlon, the creator of the Scanlon Plan, emphasized from the beginning that gainsharing fits a participative management style. In many cases, an organization must have a participative system in order for the plan to work, and in all cases, participative management enhances the potential benefits of gainsharing. Without some change in employee behavior, the gains necessary to merit a payout probably will not take place. A payout requires improved organizational performance, and that improvement requires more effective employee behavior.

Some improvement may occur simply from the incentive created by tying pay to performance. This effect is particularly likely in unskilled or independent jobs where performance depends almost exclusively on employees' efforts. In other situations, however, a gainsharing plan operating without a participative system will not produce an appreciable improvement in performance. Several factors account for the failure of gainsharing plans under these circumstances.

First, most gainsharing plans aggregate a number of people together, thus weakening the perceived relationship between individual performance and pay. The formula used is also relevant here. Some plans (for example, Improshare) use very simple formulas that focus on the relatinship between labor input and productivity, while others (like Rucker), use a comprehensive set of cost measures. Simple labor-based plans are more likely to affect motivation because they create a more direct relationship between employees' efforts and bonuses. Despite their attractiveness, simple plans do not always enhance organizational effectiveness, as will be discussed later.

Second, simple effort and good intentions alone cannot improve operating results in many cases. Improvement may require a combination of people working harder, smarter, and more effectively together. Achieving this goal often takes a formal participative system that converts the motivation to improve into actual operational changes in an organization. In the absence of new procedures or systems, these changes seem to occur rarely.

Traditional gainsharing plans emphasize participative management through a formal suggestion system with written suggestions and shop floor committees to review the suggestions. Many organizations also install a higher-level review committee that looks over recommendations which involve several parts of the organization and/or large expenditures. This sytem of committees attempts to assure that new ideas will undergo serious consideration and, where appropriate, implementation.

Some companies, such as TRW, have recently combined gainsharing with highly participative management practices to produce what is best termed high involvement management.[32] In this approach, employees make most of the operating decisions and get rewarded for their organization's effectiveness through the gainsharing plan. This approach has considerable promise since it helps increase the line of influence. It gives employees a chance to change things that determine an organization's operating results, an opportunity which is necessary for bonuses based on operating results to influence motivation.

Pros and Cons of Gainsharing

The most important research findings on gainsharing plans is that they can work.[33] Table 5 lists some of the positive results that commonly appear in research studies of gainsharing plans. As Table 5 shows, gainsharing can produce a number of benefits and research demonstrating these results dates back quite a few years. Studies on the success rates of gainsharing plans are less conclusive, but evidence suggests that such plans work in a relatively high percentage (about 70 percent) of cases.[34]

Still, gainsharing plans do some things less well than other approaches to paying for performance. Perhaps the most important weakness concerns differential attraction and retention of the best performers. Because gainsharing plans do not pay better performers more, these emloyees may lack motivation to stay. While gainsharing plans do vary costs somewhat with an organization's ability to pay, they are less effective at cost-control than profit sharing since gainsharing can provide payouts even when an organization is not profitable. Finally, gainsharing plans contribute to both integration

---

Table 5

Results of Gainsharing

1. Coordination, teamwork, and sharing of knowledge are enhanced at lower levels.

2. Social needs are recognized via participation and mutually reinforcing group behavior.

3. Attention is focused on cost savings, not just quantity of production.

4. Acceptance of change due to technology, market, and new methods is greater because higher efficiency leads to bonuses.

5. Attitudinal change occurs among workers, and they demand more efficient management and better planning.

6. Employees try to reduce overtime; to work smarter, not harder or faster.

7. Employees produce ideas as well as effort.

8. When unions are present, more flexible administration of union-management relations occurs.

9. When unions support the plan, they are strengthened because a better work situation and higher pay result.

10. Unorganized locations tend to remain nonunion.

and differentiation. They integrate the units they cover both vertically and horizontally since they treat everyone in a work unit the same. On the other hand, they tend to differentiate participants from the rest of an organization.

Quite a bit is known about how to structure gainsharing plans. A number of books and articles detail how to put together formulas, introduce plans, and manage the process side of plan design and operation.[35] As a result, "how-to-do-it" knowledge is readily available particularly with respect to the Scanlon Plan. Indeed, careful reading of the literature on this plan can enable a skilled practitioner to develop and install a plan without the help of a consultant; most plans, however, are installed by consultants.

Situational Factors Favoring Gainsharing

Research also shows that certain situational factors favor gainsharing plans.[36] The following discussion examines a number of these situational prerequisites.

Organization Size. The success of gainsharing depends on employees seeing a relationship between performance and pay. As organizations get larger, this linkage becomes more obscure. Most successful gainsharing plans cover less than 500 employees. They also tend to cover units that can operate relatively independently of other organizational units.

Performance Measurement. In some organizations, good performance measures and a reasonable performance history simply do not exist and cannot be established. This situation often arises in organizations subject to rapid technological and market changes. Under such variable conditions, gainsharing formulas are difficult to develop.

Measurement Complexity. Organizations often can measure performance only in very complex ways. As measurements grow more complicated, the connection between an individual's behavior and rewards becomes less clear and more difficult to understand. As a result, gainsharing plans work best when performance is easy to measure.

Worker Characteristics. Gainsharing depends on workers wanting greater participation and higher financial rewards. Most workers have these goals, but not all do. Unless a substantial majority of the employees wants the benefits offered by a plan, it cannot succeed.

Communication. For gainsharing to work, employees must understand and trust the plan enough to believe that their pay will increase if they perform better. Generating this belief requires a great deal of open communication and education. If an organization lacks these features, it must install them along with the plan.

Management Attitudes. Unless managers support the idea of participation, gainsharing will not fit the organization's approach to decision making. Some organizations have tried gainsharing simply as a pay incentive plan without regard to management style, and the plan has failed because of a poor fit.

Supervisory Skills. Gainsharing requires supervisors to develop new skills. Supervisors must deal with many suggestions, and they have their competence tested and questioned in new ways. Unless supervisors are prepared for and accept these changes, a gainsharing plan can fail. This point goes along with the general point that management must be prepared to manage in a different way.

Summary. As this list demonstrates, gainsharing does not fit every situation. Since manufacturing organizations often have most of these favorable conditions, it is easy to see why, for so long, gainsharing plans existed only in these businesses. However, this situation has begun to change. Some service organizations such as hotels, banks, and hospitals have recently installed gainsharing plans, and the increased use of gainsharing plans in nonmanufacturing situations appears likely to continue over the next five to ten years. Although a great deal remains to be learned about how to install such plans in nonmanufacturing environments, it appears that gainsharing can work in these settings.[37] Indeed, as long as some basic design features can be built into plans, gainsharing probably can work in many situations.

Critical Gainsharing Elements

The design of a gainsharing plan is part science and part art. Because of the wide variety in gainsharing plans, designers can easily lose track of the key elements that make for a successful gainsharing plan. One key issue in gainsharing design concerns fit. The gainsharing formula and participative management features need to fit each other and the organization. Different situations require different designs; however, some elements must appear in any plan for it to succeed. The following analysis considers each of these elements and looks at how to incorporate them into a gainsharing plan.

Credible, Trusted Development Process. Methods used to develop gainsharing plans vary widely. In some cases, a knowledgeable outside expert sells an already developed plan to the organization. In other cases, the organization establishes a representative task force to investgate different plans and recommend one for the particular situation. No right set of practices exists, but the practices must enhance employees' belief that if they perform better, they will earn more. Gainsharing plans initially require a leap of faith, since employees receive no payment until performance improves. Although relying on an outside expert may work in some cases, in most cases, a participative development process that utilizes a task force will probably lead to greater acceptance of a plan.

Understandable and Influenceable Bonuses. For a gainsharing plan to increase motivation, employees must have both a line of sight and a line of influence to the bonus. In short, they must recognize how their behavior can influence the size of the bonus. Achieving this recognition, particularly in a complex organization, is not simple. It necessitates education, communication, and the development of a good approach for determining the size of the bonus.

A typical gainsharing plan uses a formula to calculate the size of the bonus. Formula-based plans obviously offer much more objectivity than plans that rely on a discretionary decision to determine bonus size. However, situations characterized by rapid change or complexity do not lend themselves to a formula. If an organization can develop a valid, trusted decision process, it can still have an effective plan even though it cannot develop a formula. For example, some organizations have successfully used committees to make bonus decisions while others have used a trusted top manager to make them based on preset objectives.

Appropriate Measures. Any discussion of formula raises the question of what to measure. Some advocates of gainsharing push strongly for simple plans operating on the principle that simplicity always works best. For example, some plans simply measure the number units of output per labor hour. These plans can prove effective in situations where labor costs are the key issue and the business is a very simple one. In most cases, however, ignoring other costs, such as materials and supplies, can be quite dangerous and counterproductive. Focusing on any cost to the exclusion of others can lead to employees' reducing that expense while increasing others. Thus, the decision of what to measure under a gainsharing plan should focus on identifying all the controllable costs. This focus may lead to a more complex plan, but a complex plan will work better than one which ignores the true complexity of the business. Simple plans are great for simple businesses, but more complex businesses need complex plans.

Every bonus plan must have a standard that triggers payment. Many profit sharing plans use a financial break-even point or a certain return on investment. As noted earlier, gainsharing plans typically use a historical performance level. This criterion offers a number of advantages, particularly its credibility. Employees know the performance level can be achieved, and they understand where it came from. It is not an arbitrary number based on some economic concept like return on investment or someone's estimate of acceptable performance. From an organization's point of view, a gainsharing formula which requires real improvements in organizational performance makes the bonuses self funding in the sense that without improvement, there are no bonuses.

However, other performance standards may prove appropriate under certain circumstances. An organization that is on a learning curve may find that historical performance is too easy to achieve and thus, a standard based on some projections of the learning curve may prove necessary. In organizations which experience dramatic changes in products or technology, history may no longer offer a relevant standard and a more subjective approach, such as a committee decision, may be required.

Timely Bonuses. Gainsharing plans typically pay bonuses on a monthly basis, but other schedules also work. The important principle is bonuses follow the performance as closely as possible. In situations with a simple, short cycle work process, a monthly schedule may be correct. In more complex situations, a month may prove too short for an organization to complete production of a product or delivery of a service. In this case, quarterly or even semiannual bonus payments may be the right time period.

Involvement Opportunities. Employees need to have influence over the measures used to calculate the bonus. This necessity has some direct implications for the choice of a participative management model. If a formula bases bonuses on labor costs only, then a suggestion program like the one used in Scanlon plan companies often is quite appropriate. Through written suggestions, employees can develop improvements in work methods to speed production and reduce labor costs. However, a complex, multiple-cost formula will require different forms of employee involvement. In complex situations, employees should be able to influence not just direct production decisions, but decisions involving other costs, such as materials, supplies, inventory, and so forth. To accomplish this, an organization may have to install work teams and task forces to look at major business decisions, in short, develop a high involvement approach to management.

Maintenance. All gainsharing plans require maintenance. Businesses change, environments change, and as a result, gainsharing formulas and involvement approaches need to change. The success of any change in a gainsharing plan depends on its timeliness and its credibility in employees' eyes.

A typical approach to maintenance utilizes an ongoing task force which has representatives from all levels of the work force. This group regularly reviews the plan and recommends changes when necessary. To succeed, the internal group should be composed of trusted, knowledgeable individuals who understand the business and are capable of making good decisions and communicating them to the rest of the work force.

As an alternative, an organization can hire an outside expert to come in and update the plan on a regular basis. This approach can work, but it has the disadvantage of creating dependence on an outsider who may prove less credible than an internal group.

Profit Sharing

Profit sharing is better known, older, and more widely practiced than gainsharing. In the United States, for example, data indicate that at least one third of all organizations have profit sharing programs.[38] Some definitions of profit sharing include it as a form of gainsharing; however, it differs in two respects. Profit sharing often does not utilize participative management or formulas that only measure increases in employee-controlled performance. As a result, profit sharing plans typically prove much less effective in influencing motivation and in producing the kind of social and cultural outcomes listed in Table 5. These limitations particularly affect large organizations where employees have little influence and see little connection between individual performance and corporate profits.

In the typical profit sharing plan, firms (about 85 percent) defer profit sharing bonuses by putting them into retirement plans. This practice compounds the problem of tying present rewards to present controllable performance and minimizes any impact on motivation.

Advantages of Profit Sharing

Even a deferred profit sharing plan in a large corporation can accomplish three things. First, paying people based on organizational performance offers some potential symbolic and communication value. It can enhance employees' sense of belonging and emphasize the need for cooperative effort. When utilized in executive compensation plans, profit sharing can also help to align the rewards received by top management and those received by other employees. This strategy can help avoid the all too common problem of executives getting large bonuses while lower-level employees receive none, thus creating an often counterproductive vertical differentiation within an organization.

Second, some companies, most notably Hewlett Packard, have effectively used their profit sharing plans as vehicles for educating employees about the financial performance of the business. When employees actually share in the profits, they develop an interest and an understanding of what profits mean, how they are calculated, and what factors impact on profits and organizational effectiveness.

Third, and perhaps the most important, profit sharing varies labor costs according to an organization's ability to pay. When profits go down, labor costs go down, and thus labor costs become variable, at least in part. This feature proves particularly desirable for organizations that operate cyclical or seasonal businesses. In most western countries, organizations handle changes in labor costs through increasing and decreasing the size of the work force. When wages are high and fixed, work-force reductions are the only way to reduce labor costs to reflect a company's ability to pay. In contrast profit sharing allows employers to reduce costs significantly without reducing the number of employees. Most Japanese companies have used this approach to adjusting costs for decades. As businesses in Japan have shown, profit sharing enables an organization to make a much stronger commitment to employment stability and generates the advantages associated with a stable work force.

A key issue with profit sharing concerns just how much of an individual's pay should vary under a profit sharing plan. In Japan, profit sharing often determines a large percentage of a person's pay, as much as 30 percent to 40 percent. This strategy gives Japanese companies a significant cushion and helps make their guaranteed employment model work. This strategy probably risks too great an amount of employees' pay for most western businesses, but a company probably could make 10 percent to 20 percent of total compensation dependent on profit sharing.

Employee Ownership

A number of pay plans place some or all of a company's ownership into the hands of employees. These programs include stock option, stock purchase, and employee stock ownership plans. Stock ownership plans in particular have become increasingly popular. According to one study, some 11 million employees in over 8,000 businesses now own at least 15 percent of the companies employing them.[39]

Pros and Cons of Employee Ownership

The impact of stock ownership plans remains uncertain because such plans vary widely in the amount of ownership given to employees and their effect on employee behavior probably depends on the organizational situation. However, it appears that in some situations, ownership can have much the same impact as an effective gainsharing plan. In a small organization which practices participative management, a stock ownership plan has a good chance of increasing organizational performance.[40] Combining ownership with employee involvement seems critical since such plans typically produce a weaker line of influence than gainsharing and profit sharing.

In a large organization, limited employee ownership does little beyond enhancing integration, if, of course, all employees are included in the ownership plan. Unlike profit sharing, stock ownership does not adjust costs to reflect an organization's ability to pay unless it includes an approach in which stockholders share in profits. But stock ownership can help organizations raise capital and finance themselves. Indeed, most organizations probably install such plans precisely because of the tax and financing advantages they offer.[41] In addition, ownership can have a more positive impact on attraction and retention than profit sharing, particularly if ownership is difficult to sell.

In general, ownership strategies appear likely to have a positive effect in a number of situations. Their usefulness, however, depends greatly on the particular situation. For instance, in small organizations, stock ownership plans might make profit sharing and gainsharing unnecessary and if combined with employee involvement, could contribute substantially to employee motivation. A large organization, on the other hand, may use stock ownership as a supplement to other pay for performance systems even though, because of line of sight and influence problems, stock ownership appears unlikely to have a very strong impact on motivation and retention. Such a plan could, however, contribute to a positive culture and to the integration of an organization.

Design of Effective Organizational Performance Pay Systems

Ownership, gainsharing, and profit sharing all can prove useful for many organizations. Table 6 summarizes the major advantages and limitations of each approach. Employers should not view these options as competing approaches but as often compatible approaches which accomplish different, important objectives. Profit

Table 6

Pay for Organizational Performance

Organizational Impact/Fit	Gainsharing	Profit Sharing	Employee Ownership
Performance motivation	Some impact in small units	Little pay-performance relationship	Very little pay-performance relationship
Attraction	Helps with all employees	Helps with all employees	Can help lock in employees
Culture	Supports cooperation, problem solving	Knowledge of business	Sense of ownership
Organization structure	Fits small stand alone work units	Fits any company	Fits most companies
Management style	Fits participation	Works best with participation	Works best with participation
Type of work	All types	All types	All types
Costs	On-going maintenance needed operating costs variable	Relates costs to ability to pay	Cost not variable with performance

sharing can create variable costs for an organization, thus allowing it to adjust costs to its resources. Stock ownership can assist financing and help to retain employees. Like profit sharing, ownership can also affect communication patterns and culture in ways that emphasize organizational performance. Gainsharing, if correctly designed, can motivate performance and produce a culture in which people are committed to seeing their organizational unit operate effectively.

Combination Plans

The ideal system for many large corporations may combine a corporatewide profit sharing plan, a stock ownership program, and gainsharing plans in major operating plants or units. The combination of gainsharing and profit sharing deals directly with the need to vary costs and motivate employees. Gainsharing alone does not achieve these goals because it tends to focus on subunits of an organization and utilizes measures which do not include all operating costs. Thus, a gainsharing plan could pay a bonus when the organization is performing poorly. Even in such circumstances, gainsharing can enhance motivation, provided the plan utilizes accurate measures and targets performance that employees can control. However, gainsharing fails to integrate a total organization in the way an effective profit sharing plan or an effective ownership plan can. As a result, employees may erroneously feel that the organization is in good shape if they are receiving a bonus. The addition of a profit sharing plan and/or an ownership plan can help call attention to organizational performance and to the interdependencies among subunits which affect the entire organization. Profit sharing also can adjust labor costs according to an organization's ability to pay, something a gainsharing plan may not do.

When used together the size of profit sharing and gainsharing payments should vary according to a number of factors. In most cases, payouts probably should change at different levels in an organization. At the lowest level, gainsharing should offer the potential for larger payouts than profit sharing, but, actual payments should reflect performance. This strategy assumes that lower-level employees can better understand gainsharing and that it requires significant payouts in order to be motivating. At higher levels of management, the situation is different and profit sharing should have the greatest payoff potential.

Some organizational conditions also affect decisions about relative size of payout. The more interdependence among different units and the smaller the organization, the more profit sharing should come into play. The logic here recognizes that in small, highly integrated organizations, employees can easily focus on and significantly impact organizational performance.

Supportive Reward System Practices

As stated before, gainsharing, profit sharing, and stock ownership do not operate effectively in all situations. To flourish, they need to be combined with a participative approach to management and communication. In a similar way, organizations which adopt a combination of ownership, profit sharing, and gainsharing need to develop educational and reward systems to support these plans.

Employee Education. To understand how profits are measured and achieved, employees need education on the economics of the business and on how the organization works. Knowledge- or skill-based pay can facilitate this educational process. In this pay system, salaries vary according to the number of skills and amount of knowledge employees have.[42] Everyone must learn multiple skills and as individuals master new jobs, their pay increases, creating a strong incentive to learn. Organizations provide training and encourage employees to rotate jobs and to learn continually. This emphasis helps employees understand how the organization works and how they can influence its performance—key factors in making pay for organizational performance plans successful. It also instills a higher level of employee commitment to improving performance.

Job Security. Employment stability can play a critical part in the success of pay plans which are based on organizational performance. If employees fear that they will become unnecessary and will lose their jobs because productivity improves, they will lack the motivation to contribute their ideas and to work harder. Employees need at least a guarantee that layoffs will not result from the improvements that their efforts produce. If financially reasonable, an organization should assure employees that the organization will exhaust all other means of reducing costs before resorting to layoffs in economic downturns. With an employment guarantee, employees see a fair trade-off: employment stability in exchange for the fluctuating compensation inherent in profit sharing and gainsharing.

Financial Counseling. Performance-based pay can disrupt people's personal lives because it creates income variation. Although profit sharing as a cost-control device is less disruptive than layoffs, organizations should take several steps to help employees cope. Personal financial counseling and education are a must since employees may not know how to budget and manage their expenses when they have a variable income. Kaiser Steel ignored this necessity when it introduced a profit sharing plan years ago. As a result, employees suffered considerable hardship when profits dropped since they had made financial commitments they could not keep.

Flexible Benefits. Flexible benefits also complement pay based on organizational performance.[43] These plans allow employees to adjust the mix of cash and benefits they receive to fit their particular needs. Most plans allocate an amount of money which employees can take in cash or spend on any combination of company benefits, such as different kinds of health insurance and different amounts of retirement pay. With variable income, people's needs obviously will change, and it makes sense to let employees adjust their pay and benefit packages to fit their current income level.

Conclusion

Creating a pay for performance system for an organization requires a careful design process. The starting point should address the desired organizational impact of the system on such variables as costs, culture, structure, motivation, skill development, attraction, and retention. Since the pay system is not the only system that can have a positive impact in these areas, the analysis should also consider other systems that can complement and support the pay system.

An organization also should carefully assess its needs in conjunction with, or perhaps even before, the effort to identify desired outcomes of the pay system. The assessment should examine the types of work present in the organization, key interdependencies, management style, and culture. Together with the list of pay system objectives, this assessment will form the goals of and constraints on the design process.

A single approach to paying for performance probably will not accomplish all the objectives that most organizations will have for the pay system. A creative combination of different systems likely will prove necessary, in part because each approach is particularly effective at accomplishing different objectives. Fortunately, many of the pay for organizational performance approaches can be combined and are compatible with each other.

Along with combining several approaches to paying for organizational performance, organizations can combine organizational performance pay with pay for individual performance. In most cases, merit bonuses provide the best approach to reward individual performance. Incentive pay approaches tend to conflict with gainsharing in particular since they necessitate a different management style. A feasible alternative is to create a pool of money based on organizational performance but allocate these funds based upon individual performance appraisals.

Finally, employers should consider having no pay systems that base pay on either individual or organizational performance. After all, a poor pay for performance system can cause counterproductive behavior, waste time, reduce trust, split an organization into warring factions, and waste money. Having no pay for performance system is better than having a poor one. Thus, an organization needs to be sure that its situation is right for a pay for performance system and that it will put in the time and effort to make the system work. All pay for performance approaches require a substantial investment of time and effort and each pay for performance approach will work in only a limited set of circumstances. Organizational effectiveness depends on picking the right combination of pay for performance systems, given the objectives of the pay system and the characteristics of the organization.

◆

Notes

1. Peck.
2. Lawler (1971); Locke et al.; Nalbantian.
3. Lawler (1971).
4. See, e.g., Henderson; Patten; Ellig.
5. Walton.
6. Hackman and Oldham.
7. See, e.g., Lawler (1973); Mobley.
8. Macy and Mirvis.
9. Lawler (1971); Vroom.
10. Lawler (1973).
11. Lawler and Ledford.
12. Lawler (1981).
13. Lawrence and Lorsch.
14. See, e.g., Lawler (1971).
15. See, e.g., Whyte.
16. Lawler (1971).
17. Lawler (1981).
18. See, e.g., Devries, Morrison, Shullman and Gerlach; Mohrman Resnick-West and Lawler; Meyer, Kay & French.
19. Lawler (1981).
20. Prince and Lawler.
21. Lawler and Rhode.
22. Lock and Latham.
23. Lawler, Mohrman and Resnick.
24. Hackman and Oldham.
25. Lawler, Mohrman, and Resnick.
26. Meyer, Kay & French.
27. Weitzman.
28. Kanter.
29. Bullock and Lawler.
30. O'Dell.
31. Moore and Ross.
32. Lawler (1986).
33. General Accounting Office.

34. Bullock and Lawler.
35. See, e.g., Moore and Ross.
36. Lawler (1981).
37. Graham-Moore and Ross.
38. O'Dell.

39. Quarrey, Blasis and Rosen.
40. Rosen, Klein and Young.
41. Kanter.
42. Lawler and Ledford.
43. Lawler (1981).

◆

References

Bullock, R.J., and E.E. Lawler. 1984. "Gainsharing: A Few Questions and Fewer Answers." *Human Resource Management* 5: 197–212.

DeVries, D.L., A.M. Morrison, S.L. Shullman, and M.L. Gerlach. 1981. *Performance Appraisal on the Line.* New York: Wiley-Interscience.

Ellig, B.R. 1982. *Executive Compensation—A Total Pay Perspective,* New York: McGraw-Hill.

General Accounting Office. 1981. *Productivity Sharing Programs: Can They Contribute to Productivity Improvement?* Washington, D.C.: U.S. General Accounting Office.

Graham-Moore, B., and T. Ross. 1983. *Productivity Gainsharing.* Englewood Cliffs, NJ: Prentice-Hall.

Hackman, J.R., and G.R. Oldham. 1980. *Work Redesign.* Reading, MA: Addison-Wesley.

Henderson, R.I. 1985. *Compensation Management: Rewarding Performance,* 4th ed. Reston, VA.: Reston Publishing Co.

Kanter, R.M. 1987. "The Attack on Pay." *Harvard Business Review:* 65(2) 60–67.

Lawler, E.E. 1971. *Pay and Organizational Effectiveness: A Psychological View.* New York: McGraw-Hill.

————1973. *Motivation in Work Organizations.* Monterey, CA: Brooks/Cole.

————1981. *Pay and Organization Development.* Reading, MA: Addison-Wesley.

————1986. *High Involvement Management.* San Francisco: Jossey-Bass.

Lawler, E.E. and G.E. Ledford. 1985. "Skill Based Pay." *Personnel* 62(9): 30–37.

Lawler, E.E., A.M. Mohrman, and S.M. Resnick. 1984. "Performance Appraisal Revisited." *Organizational Dynamics* 13(1): 20–35.

Lawler, E.E., and J.G. Rhode. 1976. *Information and Control in Organizations.* Pacific Palisades, CA: Goodyear.

Lawrence, P.R., and J.W. Lorsch. 1967. *Organization and Environment: Managing Differentiation and Integration.* Homewood, IL: Irwin.

Locke, E.A., D.B. Feren, V.M. McCaleb, K.N. Shaw, and A. Denny. 1980. "The Relative Effectiveness of Four Methods of Motivating Employee Performance." Chapter in *Changes in Work Life,* eds. K.D. Duncan, M.M. Gruneberg, and D. Wallas. Chichester, England: John Wiley & Sons.

Locke, E.A., and G.P. Latham. 1984. *Goal Setting: A Motivational Technique That Works*. Englewood Cliffs, NJ.: Prentice-Hall.

Macy, B.A. and P.H. Mirvis. 1976. "A Methodology for Assessment of Quality of Work Life and Organizational Effectiveness in Behavior—Economic Terms." *Administrative Science Quarterly* 21: 217–226.

Meyer, H.H., E. Kay, and J.R.R. French. 1965. "Split Roles in Performance Appraisal." *Harvard Business Review* 43(1): 123–129.

Mobley, W.H. 1982. *Employee Turnover: Causes, Consequences, and Control*. Reading, MA: Addison-Wesley.

Mohrman, A.M., S.M. Resnick-West, and E.E. Lawler. 1989. *Designing Performance Appraisals Systems*. San Francisco: Jossey-Bass.

Moore, B.E. and T.L. Ross. 1978. *The Scanlon Way to Improved Productivity*. New York: Wiley Interscience.

Nalbantian, H. 1987. *Incentives, Cooperation and Risk Sharing*. Totowa, NJ: Rowman and Littlefield.

O'Dell, C. 1987. *People, Performance, and Pay*. Houston, TX: American Productivity Center.

Patten, T.H. 1977. *Pay: Employee Compensation and Incentive Plans*. New York: Free Press.

Peck, C. 1984. *Pay and Performance: The Interaction of Compensation and Performance Appraisal*, number 155 New York: The Conference Board.

Prince, J.B. and E.E. Lawler. 1986. "Does Salary Discussion Hurt the Developmental Performance Appraisal?" *Organizational Behavior and Human Decision Processes* 37: 357–375.

Quarrey, M., J. Blasi, and C. Rosen. 1986. *Taking Stock: Employee Ownership at Work*. Cambridge, MA: Ballinger.

Rosen, C., K. Klein, and K. Young. 1986. *Employee Ownership in America.* Lexington, MA: Lexington.

Walton, R.E. 1985. "From Control to Commitment in the Workplace." *Harvard Business Review* 63(2): 76–84.

Weitzman, M.L. 1984. *The Share Economy: Conquering Stagflation*. Cambridge, MA: Harvard.

Whyte, W.F., ed. 1955. *Money and Motivation: An Analysis of Incentives in Industry*. New York: Harper.

Vroom, V.H. 1964. *Work and Motivation*. New York: John Wiley & Sons.

——————— ◆ ———————

3.6

Compensation Programs for Special Employee Groups

Jerry M. Newman

A survey of compensation books demonstrates considerable agreement about which groups of employees ought to receive special compensation treatment.[1] Frequent contenders for special treatment include salespeople, foreign service personnel, engineers and scientists, and top management such as boards of directors and intrapreneurs. Despite agreement over which employee groups are "special," the criteria used to categorize these employees vary. Some authors suggest that qualititative differences in the employment exchange distinguish special groups from other employees, and hence these groups warrant different compensation treatment.[2] Other analysts argue that special groups of employees present unique compensation challenges if the compensation goals of attraction, retention, and motivation are to be met. As Table 1 indicates, these groups almost seem to have divided loyalties or built-in role conflicts. For example, foreign service personnel must carry out corporate directives in a foreign environment which may not be at all amenable to U.S. interference. The challenge for foreign service personnel is to identify compensation strategies which encourage flexible and independent decision making.

This chapter argues that employees who merit special programs share two characteristics. First, this category of employees predominantly, if not exclusively, comprises individuals with boundary-spanning functions or roles linking two or more systems that have different, and partly conflicting, goals and expectations.[3] In addition, this boundary-spanning function must be linked to a particular part of the environment that is strategically important to the organization.

Table 1

Compensation Challenges for Special Employee Groups

Group	Strategic Compensation Challenges
Supervisors	"In-the-middle" position with often conflicting duties of meeting employee needs and satisfying upper management directives. Exempt status of job may result in no overtime pay. This inequity must be recognized by developing salary differentials with subordinates.
Middle and upper management	Organizational profits presumed to be highly dependent upon quality of performance of these key decision makers. Incentive systems designed to increase motivation viewed as highly important.
Nonsupervisory professional employees	Viewed as highly mobile group with allegiances more to their profession than to any organization. Special emphasis on compensation strategies that will help to retain these employees. Payment also based on special knowledge acquired through extensive education. Compensation relative to that of managers and relative to that of younger peers with more timely (less obsolete) knowledge are particularly important concerns.
Sales personnel	Jobs often unsupervised and especially dependent upon compensation strategies designed to develop and maintain high motivational levels.
Foreign service personnel	Work in foreign countries subject to different cultural, legal, and compensation customs. Geographic distance from domestic operations requires employees capable of exercising greater independence. Equity between foreign and U.S. employees must be balanced against "normal" pay scales in area surrounding foreign subsidiary.

Source: Reprinted with permission from G.T. Milkovich and J. Newman, *Compensation*. Plano, TX: Business Publications copyright © 1987.

Absent the characteristics of boundary spanner *and* strategic importance, a job will seldom warrant special treatment. For example, purchasing agents span the boundary between suppliers and the organization's input needs. But since most organizations develop long-term contracts with these suppliers, in part to reduce environmental uncertainty, the role of purchasing agents has less strategic importance. A similar fate awaits most personnel officers, whose function somewhat resembles the role of a purchasing agent. In the past, organizations placed little emphasis on staffing because most environmental interactions with the labor market (i.e., recruitment) produced sufficient supply to satisfy corporate demand. Extended droughts in the hiring of necessary human resources might eventually change the strategic importance of the staffing function and lead to differential compensation treatment of appropriate job incumbents.

Functions of Special Employee Groups

An organization's reaction to its environment plays a crucial role in defining special groups. As one analysis has noted, environmental pressures generate task demands from which evolve specific organizational roles and structures to deal with the environment.[4] Managers seek to reduce environmental uncertainty, by modifying either the environment or the organization so that a more productive accommodation emerges. While different types of intra-organizational strategies can be employed to deal with the environment, the success of each strategy depends upon a boundary-spanning role to identify environmental opportunities and constraints.[5] The nature of this role can evolve into the following different functions.

Public Relations

Boundary spanners may represent an organization, either by shaping opinions or by negotiating with the external public or agencies. A classic example of this role is the public relations and lobbying efforts of chief executive officers. Indeed, some actions of CEOs that do not always appear economically rational,[6] may reflect the political/symbolic functions they perform. Lee Iaccocca's efforts to convince the public and the federal government that Chrysler could remain viable stands as a perfect example of this type of activity and illustrates why CEOs are treated as a preeminent special group.

Environmental Scanning

Another function of boundary spanners involves scanning and monitoring the environment for change, particularly for technological change or for new business opportunities. Two employee groups which receive special compensation treatment fit well into this boundary-spanning role. The first group, scientists and engineers, might seem like the antithesis of boundary spanners: insulated from the external world, concentrating upon scientific discoveries which might catapult the organization into technical superiority. While scientists and engineers indeed are sheltered from some external pressures, one of their main functions involves boundary spanning. These professionals monitor the scientific and engineering environment for possible technological surges and help an organization avoid technological obsolescence. The Japanese have proven particularly successful at scanning the environment for technical information on rare scientific breakthroughs and then building these scientific advances along multiple applied, and profitable, avenues.

Recent organizational competition to generate profitable technological spinoffs has resulted in the coining of the term "intrapreneurship." Intrapreneurs are charged with the task of identifying products and services which represent economically sound risks for enterprises to undertake. Because of the relative infancy of this role, the special compensation requirements are only now evolving, but as this function assumes increasing importance in the competitive strategy of organizations, the outlook is for increasingly sophisticated compensation packages for this function.

Organizational Buffers

Boundary spanners also help protect an organization from harmful environmental acts. This function resembles a car's shock absorbers, shielding an organization from the worst of what the environment may have to offer. Much to the dismay of many directors on corporate boards today, this preventive role has become an unpleasant but necessary function of board members. Before lawsuits became a favored mode for shareholders to express dissatisfaction with organizational actions, compensation strategy largely ignored boards of directors. In recent years, however, considerable debate has focused on appropriate methods to compensate directors for the risks they bear in legitimizing corporate activities which could later precipitate shareholder litigation.

Information Processing and Gatekeeping

Boundary spanning also involves interpreting and transmitting environmental information. A key part of this process includes translating information into terms compatible with corporate culture and decision-making parameters. With the proliferation of information spawned by computers, computer specialists and management information system analysts, both positions charged with ensuring proper communication of environmental information to the organization, are in high demand today.

Transactions

Some boundary-spanning roles involve the acquisition of inputs and/or the disposal of outputs through interactions with specific environmental components. The classic example is a salesperson charged with selling organizational products to consumers. This role depends heavily upon successful transactions with consumers, and sales compensation reflects this priority.

Recent changes in foreign countries also have increased the transaction role of foreign service personnel. Surges in nationalism can create, among other things, demands that goods consumed in a foreign country also be produced in that country. These demands generally produce accompanying expectations of increased employment of local citizenry. As a result, U.S. expatriates must act as ambassadors for U.S. interests, seeking profits in cultures where legal standards and social norms may present formidable barriers.

Linkage and Coordination

Boundary spanners also facilitate collaboration between an organization and its external environment or between different units within an organization. For example, supervisors must bridge the gap between organizational objectives and workers' needs. When these two interests diverge, supervisors must find a method to coordinate objectives.

Strategic Importance of Functions

Not all individuals who serve in boundary-spanning roles deserve special compensation treatment. Indeed, the interaction must take place on an environmental boundary which has strategic importance for the organization. As an example, consider the case of engineers in two different organizations, a high-technology firm with a strong research and development component, and an organization which employs a few engineers whose role is not central to the organization's mission. A survey of such differences in employee composition and organizational strategy found that research and development organizations with heavy concentrations of engineers had evolved compensation systems to respond to engineers' special needs.[7] Organizations with a different focus and with fewer engineers merged this group's compensation with the standard package offered other employees.

Compensation Strategy for Special Groups

A long-held concept in compensation characterizes employment as an exchange process.[8] Employees provide certain contributions in the form of physical or mental work, and in return receive inducements to fulfill the exchange agreement.[9] Underlying a successful exchange, however, is an evolutionary process involving successive "implicit" agreements. On one side of the exchange, the contributions expected of a boundary spanner probably vary as the environment changes over time. The role may shift among the different possible dimensions examined earlier.

On the other side of the exchange, an employee enters an employment opportunity with certain expectations about the nature of the rewards. These expectations center on a concern for equity, both in the level of rewards and in the procedures for allocating rewards. Compensation strategy for special groups can be distinguished by the great attention spent on ensuring equitable treatment. In fact, much of the work designing compensation for special groups focuses on identifying comparison groups to use in making equity determinations. Table 2 below demonstrates this concern for selected groups.

Organizations rarely focus attention on identifying a perceived equitable wage for every position. However, the strategically

Table 2

Equity Issues in Compensation of Special Groups

Special Group	Relevant Equity Issues
Supervisors	Major concern in design of compensation centers on insuring that supervisors retain reasonable compensation differential over the employees they supervise. Overtime pay for nonexempt employees may erode this differential and must be monitored closely.
Engineers and Scientists	Research suggests these groups have a cosmopolitan orientation, comparing themselves against others in their profession rather than different occupational groups in the same organization. Requires close monitoring of external salaries to ensure comparable wage progression.
Sales Personnel	Sales personnel have long been viewed as highly motivated by the cash component of compensation. Coupled with a perceived disregard for internal social pressures, this group functions well in an unmonitored work environment. Such environments maximize interactions with sales competitors and necessitate frequent monitoring of comparative wages.
Foreign Service Personnel	The major concern with foreign service personnel is deciding upon an appropriate equity standard. Should a United States Expatriate be paid wages comparable with a domestic counterpart, or to a foreign national performing the same job on the same foreign site.

important role of boundary spanning groups mandates more careful consideration of the compensation requirements which will ensure attraction, continued retention, and appropriately motivated behavior. The following discussion examines different groups of employees and the special compensation programs which have evolved to meet their needs.

Compensation Packages for Special Groups

Formal systems for compensating special groups appear to evolve after the need for some special compensation has endured for some time. For example, computer and information system specialists have presented a compensation headache to organizations for about a decade. For much of that time, employers simply elevated wages for these individuals. Organizations tolerated red circle rates, or paying above a grade maximum, in hope that the problem would prove to be transitory. As turnover in this group persisted, though, organizations began to develop special "market-sensitive" grades which maintain the internal differential between different levels of these jobs but depend heavily on external market rates for pricing level. The resulting special job cluster usually has elevated salaries relative to internally comparable jobs, but little other special treatment has evolved. Since the compensation problem continues to persist, future compensation planning will attempt to develop less patchwork solutions that focus on long-term changes with more varied and responsive group treatment.

A second short-term strategy used by employers recognizes key contributors by providing rewards from an existing program set up for that explicit purpose.[10] Centered primarily in high-technology firms, these programs focus on accurate identification of key contributors and appropriate compensation awards to signal their importance to the organization. Most of these awards are handed out after the fact (74 percent of companies surveyed) and generally consist of lump-sum bonuses ranging from $500 to $100,000. A second preferred vehicle (67 percent of companies surveyed) involves special perquisites for key contributors, such as company cars, special research funding, sabbaticals, public recognition, and general work-life improvements.

For more long-term compensation strategies, organizations have developed special programs for groups consistently identified as serving in strategically important roles. These groups include supervisors, outside directors of corporate boards, scientific and engineering employees, sales personnel and foreign service personnel.

Supervisory Compensation

As the lowest level of management in an organization, supervisors must ensure that non-exempt employees successfully perform tasks necessary for achievement of corporate goals. However, employees often may have life and work objectives which conflict with organizational goals. Consider, for example, the employee who makes plans for a family camping trip over the long Memorial Day weekend. When his supervisor asks him to work overtime that weekend because of an unexpected rush order, the extra compensation is little consolation. The supervisor has the unenviable role of linking these two groups whose needs all too frequently clash.

Given the pressures of this boundary-spanning role, one would expect special compensation treatment for supervisors. Interestingly, though, supervisors for many years were treated like lower-level management and were excluded from the overtime provisions of the Fair Labor Standards Act as exempt employees. Imagine the reaction of a non-exempt employee, who can collect time and one-half for a long stretch of overtime, when asked if he or she would like to be a supervisor. The typical response used to be, "Why should I take a pay cut for a job that's one big hassle?" Indeed, the differential between line employees and a supervisor is a major concern in the compensation of this special group.

Organizations have three strategies to deal with this problem of supervisory compensation. The most common strategy (100 percent of all companies in one survey) ensures an appropriate differential between the base salaries of supervisors and their highest-paid subordinates.[11] This differential typically ranges from 5 to 30 percent, with a mean of 15 percent across organizations.[12]

A second strategy used to maintain equitable differentials is simply to pay supervisors scheduled overtime (53 percent of organizations). Typical compensation plans stipulate a maximum overtime payment and bar extra compensation for casual overtime or self-scheduled overtime. Finally, some organizations develop special supervisory incentive and bonus plans. About 11 percent of all companies surveyed developed such incentive plans, with payouts varying between 0 to 25 percent of salary.[13]

Special compensation for supervisors indirectly recognizes the most important group in any organization: the vast majority of workers who provide the services or produce the goods which translate into organizational profits. As a group, the performance of these employees is crucial to the success of an organization, which is why the boundary-spanning role of supervisors merits special consideration of appropriate compensation strategies.

Corporate Directors

A board of directors comprises 10 to 20 individuals who meet regularly and serve a variety of roles in the interest of the corporation and its shareholders. Historically, board members were typically people affiliated in some way with the organization (retired corporate officers, suppliers, attorney and the like) and did little other than "rubber stamp" decisions made by top management. Modern corporate boards have changed considerably, with membership shifting more to outside directors (approximately two-thirds) than inside directors (e.g., CEO, corporate officers). Outside members now include unaffiliated business executives, representatives from important segments of society, and major shareholders. Along with this shift in membership to unaffiliated members has come increased accountability for decisions and for the success of the firm. This increased accountability translates into increased risks that disgruntled shareholders may bring suit for unprofitable or unpopular corporate decisions. Table 3 illustrates the types of duties assumed by corporate boards and helps to explain the increasing role of directors in managing companies, and the associated increases in potential liability.

With the increased demands and risks placed on directors has come increased compensation, generally divided into four categories: 1) base pay or retainer, 2) incentives, 3) benefits, and 4) perquisites.

Table 3

The Functions of Corporate Board Members

1. Review staffing plans for top management positions and ensure that top candidates are selected.

2. Review strategic plans of organization and ensure consistency with policies developed by the Board.

3. Evaluate performance of senior management relative to strategic objectives.

4. Evaluate overall corporate performance based on financial input and more subjective data.

5. Recommend, including occasional development of, compensation packages for senior management.

Retainer Fees or Base Pay

As might be expected, part of the retainer fee serves as compensation for the legal risks assumed by directors and for the sound advice expected from them at board meetings. The compensation also varies as a function of board member status and the sheer amount of time that members spend in board-related activities.

This base pay or retainer compensation generally ranges from $5,000 to $50,000 with 80 percent of companies paying between $10,000 and $30,000.[14] The level of this compensation seems to increase proportionate to CEO salaries and varies from industry to industry, with the pharmaceutical industry offering the highest average retainer ($26,000) and the transportation industry paying the lowest ($12,000).[15]

Incentives

Incentives serve as an extremely popular component of director compensation. The most common incentive is a meeting fee or cash payment for attendance at meetings. Obviously, since the board meetings provide the primary opportunity for input from directors, organizations try to encourage attendance. This fee, which generally varies between $750–1,000, can add up to a significant form of compensation since organizations typically have up to 10 meetings in a normal year, with 6 meetings representing a median figure.

Other forms of incentive compensation are not very popular as compensation for directors, largely because the goals of typical incentive compensation plans conflict with the role requirements of board directors. Remember, a primary function of directors is to provide strategic direction and long-term guidance in the organization's planning process. Any short-term incentive plan with yearly payouts would encourage board members to optimize the short-term goals specified by the incentive payout. Long-term incentive plans presumably would eliminate this conflict, but the viability of long-term plans for directors with short-term contracts is questionable. The average term of office for most directors is still one year, and the long-term motivational incentive effects of decisions made today for directors with fixed short-term positions is unclear.[16] However, a recent trend is toward longer terms of office for directors, with three-year terms quite popular today. If this trend continues, the viability of incentive systems may increase.

Benefits

Board directors receive an assortment of benefits which generally are narrower in scope than the benefits for regular employees. An obvious inclusion is liability insurance for directors named as defendants in shareholder legal cases. Coverage generally runs between $10 million and $1 billion.[17] Other forms of insurance also are frequently provided, including accidental death insurance for company-related business (75 percent of companies) and life insurance in the range of $50,000 to $100,000.[18]

A fast-growing minority (25 percent) of companies also provides some form of retirement benefits to directors. This benefit appears to be particularly popular among the retired business executives whose years of prior business experience represent attractive credentials for corporate boards.

Perks

Finally, directors also receive what can only be characterized as "perks" of the job. Examples include tours of overseas facilities with both expenses and per diems paid or board meetings scheduled at prominent vacation resorts. Of course, adequate time is provided between meetings so that directors may avail themselves of the leisure facilities.

Scientists and Engineers

Scientists and engineers are classified as professionals. According to the Fair Labor Standards Act, this category includes any person who has received special training of a scientific or intellectual nature and whose job is concerned primarily (80 percent) with "professional" activities.

The major growth in hiring of scientists and engineers (SEs) over the past decade has been in high-technology industries. This feature combined with unique occupational requirements gives the compensation packages of these professionals a distinctive flavor. This uniqueness can best be illustrated by looking at the characteristics of high tech firms and the characteristics of scientific/engineering jobs.

High-tech firms place primary emphasis on technology in the organization's overall business strategy. Such organizations succeed through some combination of conceptualization, innovation, and commercialization of new, technically based ideas. Corresponding to this strategic emphasis, investment in research and development activities account for a relatively high proportion of total expenditures.[19] These firms compete in high-risk, worldwide product markets where success may depend on diagnosing short product-life cycles and moving quickly to new technological frontiers.

Against this backdrop of intense activity and change are placed a contingent of scientists and engineers with equally unique characteristics. The role of these professionals is shaped in part by the need for them to act as boundary spanners between dynamic organizations and the scientific community which provides the catalyst for new ideas. These so-called knowledge workers have valuable information which quickly becomes obsolete unless bolstered by new educational infusions.[20] Scientific and engineering jobs are also characterized by nonrepetitive job tasks and unanticipated changes in job directions which reflect the dynamic nature of the organizational product market. Since both job descriptions and standard job evaluation are most effective in stable job environments, such change virtually makes standard job valuation procedures inappropriate. Instead, these traditional compensation tools are replaced by generic job descriptions that delineate broad levels of responsibilities without identifying specific duties. Scientific or engineering jobs also include large components of creativity and intense intellectual stimulation, where independent choice of a work procedure and direction are not only required but frequently mandated. Further, the results achieved by these professionals is usually difficult to quantify, particularly in the short run.[21] The relatively long lag-time from conception and design to production and marketing makes feedback on results and differentiation of performance difficult. Slow or error-laden progress can result in late introduction of a new technology. This may translate into a substantially lower market share coupled with marked impacts on the livelihoods of other workers.

These unique job characterisics combined with the strategic importance of the roles played by scientists and engineers has resulted in several interesting variations in the compensation package. Most of these variations occur in the method of determining and/or the form of base pay, incentive pay, and perquisities.

Base Pay

The base pay of scientists and engineers must respond to several challenges. First, organizations are primarily interested in the knowledge these professionals bring to the work environment and the use of this knowledge in generating new technologies. Knowledge, though, has a definite half-life, and base pay tends to reflect this fact by providing high initial pay and large early increases. Absent any efforts to stave off knowledge obsolescence, a scientist or engineer can expect these increases to moderate over time. In fact, evidence indicates that salaries of scientists and engineers top out at about 25-30 percent of the CEO's salary.[22] Couple this salary ceiling with the relatively limited opportunities for advancement within strictly scientific fields, and the occupations' bounded limitations, not surprisingly, can cause considerable dissatisfaction among scientists and engineers.[23]

Firms with large numbers of scientists and engineers have reacted to this problem by creating dual career tracks. Figure 1 illustrates a typical dual career ladder.

Dual ladders provide two different ways of progressing in an organization, each reflecting different types of values to the organization's mission. The first, or managerial, ladder delineates levels of increasing responsibility for supervision or direction of people. The professional track creates levels of increasing contributions of professional skills which do not entail much supervision of employees. Scientists and engineers have the opportunity at some stage in their careers to consider a management track or continue along the scientific track. Along with advancement opportunities, this dual-track system permits higher base pay maximums, an equally important consideration.

Another problem in base pay of scientists and engineers concerns the question of equity. The very nature of scientific knowledge and its dissemination requires relatively close association among these professionals across organizations. As a result scientists and engineers evaluate the equity of their salaries against average earnings of the age cohort who entered the labor market at the same time period. This tendency and the volatile nature of both jobs and salaries in scientific and engineering occupations, has prompted organizations to rely very heavily on external market data in pricing base pay for these employees. The form of this reliance involves the construction of maturity curves.

Maturity curves reflect the relationship between compensation and years of experience in the labor market. Surveying organizations generally ask for information about salaries as a function of years since the incumbent(s) last received a degree. This measure is intended to measure the half-life of technical obsolescence. A plot of

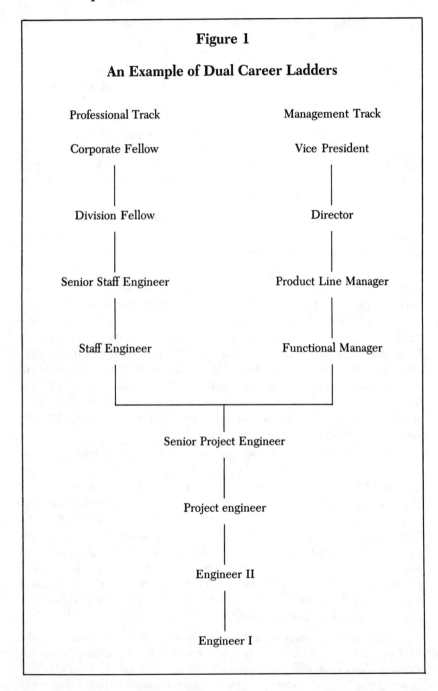

Figure 1

An Example of Dual Career Ladders

these data with appropriate smoothing to eliminate aberrations typically shows salary curves with steep increases for the first five to seven years, and then moderate increases as technical obsolescence erodes the value of these jobs. Figure 2 illustrates such a graph with somewhat greater sophistication built into it, i.e., different graphs are constructed for different levels of performance. To collect such data, the surveying organization must also ask for data broken down by broad performance levels. Notice in the illustration that high performers begin with somewhat higher salaries and the differential continues to broaden over the first few years.

Incentives

In general, high-tech firms place a great emphasis on the use of performance-based incentives.[24] To some extent, this emphasis on performance carries over to the compensation of scientists and engineers in the form of profit sharing and stock ownership incentives. Other incentives link payment of specific cash amounts to completion of specific projects on or before agreed-upon deadlines. Post hoc bonuses are also paid for such achievements as patents, publications, elections to professional societies, and attainment of professional licenses.[25] Few organizations, though, provide royalties or repeated bonuses for profitable patents (20 percent of organizations in one survey.)[26] Rights to these profits are assigned to the company as part of the initial employment contract.

Perks

Finally, organizations have devoted considerable creative energy to development of "perks" which satisfy the unique needs of scientists and engineers. This grouping includes flexible work schedules, large offices, campus-like environments, and lavish athletic facilities. The strategic importance of these groups dictates that both mind and body be kept active.

High-tech firms also have assumed an important role in shaping the compensation of an emerging special group: intrapreneurs. Rapid response to changing environments has not been a characteristic strength of organizations burdened by large bureaucracies. To counter this inherent disadvantage that large technical corporations face in competing against their smaller and more flexible

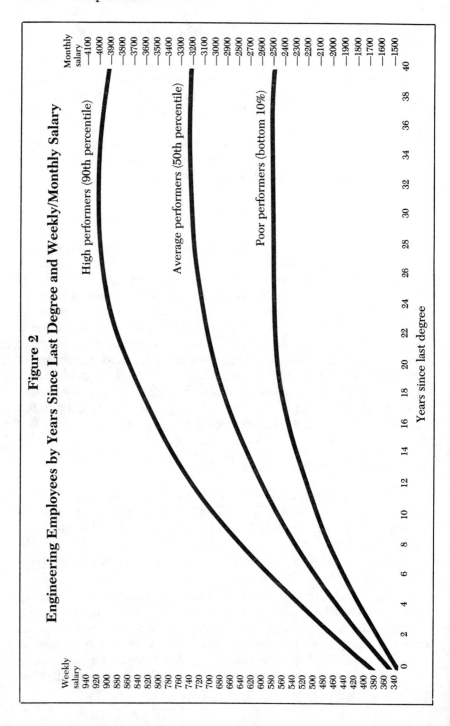

Figure 2

Engineering Employees by Years Since Last Degree and Weekly/Monthly Salary

competition, the concept of intrapreneurship has emerged. Intra-preneurs are charged with identifying, planning, and then achieving internal funding for new business ventures which are compatible with the organization's resources and strategic directions. Some high-tech firms are beginning to offer internal venture funding programs, incentives, royalty arrangements, team bonuses, and promotions to successful intrapreneurs and intrapreneur teams.[27] With the emphasis on rapid response to changing product markets and the need for flexible adaptation to new lines, such programs no doubt will grow in number and sophistication in the future.

Sales Force Compensation

The sales staff spans the all-important boundary between an organization and consumers of the organization's goods or services. Besides the sales function, or even as part of selling, the sales staff must be sensitive to changing consumer tastes and provide rapid feedback to appropriate departments. This role requires individuals with high initiative who can work under low supervison for extended periods of time. The standard compensation system, which orders jobs based on commonly shared characteristics that reflect internal values of the organization, is not designed for this type of job. The factors determining the value of sales jobs are largely external to the organization and driven by market forces.[28] The goal of an organization's sales compensation system is to identify the level and form of compensation which will direct sales behavior towards desired organizational ends.

Factors in Motivation and Performance

While financial compensation and incentives certainly play an important role in motivating the sales force, other considerations affect sales force performance. First, and perhaps most obviously, an organization must design selection systems which identify individuals possessing both the aptitude and ability required in the job. While a compensation system can attract applicants with the "right stuff," selection tools must follow through with correct identification.

In addition, organizational factors shape performance requirements and hence the types of compensation tools which should be used. The importance of this factor becomes apparent in the following discussion of designing a sales compensation plan.

Sales Compensation Design

A sales compensation plan should link desired behaviors of salespeople to the organization's strategy. As boundary spanners, salespeople must know which environmental changes are particularly important to the organization, which products to stress in customer calls, when to stress customer service and when to stress volume sales, and countless other decision alternatives influenced by organizational strategy. As an example, consider the following features in a model of strategic planning.[29]

Conducting an Environmental Scan. A key element in this model involves environmental scans to determine viability of different strategies. In the external environment, the organization reviews actions of both customers and competitors. For example, increased centralization of buying and merchandising decisions by customers mandates more individualized sales calls at the central office. This strategy lowers the need for routine calls placed by low-level sales staff and increases the emphasis on staff experienced in making tailored calls. Internally, the compensation system must be adjusted so as to identify individual contributions to gross sales under centralized decision making, and it must be structured to attract and retain higher-level sales personnel.

Competitor practices also influence the design of compensation systems. Data on competitor compensation level, types of packages offered, and degree of sales success will help in designing compensation packages and warding off unwanted turnover.

After completion of an external and internal scan, an organization may tentatively develop strategic plans that trigger subsequent sales plans. Will the organization focus on gross margin or profit attainment or some measure of improvement? Will market share dominate strategic discussions or will introduction of a new product command most of the sales planning sessions? Depending on which objective is preeminent, different incentive strategies should evolve.

Selecting Performance Measures. After linking the strategic plan to sales compensation, the compensation analyst must determine which performance measurement is appropriate. Typical performance measures include overall territory volume, market share, number of product placements in retail stores, number of new accounts, gross profit, percentage of list price attainment (relative to other salespeople in organization), consistency of sales results, expense control productivity per square foot (especially popular in

---

Table 4

Alternative Sales Compensation Plans

Method	Percentage of companies using this plan	
	1985	1984
Straight salary	17.4	17.1
Draw against commission	6.5	6.8
Salary plus commission	30.7	29.0
Salary plus individual bonus	33.7	33.6
Salary plus group bonus	2.7	2.3
Salary plus commission plus bonus	9.0	11.2

Source: Reprinted with permission from *Quantitative Analysis for Compensation Decision Making.* Scottsdale, AZ: American Compensation Association, copyright © 1989, pp. 4.7–4.9.

---

retail stores), and bad debt generated by sales.[30] Each measure, of course, corresponds to a different business goal. For example, an organization might use some volume measure such as number of units, orders, invoices, or cash received if the business goal is to increase sales growth. Alternatively, if the goal is profit improvement, the appropriate measurement would be gross margin on sales or price per unit. Percentage account erosion would be stressed if improved account retention became a major focus of attention, while sales per account might be stressed when account penetration becomes a major organizational goal.

Reviewing Alternatives. The third step in design of a compensation plan includes a review of alternatives.[31] Table 4 identifies the major alternatives used by organizations today in designing salesforce compensation systems.

Selecting a Plan

Which of these alternatives an organization uses depends upon the overall plan design. This final step of designing a sales compensation package covers issues of compensation levels, differentials, plan choice relative to business objectives, and other reward considerations.

Popular stereotypes of salespeople characterize them as heavily motivated by financial compensation. A recent study supports this perception, with pay ranked significantly higher than five other forms of reward for a sample of 108 salespeople.[32] As a source of satisfaction, pay received a mean rating of 83.7 on a 100-point scale. Promotional opportunities, sense of accomplishment, personal growth, recognition, and job security were all less highly regarded.

This finding confirms that sales compensation should stress financial incentives over other forms of psychological rewards. In selecting an appropriate pay level, organizations should recognize that external competitiveness is essential. In their quest for potential customers, sales competitors will inevitably cross paths and have the opportunity to compare compensation packages. To ensure favorable comparisons, an organization should identify a compensation level strategy that explicitly indicates target salaries for different sales groups and performance levels. Since sales compensation can vary widely, it is possible to be competitive for one level of sales personnel or level of competency and noncompetitive at other levels.[33] The incentive plan should be designed to ensure that low, moderate, and high achievers at each step of the career ladder all fall in the policy-determined pay range.

An organization should also recognize that sales compensation varies across individuals for reasons other than just sales ability. Factors that may not be totally under the control of sales staff can influence the level of sales, and organizations may wish to consider these factors in assigning sales people and in determining reward differentials. The first factor to consider is the kind of product sold. For some higher-level sales positions, the consumer goods industry yields higher compensation than for sales of industrial goods. This pattern reverses itself for lower-level sales staff, with industrial products proving more lucrative than consumer products. As a second example, sales personnel in technical product markets earn more than their counterparts in non-technical markets. The geographic size of the selling market and the potential customer density also influence potential level of sales and hence compensation.

One strategy for incorporating these factors in a compensation package is outlined in Figure 3. A company should assess the importance of sales ability (as opposed to the natural potential of the market) in closing a sale relative to the level of technical skill needed for the type of selling situation. For product lines requiring highly technical sales pitches, the type of compensation necessary to attract, retain, and motivate a legitimate prospect might have to be structured differently.

Figure 3

Designing a Sales Compensation Package

		Importance of "sales" ability in closing sale.	
		High	Low
	High	high starting salary to attract, large incentive to motivate.	high salary to attract, no incentive necessary.
Probability that job has highly technical dimension requiring skills not readily available in population			
	Low	lower starting salary, but large incentive.	salary only, and not at high level

Designing a sales compensation plan also requires selecting from among the alternative packages noted in Table 4. Depending on sales objectives, different behaviors can be stressed by the three generic variants: 1) straight salary plan, 2) a straight commission plan, and 3) a plan combining elements of both these types.

Straight Salary Plans. In a straight salary plan, the sales force is paid a fixed income independent of sales volume. This strategy is appropriate when the organization wants to emphasize customer service and sales prospecting in low-potential areas. In a traditional plan, the incentive is placed upon sales volume in some manner, and customer service is viewed as an imposition. And woe be to the sales supervisor who assigns a commission-based salesperson in a market with low sales potential.

Salary plans are also appropriate where individual sales performance is difficult to measure. This circumstance arises when sales volume is based on group effort or when traditional sales volume measures are inappropriate such as in positions that require a large training component.

Straight Commission Plans. At the other end of the continuum are straight commission plans. Such plans are appropriate where company's objectives focus on motivating sales volume, or where cost accounting procedures stress the importance of strict controls over the ratio of sales cost to sales volume.

Combination Plans. Most jobs do not fit the ideal specifications for the two extremes of straight salary or straight commission plans. A combination plan is intended to capture the best of both alternatives. A guaranteed straight salary can be linked to performance of non-sales functions (e.g., customer service), while a commission for sales volume yields the incentive to sell. A plan combining these two features signals the intent of the organization to ensure that both types of activities occur in the organization.

A recent survey of organizations indicates that sales plans with an incentive component will continue to be popular into the foreseeable future. Over 90 percent of all companies surveyed stated that sales incentive plans will have as large or larger a budget in the future as in the past.[34] Other forms of rewards, however, continue to play a role, albeit small, in the total compensation package of salespeople. For example, some companies develop formal recognition programs for high sales performers (e.g., 44 percent of those surveyed). More popular forms of recognition, though, focus on more tangible incentives, such as merchandise and travel for outstanding performance (61 percent of those surveyed). Along with standard benefits, organizations offer salespeople additional features such as company cars and expense accounts to recognize the distinctive feature of the jobs performed by this special group.

Compensation of Foreign Service Personnel

When multinational organizations decide to open facilities in a foreign location, one of the many decisions faced involves the type of personnel to hire. Foreign subsidiaries also choose among a mix of United States expatriates (USEs), third country nationals (TCNs), and local country nationals (LCNs). (See ASPA-BNA Series, Volume 1, Chapter 1.6 for further information on international HRM.) One obvious choice is to staff the subsidiary with citizens of the country in which the subsidiary is located. This staffing option eliminates relocation expenses, avoids concerns about "fitting in" with the local culture, and satisfies nationalistic demands for hiring of locals. Only about 5 percent of the time do organizations decide against hiring of locals in favor of employing U.S. expatriates or third-country nationals.[35] Typical reasons for such a decision include the following: 1) the foreign assignment represents an opportunity to develop the international perspective of selected United States expatriates, 2) the position involves confidential information that is only entrusted to a proven domestic veteran, 3) the particular talent demanded by a position is not available in the local pool, 4) the necessary talent is available locally but in insufficient quantities, or 5) past hiring of local country nationals has resulted in "pirating" by other local firms after the foreign enterprise has provided costly training. When one of these situations arises the foreign subsidiary either transfers an American citizen to the foreign subsidiary (USEs) or hires an individual whose home country is neither American nor the host country (TCN).

The compensation package offered each of these groups must be balanced in three ways.[36] First, the compensation must be high enough to attract qualified applicants. Second, compensation costs must be balanced so that foreign production remains comparatively profitable. And most importantly, the compensation package must be equitable for the three groups. This last concern is the factor which yields special compensation treatment for foreign service personnel. For example, equity for U.S. expatriates requires providing both salaries comparable to those of their American-based counterparts and an incentive wage for accepting employment in an unfamiliar, and perhaps less comfortable, environment. Equity concerns for both local- and third-country nationals center on the appropriate compensation standard for comparative purposes: For example, should third-country nationals be paid according to home country norms, United States norms, or local country norms? Typical multinational practice pegs salaries of U.S. expatriates to those of domestic counterparts (72 percent of companies follow this practice) and salaries of third-country nationals to either home country wages (36 percent) or some combination of home country and local standards (35 percent).[37] Not surprisingly, local-country nationals typically receive wages tied to local norms.

Each of these three standards for setting wages presents different advantages. Using the home-country salary as a basis of equitable comparison probably best corresponds to the equity standard held by each of these three groups, plus it probably facilitates home country repatriation. In contrast, a host-country standard probably helps to establish a psychological bond with the local environment, facilitating the transition to a foreign work setting.[38] Finally, wages based on some combination of different countries' standards are typically employed to facilitate transfer within certain geographic areas, most notably among the Common Market countries.[39] More explicit statements on the compensation packages for the three groups of employees are covered below.

United States Expatriates

Maintaining equity for U.S. expatriates while serving in a foreign subsidiary typically requires a three-component compensation package, including a base salary, incentives, and equalization components. All three parts of the package are guided by the principle of keeping the workers "whole." This requirement means that compensation is allocated for both the psychological and real costs borne by foreign subsidiary employees in excess of costs they would have incurred in the home country.

Base Salary. The base salary of U.S. expatriates depends upon job worth, which is typically assessed using the same job evaluation system and surveys employed for domestic workers. Beyond this base wage, expatriates also receive an incentive and an equalization component.

Incentives. The incentive component, or foreign service premium, reflects the unique requirements placed on expatriates to work with less supervision than an American counterpart; to live and work in strange and, in some cases, uncongenial surroundings; and to represent the U.S. employer in the host country. The size of the premium varies relative to the expected hardship to be endured in the host country and the type of expatriate employed. As the hardship increases, the size of the foreign service premium increases. For example, an assignment in Brussels would yield little or no foreign service premium, while one in Peking might warrant a considerably larger incentive. This hardship component is balanced against considerations of the role played by the U.S. expatriate.[40] For example, career international employees are less likely to receive a foreign service premium, largely because their choice of an international career eliminates the need to provide transfer incentives. Foreign service premiums also are less prevalent in organizations where foreign assignments are viewed as a necessary career stage, preparatory to assumption of top-level positions in the multinational organization. For more traditional international assignments with neutral career implications, incentives may be necessary to attract these boundary spanners to the geographic frontiers of the organization.

Equalization Allowances. A third component of the compensation package for U.S. expatriates includes four equalization allowances. The intent of these allowances is to keep the worker whole financially when an overseas assignment is accepted. The first income source is a tax equalization allowance. Income earned in foreign countries has two potential tax liabilities. With few exceptions (Saudia Arabia is one), foreign income tax liabilities are incurred on foreign-earned income. The United States also taxes foreign-earned income in excess of $70,000. Tax equalization allowances provide for employer payment of tax liabilities at a rate sufficient to ensure that a U.S. expatriate does not have any positive or negative tax impact from employment in a foreign country.

A second allowance covers housing costs in the host country. These payments are intended to compensate for cost differences between U.S. housing and comparable foreign housing. The alternative to providing this allowance is to provide an expatriate housing complex. This option is only considered when the contingent of U.S. expatriates is large enough to warrant a separate housing complex.

Many organizations pay for language training of the expatriate and any family members who also make the move. In addition, companies will provide educational allowances to ensure that the quality of children's education is equivalent to the opportunity missed in the home country.

Finally, cost-of-living allowances are intended to equalize the differential for a market basket of goods that a U.S. expatriate might be expected to purchase. These adjustments tend to be a major source of complaints in expatriate compensation. High-quality and readily available goods in the United States may be extremely costly or unavailable in the foreign subsidiary. Money alone cannot compensate for the life-style changes necessitated by differences in the quality and type of goods available. Despite the inherent difficulties of comparing apples and oranges, most companies use some index of living costs abroad, typically provided either by a consulting firm or by the State Department.

Third-Country Nationals

Third-country nationals can be paid off a local standard, a home country standard, or off a U.S. standard. Any of the three have legitimacy, particularly when the third-country national is working alongside a U.S. expatriate receiving U.S.-based compensation and a local-country national receiving compensation pegged off local rates. Organizations should ask two questions before selecting an appropriate standard. First, is the person hired by the corporation as part of an international reservoir of talent, or by a subsidiary to satisfy local needs? As part of an international contingent, the appropriate standard might be the home country or the United States. If the employee is hired to satisfy local needs, the standard might be the local pay scale. Second, does the employee plan on retiring at home or in the local country? As an indicator of the allegiances of a third-country national, the answer would either dictate home country or local pay scales, respectively.

Local-Country Nationals

Although a growing trend is to pay all employees on the same scale, the prevalent compensation standard for local-country nationals continues to be the local pay scale. The major difficulty with this arrangement arises when compensation is pegged to the value of the U.S. dollar. If the dollar changes in value relative to local currency, the compensation system must be flexible to ensure that the fluctuation doesn't penalize or provide windfall salary levels.

Integrating Special Compensation Groups With the Total System

The traditional perspective on compensation of special groups portrays these decisions as made in isolation, independent of the system-wide compensation decisions made by an organization. In fact, compensation of special groups must be integrated into the overall policy-making framework guiding compensation. To demonstrate how policy making is affected by compensation of special groups, the four broad policy decision areas confronting organizations are outlined below, coupled with a consideration of issues relevant to special employee groups.

General Policy Issues

Policy questions can be broken into four broad areas:[41] 1) determining external competitiveness, 2) assessing internal consistency, 3) identifying an appropriate role for employee contributions in wage setting, and 4) identifying fair administrative procedures.

External Competitiveness

Organizations make decisions about the appropriate level of wages relative to external competition. Should an organization lead the market, lag the market, or pay wages at the market rate? Sometimes, the strategy varies for different levels in the organizational hierarchy. As an example, an organization may choose to lead the market for top jobs and pay at the market for other jobs. In rare instances, organizations may choose to establish different competitive policies for specific occupations, paying above the market, for example, in the engineering occupations, but at the market for all other positions.

All of these decisions presumably are based upon an assessment of the costs associated with a particular market position relative to the presumed benefits. A market-leading position, for example, engenders higher wage costs that are hopefully balanced against higher productivity, lower turnover, and lower training costs. In fact, the role of special groups in an organization should be assessed against both the market rate and the chosen policy for the remaining positions in the organization. The choice of a competitive stance for special groups should be linked to the boundary-spanning role assumed by these occupations. In other words, the relative market position should vary as a function of the importance attached to the environmental scanning function performed by the different groups.

As the importance of analyzing and interacting with the environment becomes strategically more or less important, the competitive pay level also should fluctuate. While this decision may require case-by-case analysis, some broad generalizations can guide policy making. The role of special groups as boundary spanners should vary in part as a function of an organization's life-cycle stage. In the growth phase, an organization attaches particular importance to moving quickly to capitalize on perceived demand for organizational products and services. This strategy probably requires rapid response from all agents scanning the environment to ensure that the growth phase does not stall prematurely. Special groups are particularly important in this phase, and the compensation policy should reflect the relative importance of boundary-spanning functions.

In a relative sense, boundary spanning becomes less important when an organization reaches the mature phase of its life cycle. Products are known and accepted in the marketplace. Growth curves are relatively level and the organization can be characterized by a steady-state which is sufficiently profitable to warrant continued operation. Under these conditions, the role of boundary spanners tends to become more protective, ensuring that an existing market niche isn't upset. The relative importance of special groups in this phase might be somewhat less.

Interestingly, the greatest importance of boundary scanners might occur when an organization enters a declining phase of its life cycle. To avoid continued decline and eventual demise, an organization must rely heavily on boundary spanners to identify new market opportunities. Environmental scanners need to identify relevant market information which might suggest alternative survival paths, transmit this information to the organization, test the viability of an organization's potential response with appropriate environmental agents. The obvious dependence on highly qualified boundary spanners may signal the need for particularly attractive compensation packages.

Internal Consistency

Is the reward pie cut up fairly from the perspective of employees? Sometimes the special treatment afforded special groups remains relatively unknown to the majority of workers by the very nature of boundary-spanning roles. Many of these special groups have less opportunity to interact with other workers simply because the job entails considerable interaction with external agents. However, certain boundary-spanning jobs, by the nature of the environmental interaction, actually are more visible. The classic example is computer programming and systems analyst positions. The role of processing information and making sense of the overload involves a strong component of interaction with organization members at the end transmission stages. As a result, the special compensation treatment of these special groups causes considerable discussion and occasional discontent in organizations.

Effective communication of the role of special groups can prevent resentment among other employees. Organizations often make the mistake of communicating that the special treatment is a temporary aberration precipitated by short-term imbalances in supply and demand. This explanation overlooks the importance associated with information system positions and clearly signals internal inconsistency in the compensation package. Equity in the employment exchange necessitates a perceived balance between inputs and outcomes relative to other employees. Appropriate communication of the special treatment given information system employees should stress the importance of the boundary-spanning role played by this group and the added responsibilities assumed by the employees.

This perspective should also appear in an organization's job evaluation system. Very few job evaluation systems adequately tap the functions and organizational importance of boundary-spanning roles. As a consequence, the compensable factors communicated as important to employees don't account for the large wage disparity of such special groups as computer programmers. Job evaluation systems that incorporate environmental-scanning functions and increased prominence as compensable factors (i.e., increased factor weight) would signal that higher wages reflect higher inputs, a perfectly legitimate and equitable transaction.

Employee Contributions

Special groups are seldom singled out for differential treatment in the distribution of reward increases based upon employee contributions. Organizational decisions about whether to tie pay to performance or to base increases on some other criterion (e.g., seniority) seldom differentiate across groups. Nor is much thought given to variable treatment for special groups within a broadly applied increase guideline. Organizations may want to consider such differential treatment, particularly when the increase guideline is based upon performance. By their very nature, special groups perform unique, strategically important functions for the organization. Failure to weed out poor performers quickly can have pronounced relative impacts upon the organization. Merit scales with large differentials between high and low performers would be a first reward signal that inadequate performance has occurred and is unacceptable. Such rapid reaction to both poor and superior performance is particularly important in jobs critical to organizational success.

Administrative Procedures

The nature of special group roles, as noted earlier, brings incumbents into contact with comparison groups not typically encountered by other employees in the organization. A key element of equitable treatment for these special groups involves identification of the appropriate comparison group. Even though a company may treat its engineering staff better than most employees, the appropriate comparison is not other internal employees, but other engineers in outside firms. Because boundary spanners spend considerable time interacting in external environments, they are influenced by the procedures and practices evident in these environments. It becomes particularly important for internal procedures to compare favorably with policies in the scanned environment. Attempts to shelter boundary-spanning jobs from the external market and to construct internal equity considerations is difficult. As a consequence, the most important practice to ensure perceptions of procedural justice is to monitor practices in the external market and make adjustments where necessary.

Conclusion

Special groups are portrayed here as sharing one common characteristic: They all perform boundary-spanning functions which, in multiple ways, help the organization to deal with its environments. While the importance of this function may vary depending upon the environment scanned, its strategic importance, and an organization's life-cycle stage, special groups clearly receive different compensation treatment largely because of the importance attached to the boundary-spanning role. Unfortunately, most of this compensation differentiation is prescriptive in nature. Little is known about the specific roles assumed by boundary spanners and the functions that compensation should assume in motivating appropriate performance. Future practice and research should focus on answering these questions.

◆

Notes

1. Belcher; Rock; Hills; Milkovich and Newman.
2. Belcher; Hills; Milkovich and Newman.
3. Miles.
4. Lawrence and Lorsch.
5. Thompson; Robbins.
6. Ungson and Steers.
7. Crim (1978a and 1978b).
8. Barnard.
9. March and Simon.
10. Spratt and Steele.
11. Miller.
12. Ibid.
13. Ibid.
14. Tauber.

15. Bacon.
16. Tauber.
17. Ibid.
18. Ibid.
19. Milkovich.
20. Gregerman.
21. Kail.
22. Crim (1978b).
23. Gomez-Mejia and Balkin.
24. Milkovich.
25. Northrup and Malin.
26. Ibid.
27. Intrapreneurial Excellence.
28. Schultz.
29. Hofer and Schendel.
30. Weiss and Langer; Freedman.
31. Executive Compensation Services.
32. Ford, Walker, and Churchill.
33. Schultz.
34. Urbanski.
35. Sym-Smith.
36. Business International Corporation.
37. Teague.
38. Business International Corporation.
39. Sym-Smith.
40. Ibid.
41. Milkovich and Newman.

Editor's Notes: In addition to the References shown below, there are other significant sources of information and ideas on compensation Programs for special employee groups.

Books

Analog Devices. 1985. "Parallel Ladder Program and New Products Bonus Program." *Analog Devices*. Norwood, MA: Analog Devices.

Guerci, H. 1984. "Compensation Programs for Scientists and Professionals in Business." *Handbook of Wage & Salary Administration*. New York: McGraw Hill.

Henderson, R.I. 1985. *Compensation Management*. Reston, VA: Reston Publishing.

Hodge, B.J. and W. Anthony. 1984. *Organization Theory*. Boston: Allyn & Bacon.

Jamison, R.G. 1984. "Designing an Integrated Sales Compensation Program." In *Handbook of Wage and Salary Administration*, ed. M. Rock. New York: McGraw-Hill.

Leavitt, H., W. Dill and H. Eyring. 1973. *The Organizational World*. New York: Harcourt Brace Jovanovich.

Nemerov, D.S. 1987. "Managing the Sales Compensation Program: Integrating Factors for Success" In *New Perspectives in Compensation*, ed. D.B. Balkin and L.R. Gomez-Mejia. Englewood Cliffs, NJ: Prentice-Hall.

Articles

Brook, B. 1985. "Long-Term Incentives for the Foreign-Based Executive." *Compensation and Benefits Review* 17(3): 46–53.

Ellig, B. 1983. "Compensating the Board of Directors." *Compensation Review* 3: 15–28.

Hansen, A.S. 1987. "Survey of Selling Costs." *Sales and Marketing Management*, 138, 3: 57.

League, B. 1982. "Compensation Foreign Service Personnel Conference Board Report No. 818. New York: Conference Board.

◆

References

Bacon, J. 1984. *Corporate Directors Compensation*. New York: Conference Board.

Barnard, C.I. 1938. *The Functions of the Executive*. Cambridge, MA: Harvard University Press.

Belcher, D. 1974. *Compensation Administration*. Englewood Cliffs, NJ: Prentice-Hall.

Business International Corporation. 1982. *Worldwide Executive Compensation and Human Resources Planning*. New York: Business International Corporation.

Crim, J.W. 1978a. "A Shortage of Professional Employees? A Note on Corporate Compensation." *University of Michigan Business Review* 23 (May): 22–31.

————. 1978b. *Compensating Non-Supervisory Professional Employees*. Ann Arbor, MI: Research Press.

Executive Compensation Services. 1986. "Survey of Selling Costs." *Sales and Marketing Management* 135 (March): 54.

Ford, N., O. Walker, and G. Churchill. 1985. "Differences in the Attractiveness of Alternative Rewards among Industrial Salespeople: Additional Evidence." *Sales Force Performance*. Lexington, MA: D.C. Heath & Co.

Freedman, R. 1986. "How to Develop a Sales Compensation Plan." *Compensation and Benefits Review* 18 (February): 41–48.

Gomez-Mejia, L.R. and D. Balkin. 1988. *The Effectiveness of Aggregate and Individual Incentives for R&D Workers*. Unpublished technical report, University of Colorado.

Gregerman, I.B. 1978. *Knowledge Worker Productivity*. New York: AMACOM.

Hills, F.S. 1987. *Compensation Decision Making*. Hinsdale, IL: The Dryden Press.

Hofer, C.F. and D. Schendel. 1978. *Strategy Formulation: Analytical Concepts*. St. Paul, MN: West Publishing Co.

Intrapreneurial Excellence. 1986. "Baiting the Intrapreneurial Hook." *Compensation and Benefits Review* 18 (June): 63–68.

Kail, J.C. 1987. "Compensating Scientists and Engineers." In *New Perspectives on Compensation*, ed. D.B. Balkin and L.R. Gomez-Mejia. Englewood Cliffs, NJ: Prentice-Hall.

Lawrence, P. and J. Lorsch. 1967. *Organizations and Environment*. Cambridge, MA: Harvard University Press.

March, J. and H. Simon. 1958. *Organizations*. New York: John Wiley & Sons.

Miles, R. 1980. *Macro Organizational Behavior*. Santa Monica, CA: Goodyear.

Milkovich, G. 1987. "Compensation Systems in High Technology Companies." In *New Perspectives on Compensation*, ed. D.B. Balkin and L.R. Gomez-Mejia. Englewood Cliffs, NJ: Prentice-Hall.

Milkovich, G. and J. Newman. 1987. *Compensation*. Plano, TX: Business Publications.

Miller, E.C. 1978. "Supervisory Overtime, Incentive, and Bonus Practices." *Compensation Review* 10 (April): 12–25.

Northrup, H. and M. Malin. 1985. *Personnel Policies for Engineers and Scientists*. Philadelphia: University of Pennsylvania.

Robbins, S. 1983. *Organization Theory: The Structure and Design of Organizations*. Englewood Cliffs, NJ: Prentice-Hall.

Rock, M., ed. 1984. *Handbook of Wage and Salary Administration*. New York: McGraw-Hill.

Schultz, C.F. 1987. "Compensating the Sales Professional." In *New Perspectives on Compensation*, ed. D.B. Balkin and L.R. Gomez-Mejia. Englewood Cliffs, NJ: Prentice-Hall.

Spratt, M. and B. Steele. 1986. "Rewarding Key Contributors." *Compensation and Benefits Review* 17 (March): 24–37.

Sym-Smith, C.I. 1984. "Compensation Programs for International Organizations." In *Handbook of Wage and Salary Administration*, ed. M. Rock. New York: McGraw-Hill.

Tauber, Y. 1986. "Trends in Compensation for Outside Directors." *Compensation and Benefits Review* 18 (January): 43–52.

Teague, B. 1982. *Compensating Foreign Service Personnel*. Conference Board Report 818. New York: The Conference Board.

Thompson, J.D. 1967. *Organizations in America*. New York: McGraw-Hill.

Ungson, G.R. and R. Steers. 1984. "Motivation and Politics in Executive Compensation." *Academy of Management Review* 9 (April): 313–323.

Urbanski, A. 1986. "Incentives Get Specific." *Sales Marketing Management* 136 (May): 98–102.

Weiss, H., and A. Langer. 1984. "Compensation for Retail Sales Personnel." In *Handbook of Wage and Salary Administration*, ed. M. Rock. New York: McGraw-Hill.

——————— ◆ ———————

3.7

Strategic Design of Executive Compensation Programs

Luis R. Gomez-Mejia
Theresa M. Welbourne

Top executives tackle the awesome responsibility of charting the future direction of an enterprise and implementing organizational strategies through effective management of human resources and capital. Their foresight and talent are essential to assure maximum corporate performance. As a result, the systems that motivate these key individuals to perform and remain committed to the firm are of prime concern to every business, regardless of size. External competition, internal pressures, accounting procedures, tax laws, and many unknowns can make executive compensation a bewildering and difficult task. The cost of error in designing and updating executive pay programs is immense. This chapter will examine research findings, strategic issues, and current trends that influence the design of a successful executive compensation program.

Unique Characteristics of Executive Compensation

A chief executive officer (CEO) "sets the tone, defines the style, and becomes the company's public face."[1] This role requires a tremendous commitment of time and energy, and the pay package must reward the individual for this extraordinary effort. A recent survey shows that only 2.7 percent of the CEOs in Fortune 500 companies work between 35 and 44 hours per week, while the largest percent (45.9%) work between 55 and 64 hours per week.[2] A CEO job demands someone who is willing to give up much personal time to tackle the challenges facing the leader of a corporation.

Qualified candidates are "one of a kind" and difficult to recruit because of the fierce competition for these few individuals.

Traditional job evaluation plans are totally inappropriate for executive compensation. Job descriptions for chief executive officers are hard to prepare because a complex interaction exists between the person and the job. The particular style of the incumbent defines the executive's course of responsibilities. This difficulty in separating the job from the person complicates the task facing designers of executive compensation packages. Each deal is likely to be highly individualized, similar to the contracts offered movie stars or free-agent football players. The resulting pay package will depend on the idiosyncrasies of the situation and the negotiation skills of both parties.

Use of Pay to Control Executive Behavior

Unlike most employees, top executives enjoy much discretion and are subject to minimal supervision. Shareholders place an incredible amount of trust in the CEO. Although a CEO reports to the board of directors, which represents the shareholders, many observers argue that the board is, in general, ineffective in monitoring a CEO's performance.[3] Others hold the opinion that the CEO sets his or her own pay and that the boards merely "rubber stamp" pay actions implemented by the executive.[4] Executives may be tempted to maximize their personal wealth rather than the shareholders' returns (e.g., by engaging in mergers and acquisitions to justify higher pay), yet close monitoring of a CEO's diverse activities by the board is difficult, if not impossible. As a result, the compensation system must serve as the primary mechanism that aligns the CEO's interests to the shareholders' welfare by linking incentives to desired managerial actions and firm outcomes.[5]

Complexity of Executive Pay Packages

A myriad of constantly changing issues affects executive compensation practices. The astute designer of executive pay must continuously scan the environment to anticipate the potential effects of volatile tax codes and accounting procedures. For example, the Tax Reform Act of 1986 (TRA 1986) has impacted virtually every component of executive compensation, including the amount of net pay received by executives and the cost of such pay packages to employers.[6] These changes result in adjustments to the accounting statements, which ultimately affect stock prices. As a second example, the Financial Accounting Standards Board is expected to require expensing of stock options for computing book value.[7] This requirement will have a significant impact on corporations that are utilizing stock options. Lack of awareness of these issues could severely impact a corporation and its shareholders.

The information available to designers of executive compensation is in itself overwhelming. David McLaughlin, a principal in McKinsey & Company, has commented that 200 to 300 different types of salary survey data on executive compensation are available.[8] Sorting through this amount of data is almost insurmountable and requires very special skills on the part of compensation professionals.

High Visibility of Executive Pay

Federal law requires detailed reporting of executive compensation in most companies, so firms can seldom hide these decisions from the mass media. The publicity surrounding executive compensation recently has brought the topic to the "kitchen table." News of layoffs and poor international competitiveness disheartens readers who learn that Jim P. Manzi (chairman of Lotus Development Corporation) had earnings of $26.3 million during 1987.[9] The inequity of the situation hits home to the many employees who are experiencing layoffs, watching jobs go overseas, and reading about corporate losses.[10]

Fostering teamwork has become a slogan in many boardrooms, yet, the trend of increasing executive compensation may cause stress between workers and management.[11] Marc Stepp, vice president of the United Auto Workers, claims that executive compensation is "an incredible ripoff," noting that executives at Chrysler Corporation earn approximately 615 times more money than the typical assembler.[12] This figure compares to a ratio of 10 to 1 between a CEO's income and the lowest pay classification in most Japanese firms.[13] The United Auto Workers' analysis that Lee Iacocca receives $8,608 per hour versus $14 per hour for the typical assembler has prompted the union to place executive compensation on the agenda for contract negotiations. The potential for conflict and lower morale resulting from perceived pay inequities could make implementation of concepts such as "teamwork" less successful and a mockery in employees' eyes.

Future government intervention also could result from negative public views of executive compensation packages. Congress reacted harshly to seemingly excessive golden parachute payments by imposing increased tax liability on executives and limiting employers' ability to utilize tax deductions through the Tax Reform Act of 1986.[14] Could Congress react with additional vigor to "excessive" executive pay packages, particularly given claims that executive pay is not linked to corporate performance?

The designers of executive pay must also consider how stockholders will perceive such plans and their subsequent payout. Shareholders are responding to what they perceive as inequitable compensation packages with numerous lawsuits against management.[15] Ponderosa's stockholders were certainly not pleased to read the concluding line in a report reviewing the company's performance and the executives' salaries: "Here's a company where management comes first, and the shareholders, if they come in at all, are way at the end of the cafeteria line."[16]

The total cost of executive compensation is high, making it an easy target of criticism by multiple constituencies. Many observers have noted that a major culprit behind U.S. firms' obsession with short-term gains at the expense of long-term results lies in the incentive structure of CEO compensation activities.[17] Others have blamed executive pay policies that tie CEO compensation to firm size as a prime reason for the flurry of merger and acquisition activities in the United States.[18] The complex issues surrounding development, implementation, and administration of executive pay within a rapidly changing environment require that these packages receive detailed attention. Compensation designers must consider the perceived impact of such contracts on the recipient and the company, as well as the perceived effects on shareholders, government, general public, employee population, and other businesses.

The remainder of this chapter will briefly review the literature and research findings on executive compensation in addition to addressing the pertinent issues of structuring the CEO compensation package from a strategic perspective.

Major Determinants of Executive Compensation

Research on executive compensation dates back to at least the mid-1920s.[19] U.S. accounting regulations that require publication of executive compensation data have provided fertile grounds for analysts interested in testing theory, asking questions, promoting debate, and trying to explain the consistently large salaries earned by the minority of people who are top executives. A rich debate has been accelerating between those who feel that executives are worth what they are being paid and those who proclaim that executives are extremely overpaid and do not deserve what they earn.

Ongoing interest in these issues is evidenced by the front-page stories and surveys on executive compensation that Fortune, Inc., and Business Week (all well-circulated business magazines) have published during the past three years. The topic has also spurred a flurry of recent studies in the academic community; at least 50 articles on executive compensation can be found during the past five years in such journals as *Academy of Management Journal, Journal of Taxation, Journal of Accounting and Economics,* and *Compensation and Benefits Review,* to name a few.

Everyone seems to be asking the same question: "Why is executive pay so high and to what does it relate?" To date, the debate has produced no conclusive answer, merely suggestive research that often contradicts itself. While statistically significant relationships between CEO pay and other variables (such as profitability) are not hard to find, the vast majority of variance goes unexplained; few studies account for more than 25 percent of the variance in executive compensation.[20] The existing research, however, while leaving much to be desired, suggests that a number of factors influence executive compensation. This literature is summarized below.

Size vs. Performance as Predictors of Executive Compensation

According to traditional economic theory, managers will operate a firm in the most efficient manner to maximize profits. Neoclassical economists conclude, based on deductive reasoning, that executive pay should reward performance that maximizes profit. This basic assumption was first challenged by a 1959 study suggesting that executive compensation is more closely linked to corporate size or scale of operations than to profits.[21] The debate began: Does executive compensation reward management's ability to increase corporate size or to increase profitability? The question led to a series of research studies, which unfortunately supported both sides of the issue.

The first researchers to test this issue found that sales volume was more predictive of CEO pay than profit.[22] Thus, this research supported assertions that executives pursued the prestigious (and more financially rewarding) goal of increasing the size of their firms. However, later research backed the alternate hypothesis that profit was related to executive compensation, and found that after parceling out the effects of profits, size had no impact.[23]

Researchers have refined their measurement processes, changed the operationalization of the key variables, used larger and more diverse samples, but have failed to provide conclusive evidence on either side of the debate. Even the most recent research is inconclusive. A 1987 study found support for the position that size serves as the best predictor of executive compensation, while a 1988 investigation concluded that executive compensation was related (but very weakly) to profits measured as a percentage of sales.[24]

The debate has been fueled by those who view reported profit as a contaminated criterion of performance and who have developed sophisticated alternative measures based on the firm's stock value. Two of these investigations found that executive compensation related more strongly to stock performance than accounting measures. However, another study concluded that although statistically significant, stock market data alone explained only 5.4 percent of the variance in executive compensation.[25] To make matters more confusing, a 1987 analysis concluded that "in general, boards of directors do not consider performance of a firm's stock when changing CEO's salaries and bonuses. Neither overall market movements nor abnormal [stock] returns were associated with adjustments in compensation."[26] This pessimistic view of the explanatory value of stock market data also has appeared in other studies.[27]

A third group of researchers, rather than taking sides in the debate, have provided evidence that both size and performance (profits or stockholder value) can predict executive compensation.[28] Instead of viewing these two perspectives as contradictory, these "middle of the roaders" argue that both measures should be employed to provide a better understanding of the determinants of CEO pay.[29]

While it seems reasonable to expect that executives should be paid for both firm size (which reflects the complexity of the job), as well as performance (which is an outcome measure), problems remain. Both measures combined will explain relatively little of the variance in CEO pay, and performance typically lags behind size as a predictor of CEO compensation. A recent empirical study, appropriately titled "The Wacky, Wacky World of CEO Pay," provides a sense of despair by concluding "just about all the rational factors you can think of, taken together, don't play a big role in determining CEO pay . . . top-level compensation doesn't make much sense."[30] The next section specifically addresses some of these other factors.

Secondary Influences on Executive Compensation

Several innovative approaches have been tried in an attempt to understand variables that moderate the relationship between CEO pay and firm size or performance. Researchers have examined the effects of personal characteristics, political considerations, and factors within a firm such as the internal hierarchy. Findings of these investigations are briefly discussed below.

Owner Control vs. Management Control

Since A.A. Berle and G.C. Means published their classic book in 1932, a large literature has explored its central thesis:

> The separation of ownership from control produces a condition where the interests of owner and of ultimate manager may, and often do, diverge, and where many of the checks which formerly operated to limit the use of power disappear. . . .[31]

Most of the work testing this proposition in relation to executive pay comes under the rubric of "agency theory."[32] In a highly simplified fashion, agency theory can be described as follows: Owners of a firm hire managers to act as their agents. Since these agents may be tempted to engage in behaviors that maximize their own personal wealth, perhaps at the expense of owners, owners therefore will develop mechanisms to monitor the performance of the agents and to align their interests to those of the firm. Several authors have argued that shareholders do in fact accomplish this objective rather efficiently.[33] However, an overwhelming amount of empirical research in recent years suggests that the situation is not quite so rosy.

Studies have found that in organizations with less stockholder (owner) control, executives' personal income increases with very little relation to the performance of the firm.[34] In contrast, if a major stockholder exerts control over the executives, CEO pay correlates more highly with performance variables. Among management-controlled firms, on the other hand, where stock holdings are highly diluted so there is no dominant owner, size appears to be the crucial determinant of executive pay.

Other evidence also suggests that "agency problems" are very real indeed. Executives in management-controlled firms are more likely to engage in mergers and acquisitions to justify higher executive pay, even if these activities lower overall corporate performance.[35] Information asymmetries exist that may give an advantage to managers vis-à-vis owners.[36] Executives may succeed in "passing amendments to corporate charters to maximize their own welfare, sometimes to the detriment of stockholders."[37] In short, the evidence suggests that the distribution of ownership across firms is an important determinant of executive pay.

Industry

The relationship between size and executive pay also varies between industries.[38] For example, size accounts for 66 percent of the total variance in executive pay in commercial banking, but explains only 32 percent of the variance in publicly traded construction industries. One study even concluded that market variables (industry) were better predictors of CEO pay than either size or profits.[39] In general, the more competitive the industry, the more likely executive pay is linked to corporate performance.

Organizational Strategy

A 1975 study investigated the relationship between pay and performance within firms with varying strategies.[40] Firms were categorized as using either dominant, related, or unrelated products strategies. Companies that acquire their sales from a single business, such as Alcoa, B.F. Goodrich, and Firestone, use the dominant product strategy. The related products strategy, utilized by firms like Bristol-Myers, Eastman Kodak, and Procter and Gamble, is characterized by growth through the acquisition of businesses related to the company's original products. Unrelated products firms are defined as companies that grow by acquiring businesses that are dissimilar to the organization's current products. This category includes large conglomerates like Martin Marietta, TRW, and FMC.

The investigators found low correlations between pay and financial performance in firms that used a dominant product strategy. Higher relationships between top management compensation and firm performance were noted in the unrelated and related products firms.

One probable explanation for these findings is that the role of a CEO presumably changes as a firm acquires businesses unrelated to the original product. The executive's duties evolve from a "hands on" management style to a more distant one where the primary goal is allocating resources to the various divisions. In addition, as board members evaluate the unrelated business' performance, they may rely more on traditional financial measures, rather than subjective, qualitative indicators of performance, because they are unfamiliar with the products. These same quantitative financial indices are then employed to evaluate the executive's performance. Thus, the link between accounting performance indicators and executive pay is more visible in firms that have followed the unrelated products strategy.

A similar stream of research has evaluated the level of autonomy given to divisional managers and how that autonomy or dependence translates into reward systems. One study found that managers in external acquisitions, and in divisions whose products are unrelated to the major business, have more autonomy than those in divisions developing products linked to headquarters.[41] Top executives in more autonomous business units are rewarded based on quantitative, formula-based criteria for the division. Those in less autonomous business units are evaluated based on both division and corporate performance, which makes objective division performance measures less crucial for pay decisions. Divisional managers of related products firms are evaluated by more qualitative measures that recognize the division's dependence on the corporation.

Personal Characteristics

In addition to the corporate financial measures frequently used to predict executive compensation, personal characteristics of executives have been employed as potential determinants of their pay. One study looked at age and executive mobility in relationship to pay.[42] It found that through their mid-40s, highly mobile executives earned lower salaries than less mobile executives. However, the mobile strategy paid off after middle age, when the highly mobile group, now in their mid-50s, had higher compensation packages. Executives in the highly mobile group were characterized as risk takers who were less resistant to change.

Another study noted that internal work experience better predicted executive pay than external work experience. Compensation of internal candidates appears to be more easily controlled than pay packages for outsiders since a recruitment premium is not needed for insiders.[43] As a result, individuals groomed within a company will eventually cost less than executives brought in from the outside. Other research has found that executives recruited from outside the company earn more than those placed from within, but both groups make more money than the original founders. This study also found that age and length of service have little effect in predicting executive compensation.[44]

Interpersonal skills of executives vary, and greater organizational savvy may promote more favorable financial terms for an incumbent. In particular, a CEO's relationship to the board of directors might serve as an important determinant of how generously the board rewards the executive.[45] The nature of this relationship might well provide insight as to the level of CEO pay and the design of the CEO pay package in terms of salary, bonus, and long-term income.

A recent research study found that successful managers (defined as those who moved rapidly to the top levels of the organization) were not the most effective managers (those who have satisfied, committed subordinates and high-performing units).[46] The difference between the two groups was that the successful executives were very good at creating a favorable image with their superiors and peers. This finding might help explain why so many companies with poor financial figures grant large pay packages to their executives. It could be that shrewd executives, who have refined the art of "impression management," manage to negotiate large compensation packages despite their poor performance.[47] This aspect of executive compensation warrants more attention.

Political Duties

Some analysts have speculated that "CEO rewards may be more a function of political than of economic variables."[48] As a political figurehead and strategist, the CEO represents a firm at various social, legal, and ceremonial functions,[49] and manages constituencies both inside and outside the organization.[50] Winning board approval for a new acquisition, gaining local government support for building a plant, or acquiring union support for wage concessions are all examples of how a political strategist can enhance a firm's short- and long-term goals.

Skillful execution of political duties is crucial to a firm's success, particularly in larger organizations that operate in diverse, international markets. However, designers of CEO reward packages find it very difficult to assess how well someone is handling the political duties of the job. To further complicate this measurement problem, a CEO's relationship with the board will likely have a halo effect on how the board perceives the CEO's effectiveness as a political strategist and figurehead.

Organizational Structure

An alternative sociological view of executive compensation suggests that salaries are determined by the internal hierarchy of the organization.[51] This linkage results from firms' attempts to maintain appropriate compensation differentials between management levels and to establish those pay differentials not in absolute terms, but as ratios. As a result, CEO compensation should be greater in firms with taller organizational structures because they tend to have more executive levels. One analyst has suggested that these ratios are consistent across firms, with approximately a 33 percent pay differential between levels in the hierarchy.[52] Recent research confirms this proposition by demonstrating that the pay relationship among the five highest paid executives differs little by type of business.[53] For example, on average, the second highest paid executive typically receives 67 to 78 percent of the highest paid executive's salary and the third highest receives approximately 55 percent of the top executive's pay.

Problems in Research on Executive Compensation

Readers should recognize the methodological problems which limit the usefulness of these research findings. The most frequently noted flaws arise from differences among studies in terms of samples, time periods, statistical methods, and definitions of key variables.

Differing Definitions of "Executives"

Researchers commonly use the term "executive" but few elaborate exactly to whom this phrase refers. Does "executive" refer only to the CEO, or does it include the entire top management team? While the Securities and Exchange Commission requires disclosure of the five highest salaries within a company, most investigators choose to focus only on CEO compensation. Very few studies make use of SEC disclosure data on the five highest paid executives, and even fewer examine the entire top management team.[55]

Limited Data

Accessibility of accounting data limits most investigations to Fortune 500 firms or other large corporations. Data limitations also restricts the type and number of predictors in a study to data required by the federal government. These data problems make it difficult to provide a thorough understanding of executive compensation. For example, public data provides no means for predicting performance outcomes under alternative stewardships.

Unclear Relationship Between Executive Compensation and Organizational Performance

Mounting evidence suggests that executives have little direct impact over organizational performance and that environmental influences play a greater role.[56] In fact, one study indicates that managerial actions account for as little as 10 percent of the variance in organizational performance.[57] If this finding holds true, formulating a direct connection between organizational performance and executive compensation may prove elusive.

The time period used in an investigation may contribute to this problem. Studies vary from one to ten years in duration, and researchers disagree over how long a study should last to determine whether a genuine link exists between performance and compensation. For example, poor performance by the CEO of a large company should have less disastrous short-term consequences, since largeness and diversification tend to minimize any single individual's impact on overall performance.[58] In addition, compensation earned during a given period may reflect not only the executive's performance during that period, but also his or her past performance and future potential. Thus, the linkage between performance and rewards may not be synchronized chronologically.[59]

Unclear Concepts of "Compensation"

Few studies define executive compensation in a way that distinguishes between recruitment packages and reward programs. Moreover, most researchers ignore long-term income plans and use salary plus bonuses as the total pay package. This substitution is usually done to circumvent difficulties in calculating the present value of long-range programs.[60] However, estimates of total executive compensation including long-term income correlate poorly with salary plus bonus.[61] Therefore, many studies may lead to erroneous conclusions since typically 20–50 percent of an executive's compensation package consists of long-term incentives.[62]

Biased Accounting Measures

Net profit results from choices made by executives which affect the treatment of various depreciation, costing, and inventory accounting methods. Since executives can manipulate these indicators to make themselves look good, profitability data may not reflect a firm's true underlying value or performance.[63] Stock price data is no panacea for this problem, since they are very sensitive to external events which may have little bearing on actual performance and which may be totally beyond management's control.[64] Stock prices also respond to corporate announcements, such as a merger proposal, irrespective of final outcomes.[65]

Summary of Research on Executive Compensation

Table 1 summarizes the various potential determinants of executive compensation in terms of personal, corporate, and external dimensions. The majority of research conducted to date has concentrated on financial measures of firm size and performance and how these relate to executive compensation. The results are conflicting and even when statistical significance is demonstrated, the magnitude of the observed relationship tends to be surprisingly low. Variables other than firm size and performance have been suggested as determinants of CEO pay, but they are not as rationally obvious to employees and outsiders to justify the high level of executive compensation. As a result, this literature provides limited guidance to the compensation practitioner who must legitimize executive pay plans to multiple constituencies.

The overreliance on published data by investigators seems to have led us into a blind alley. What is needed is more intensive study of the process—how do the compensation committees go about setting executive pay packages for recruiting new executives and for rewarding current incumbents? What are the goals of the board for the CEO? Do the goals encompass only financial outcomes or more elusive objectives such as those discussed under political

Table 1

Summary of Research on Executive Pay Determinants

Propositions	Research Evidence
Firm size is an important determinant of executive pay.	Generally strong and consistent.
The greater the distribution of ownership in a firm, the more executives are paid for firm size.	Generally strong and consistent.
Executive pay is more responsive to firm performance when ownership is highly concentrated in a few stockholders.	Generally strong.
Taller organizational structures with multiple management levels are associated with greater top executive pay than those with flat structures.	Generally strong.
Executives are more likely to engage in behaviors that increase firm size even if it is detrimental to shareholders when ownership is widely dispersed.	Generally strong but limited evidence.
The more competitive the industry, the more executive pay is linked to firm performance.	Generally strong but limited evidence.
There is a weak relationship between executive pay and company performance in firms that follow a "dominant product strategy"	Generally strong but limited evidence.
There is a closer connection between top management compensation and firm performance in "unrelated" and "related" product firms.	Generally strong but limited evidence.
Highly mobile executives willing to change jobs and accept risks earn more money as they get older.	Generally strong but limited evidence.
Internal executive hires are paid less than those recruited from external labor market.	Generally strong but limited evidence.
Age and length of service have little effect on executive pay.	Generally strong but limited evidence.
Successful executives in terms of income level and career mobility are not necessarily the most effective managers but those who can create positive impressions.	Very limited evidence but some support.
Firm performance is an important determinant of executive pay.	Weak and mixed.
Executive pay is more strongly related to stock-related performance criteria than to accounting measures.	Weak and mixed.

Table 1 continued

| The Board of Directors plays an active and independent role in establishing and monitoring executive compensation practices. | Inconsistent but generally weak. Very limited research. |
| Executive pay is more a function of political factors (i.e. how well executive represents firm in socio, legal and economic environment) than economic variables. | Very little, if any, empirical research conducted. |

duties? Is the design of the CEO compensation package based on the firm's strategic plans? Answers to questions such as these call for very different research approaches involving qualitative field studies and "clinical" assessments that cannot be easily made by "number crunching" existing data bases.

Strategic Perspectives on Executive Compensation

Decisions concerning growth or cutbacks, expansion into new or similar product lines, and whether to invest in capital or research are made daily by members of top management. These decisions take place based on shared assumptions about the future direction of the firm. Strategy formulation may develop through formal planning procedures, or it might result from the insight of key officers and their ability to take advantage of environmental opportunities.[66] Nowhere else in the firm is there a closer tie between compensation and organizational strategies than at the top executive level.

Need for a Strategic Perspective

Many authors have suggested that the compensation strategy of a firm should fit or link with the organization's business strategy in order to maximize productivity and corporate performance.[67] Compensation strategy has been defined as "the patterns of compensation decisions that are critical to the performance of the organization and which may vary by employee groups within the organization."[68] Therefore, not only is overall compensation strategy considered critical for success, but strategies aimed at specific target groups of employees are also recommended.

Executive pay strategy is the most critical element of the compensation program. It directly and indirectly drives both the formal compensation plan for the remainder of the employees and how they perceive the reward system's link to their own performance.[69] The top management team develops the pay package for the entire organization and determines which activities to reward based on what they perceive as important for corporate success. The management team, which is acting based on their own incentive system, will enforce their own priorities with their subordinates. As a result, goals and objectives built into the executive compensation plan can affect the behavior of the entire work force.

In other words, compensation strategy is critical because the reward system signals to the employees the type of behavior that is essential for corporate and personal success. Behavioral scientists agree that performance-based pay is a motivator, or more importantly, when the employees perceive that pay is linked to performance. As one analysis stated, the major compensation issue facing boards and top management is not pay for performance but pay for *what* performance.[70] The designers of executive rewards can play a major role in defining what constitutes desired behaviors throughout the organization.

Managers act in their own self-interest; a successful rewards program should link a manager's self-interest to the strategic goals of the corporation.[71] Executives' self-interest might encompass many goals outside of pure pecuniary satisfaction, such as self-esteem, power, independence, and authority. However, money is the one, unarguable measure of whether an executive has attained many of these less objective signposts of success. Money is important not only in its own right but as a yardstick to measure the executive's success at meeting many other essential goals.

While many organizations rely on the market as the basis for compensation decisions, such policies deny corporations flexibility to design reward systems that will enhance their strategy. Regardless of industry trends, most companies find themselves with changing goals at different points in time.[72] A firm's idiosyncrasies should be recognized in the design of the executive compensation package. In fact, some analysts recommend giving higher priority to corporate strategy than industry trends when developing executive pay plans.[73] For example, a firm trying to encourage technological change may include innovation rate, product life cycle, and variable manufacturing costs as part of the managerial performance measurement process. Linking pay to these measures signals employees that the goals of the corporation have changed, and rewards will be based on contributions to the firm's new strategic moves.

Strategic Choices Essential to Executive Compensation

An array of strategic pay choices should be considered when designing executive compensation programs. If these options are not explicitly addressed in the design phase, the compensation system may be decoupled from the organization's strategic orientation, and by implication, become less effective or even counterproductive. The following pay policy dimensions should be taken into account:

Who to Cover

The question of who should be included in an executive compensation program to ensure maximal alignment of corporate and individual goals is complex and unique to each organization. Packages which cover fewer employees permit a more personalized design and will reinforce a more authoritarian, hierarchical type of culture within the firm. However, the trend appears to be to include more employees in long-term incentive programs.[74] The *Wall Street Journal* recently reported that the median salary of employees eligible for stock options dropped 10 percent to $68,900 in the past twelve months.[73] The report concluded that this expansion of stock options to lower pay levels is an attempt to propel productivity and improve loyalty to the firm.

R.C. Ochsner, a senior vice president of Hay and Associates, also has noted that a greater percentage of employees are now being covered in executive compensation programs.[76] This trend, he suggests, results from today's smaller, leaner, and flatter organizational hierarchies in which executives are not as far from the bottom as they were in previous years. If this observation is accurate, compensation professionals may become more intimately involved in formulating and implementing strategic decisions that directly affect corporate success through the reward system.

Attraction and Retention Goals

Organizations often view turnover negatively, and HR systems are constantly undergoing revisions to increase tenure and decrease attrition. But turnover is not always undesirable, and firms must understand the type of turnover that will help achieve organizational goals.

In some companies, the strenuous demands placed on the top executive may limit maximum productive tenure to five years. Or a firm's environment and business might change so dramatically that an individual hired a few years ago no longer suits the current business climate. In these cases, turnover might prove more productive than extended tenure. On the other hand, a corporation might value loyalty and feel that long-term tenure on the part of the executives communicates to other employees that stability is an expected and rewarded norm within the organization.

Once the goals of tenure are understood, an organization can make better decisions regarding the mix of short- versus long-term incentives. More importantly, the extent to which long-term income plans deliberately include a tenure factor in the pay-out formula should reflect a firm's strategic needs.

Group vs. Individual Performance Measures

A group performance reward system utilized by many firms is profit sharing. This system allows all employees in the corporation to share the benefits of net profits produced by all members of the firm. While no one person can take credit for changes in net profit, many executive compensation packages employ net profit or other accounting measures to evaluate an individual executive's performance. In fact, many commonly used criteria for incentive compensation are based on group performance, despite evidence that individual performance indicators are the best motivators[77] and that the top executive has minimal impact on organizational performance in many firms.[78]

The reliance on group performance indicators in executive compensation emanates from the objectivity and easy accessibility of these measures. To justify large sums of money allocated to executive pay, board members must be able to communicate the reasons why management earned such amounts. These companywide financial indices should factor into the performance evaluation process for executives, but innovative measures of individual contributions are also needed. For example, an executive could do an outstanding job during bad times, even when financial indicators would make him/her look like a dismal failure.[79]

Accounting vs. Stockholders' Welfare Measures

As noted earlier, one of the most controversial issues in executive compensation revolves around how to measure firm performance. Some would argue that profitability figures are easily manipulated through creative accounting procedures. For example, perfectly legal "tricks" that can inflate the bottom line include accelerated versus straight-line depreciation; FIFO versus LIFO inventory reports; use of short-term, non-capitalized leases for plant and equipment; and window-dressing techniques, such as holding borrowed money as cash until the end of the year so a balance sheet looks good. These practices obviously could have dysfunctional effects for the organization. The importance that management attaches to showing good profitability figures could lead to deliberate bypassing of excellent investment opportunities or to economically inefficient decisions. As one observer noted, use of such measures as earnings per share as a basis for executive pay may create a situation where "what is economically rational from the corporate or social viewpoint may, however, be an irrational course of action for the executives charged with decision making."[80]

Some critics of profitability measures prefer to use such criteria as increases in stock price, dividends paid, or "abnormal market rate returns"[81] as a basis for executive pay because these indices of stockholders' welfare are more difficult to manipulate. On the other hand, these measures also have their foes. A recent review of these counterarguments noted that "paying out cash dividends will tend to raise a stock's price. However, raising cash dividends decreases funds available for reinvestment and for research and development, which lowers expected growth rate and depresses the price of a stock in the long run—with effects perhaps occurring at a time when another executive will bear the brunt of the problem. . . . Stock prices are also very sensitive to external events that may have little to do with how efficiently a firm is being run and that are totally beyond management's control."[82] Because of problems with stock-related indicators, several well-known compensation practitioners recommend use of accounting measures as proxies for performance, or a combination of stock price and profitability data.[83]

Incorporating both types of measures in the criteria to determine executive pay seems to make the most sense for two important reasons. First, using multiple indices leads to a better estimate of "true" firm performance because any single measure may arouse criticism.[84] Second, these different measures are likely to be correlated; indeed, analysis research shows that the most frequently used indicators of firm performance all tend to load on a single factor.[85] In other words, these indices all tend to measure a similar performance dimension. The following rationale has been provided for these findings:[86]

> Changes in levels of sales affect net income, the common denominator of the ROE [return on equity] and EPS [earnings per share] ratios. A firm's ability to pay dividends depends on its earnings. In financial markets, investors and credit analysts use the information contained in annual reports to form expectations about future earnings, thereby affecting stock prices. Changes in stock prices tend to follow the announcement of EPS, ROE, and dividend actions, indicating that the reports have important signaling effects. If the profitability ratios are all good, a stock price will probably be as high as is possible.

Internal vs. External Equity

A major goal of an HR system, and of compensation systems, is to attract and retain managers who make useful contributions, as well as to provide methods by which to terminate those who fail to accomplish desired objectives.[87] Compensation programs that excel in attracting key executives and keeping up with the market will not necessarily provide the most effective method for retaining the current top management team. If a newcomer's salary is excessively higher than that of the current top management team, the firm will signal that persons from the outside have more value than internal employees. Wise executives will find that they too can quickly become newcomers at a different firm and command a much higher salary. In this situation, loyalty and long-term tenure are not rewarded, and the executive willing to make changes in employment will receive a better compensation package than the manager who elects to stay with one employer.

Innovative compensation packages often utilize detailed salary survey data in order to keep up with the competition and allow the firm to recruit new top management talent. Survey findings indicate that executives cite compensation more often as a reason for joining a company than as a reason for leaving.[88] In executive compensation, this attention to designing rewards to recruit new talent has led to an emphasis on external equity, with escalating salary, bonus, and incentive payments as consequences.

Succession planning has many benefits to employers, including lower compensation costs. For example, internal hires are already familiar with the firm's culture and have been "groomed" specifically for the positions that they will attain. Compensation programs that are not totally dominated by market concerns may better synthesize the corporation's strategic goals and those of the pay system.

Long- vs. Short-Term Performance Measures

Critics see executive compensation as one reason that management is primarily interested in maximizing short-term gains, often at the expense of long-term performance. This short-sightedness should not come as a surprise, given that very few firms actually design rewards that balance both short- and long-term goals.[89] Decisions regarding investments in capital equipment and research and development are often made with short-term financial statements in mind.[90] Indeed, many analysts have cited the concern for short-term profits at the expense of long-term competitiveness and innovation as the primary reason the United States is losing business in the international arena.

Organizations have attempted to correct this problem, with mixed success. Ford Motor Company found that its executive compensation plan communicated an extensive emphasis on short-term performance.[91] In order to redirect management's efforts toward long-term directives, Ford changed its compensation plan to incorporate five-year performance measures. In addition, the new plan utilized qualitative measures to tap how well the executives were managing. On the other hand, General Motors retooled its incentive package to emphasize long-term performance, but gave executives short-term rewards in the final plan. Restricted stock grants (discussed later in this chapter) were utilized in an effort to encourage a long-term orientation, but the designers allowed one-third of the stocks to become vested after one month—thus diluting the long-term motivational effect of the reward.[92]

Long-term measures of performance can evaluate not only financial criteria but the more subjective goals and objectives that are critical to corporate success. Achievement of long-term goals also might serve as a surrogate for political success, which is an essential component of the executive's responsibilities.[93] In order for a corporation to instill a long-term orientation among top management, its compensation system must measure and reward progress toward long-term goals, in addition to short-term performance.[94]

Risk Aversion vs. Risk Taking

One commentator has noted that executives, acting as agents of the shareholders, have a much lower tolerance for risk than do the owners of the corporation.[95] Executives' penalty for failing to accomplish minimal goals and objectives of the corporation is termination of employment. Their employment situation and earnings are not diversified in the same manner that most stockholders' portfolios are. Executives usually cannot afford a loss in earnings to the same degree that the owners of a corporation can afford fluctuations in income. Management's only method of spreading personal risk is through various projects within the firm or through acquisitions. Therefore, pay systems must induce executives to assume the degree of risk that is necessary to meet a company's strategic goals and is desired by shareholders.

Compensation plans are designed to provide some sense of security to employees in an effort to enhance loyalty and long-term tenure. The Japanese believe that reducing variability in an individual's income frees that person from the burden of considering the results each decision will have on personal income.[96] In contrast, U.S. corporations have tended to increase variable income to create a sense of entrepreneurship in the managerial cadre. The underlying rationale for this trend is that if managers share the risk, they might strive to produce exceptional results. Each strategy, emphasizing either security or risk taking, can work but it must reflect the needs and nature of the individuals involved and the demands of the organization's strategy.

Younger executives who have less financial commitments are often motivated by an entrepreneurial climate with a high degree of risk taking.[97] The companies that employ this compensation strategy tend to be fast-growing firms that need individuals who are willing to sacrifice income in the early stages, when capital is limited, in exchange for large potential payoffs if the company succeeds. Mature firms, on the other hand, tend to prefer executives who emphasize "harvesting" the current product, follow existing methods of operation, and show less interest in experimenting or risking money and capital with new ventures.[98] The base salaries of executives in mature firms are high enough that their opportunity costs are not prohibitive. Their "down-side risk" usually is nonexistent, particularly if an executive has a large golden parachute contract.

Corporate Culture

The reward system contributes to the formation of employees' attitudes, their motivation to perform, and their willingness to cooperate with each other.[99] The result of these attitudes and behaviors is the organization's culture.[100] The role of reward systems in integrating culture and strategy should be considered when developing a compensation program.

The relative emphasis on executive compensation versus the pay programs for other employees is one indication of culture. In an attempt to minimize status differentials, an increasing number of other corporations have deleted many of the perquisites once reserved for top management. For example, executive cafeterias and preferential parking may be eliminated to enhance atmospheres of teamwork and equality.

Investigations into the linkage between compensation and culture have posited two types of reward systems, each of which produces a different type of culture.[101] These cultures represent extreme poles on a continuum of different persuasions in the way that corporations view themselves. Certain firms can find that their culture resembles one of these two extremes, while others find that they fall somewhere in between, borrowing concepts and values from both systems. A hierarchy-based reward system, described as flexible with both qualitative and quantitative performance measures, results in a "clan culture." This clan culture promotes unity within an organization through support of social and long-term relations between employees and departments. A performance-based reward system utilizes primarily objective measures of performance and precisely defined job descriptions. This system produces a "market culture," which encourages a strong sense of independence and individuality. Employees within this culture are encouraged to pursue their own individual interests rather than team goals.

While an organization's culture may determine its compensation style, pay systems also can be changed to either cause strategic and cultural change or assist in the implementation of such change.[102] For example, Colgate-Palmolive Company's new chief executive officer, Reuben Mark, has specifically addressed executive compensation as one method to change the company's culture from a "family-oriented" philosophy to one that emphasizes independence and entrepreneurial attitudes.[103] Management's awareness of the current culture and understanding of whether it should be enhanced with the compensation system or changed through alterations in pay programs is essential to implementing the organization's strategy.

Objective vs. Subjective Performance Measures

The notion of pay for performance rests on the assumption that somehow performance can be measured. The issue of measurement is at the root of many problems associated with pay administration. Employees often do not perceive a strong relationship between pay and performance because objective measures of performance are extremely difficult to obtain. Quantitative measures, such as financial and accounting data, appear objective, but often do not truly measure the performance of one individual, department, or company. As noted earlier, these figures could be manipulated through creative accounting procedures. In addition, many factors external to the individual or group, such as tax legislation and accounting standards, affect financial performance as well as stock prices.

The availability of accurate performance criteria and the ability of a board to accumulate such information will determine the strength of a pay-performance link in an executive compensation program. Boards need to utilize objective measures of performance so they can justify executive pay packages to external and internal constituencies such as unions, stockholders, and the general public.[104] Unfortunately, many of these financial measures will not increase shareholder value or lead to long-term success of the corporation.[105] In addition, the emphasis on quantitative, objective measures of performance has accelerated the problem of focusing on short-term objectives.[106]

Utilizing both quantitative and qualitative measures of performance can maximize desired performance and adherence to strategic goals.[107] However, pursuing this objective will require an increased amount of time by compensation committees, boards of directors, and top management who must make judgment calls based on incomplete data and even conflicting sources of information.

Integrating Compensation and Organizational Strategies

A variety of mechanisms and tools are available to the designers of executive compensation to facilitate linkage of corporate and compensation strategies. This section will address a number of operational and legal concerns that HR managers should take into account when designing an executive pay package. The next section will focus on the actual compensation tools available for strategy implementation.

Compensation Committees

The formality of the pay-setting process for executives increases with the size of the firm. For example, in interviews conducted during the summer of 1987, the authors found that venture capitalists often negotiate salary terms that "feel right" to them with the founders of small companies over dinner or drinks.[108] As these start-up companies expand and the venture capitalists seek new talent, they utilize executive recruiters and consultants who assist in refining the compensation-setting process. Most publicly traded firms in the United States utilize compensation committees for the purpose of recommending pay programs for the executive team. As discussed below, the role of a compensation committee varies among firms, and its responsibilities appear to be evolving.

Committee Structure and Purpose

The ultimate responsibility for approving executive pay lies with the board of directors, who will vote on a final recommendation, usually submitted by the compensation committee. An organization may have one or several compensation committees. Some larger corporations utilize one committee to administer the salary and bonus (non-stock) components of the rewards package and a second committee to oversee the stock options granted. Other organizations will combine these two functions into a single committee.[109]

The actual procedure used for gathering information, reviewing data, and making pay recommendations varies from firm to firm, but a general process is outlined as follows:[110] The vice president or other high-level officer of the personnel department reviews salary surveys within the industry to determine appropriate compensation packages for new executives or adjustments to the current system for active officers. In companies where the compensation committee has more experience and greater involvement in the process, the personnel officer might only acquire the appropriate surveys and forward them to the committee for further study. In many cases, an outside consultant may be utilized to review salary data and make recommendations.

The compensation committee is usually composed of outside directors to assure conflicts of interest do not occur. Even when inside directors sit on the committee, the outside directors form at least a majority. The committee sifts through recommendations, discusses alternatives, and makes a final endorsement to the board of directors. The board of directors then votes on the package and informs the chief executive officer of the results after the decision has been finalized.

Control Over Executive Compensation

The above process for setting executive pay can create several problems. Consider the reporting structure of individuals involved in making recommendations. The personnel officer reports to the top executive and has a vested interest in maintaining an ongoing positive relationship with that individual. The consultant is usually hired by the personnel officer and also wishes to maintain a relationship with the firm that is conducive to future business. The directors who serve on the compensation committee often head up other firms and strongly identify with the executive position and its associated rewards. The chief executive officer is usually an active member of the board of directors, and might also serve on the compensation committee or get invited to attend its sessions.

All of these issues have led critics to point out that the board of directors and the compensation committee are used mostly for window dressing and that top management actually controls the board.[111] Harold S. Geneen, the chief executive officer of ITT for 15 years, recently lamented, "In most corporations, most of the time, the board of directors has little choice but to follow meekly where the Chief Executive leads."[112] Myles Mace, who studied boards of directors for 25 years, concluded in a 1975 interview that boards are ineffective in evaluating, appraising, and measuring a company's president until the financial results are fatal and they are forced to take action against the president.[113] Other researchers who have empirically studied the relationship between chief executive officers and boards of directors have also concluded that although the board has formal power over management, management in fact dominates the board.[114]

Individuals on the other side of the argument claim that a cooperative relationship between the board and the top executive is necessary for corporate success, but deny that this association puts the executive in command of the pay-setting process.[115] David McLaughlin, during a symposium on executive compensation, commented that while executives might have controlled the process in the past, the new trend is for compensation committees to become active and aggressive in their responsibilities to the stockholders.[116] In addition, McLaughlin feels that the directors serving on these committees are better qualified for the job. They often serve on several compensation committees and can use this experience to contribute to the goals of the committee. Ulrich E. Laudauer, in the same session, agreed and stated that the trend is particularly evident within larger organizations.

While some of these fears regarding the executive pay process may be exaggerated, compensation professionals must learn to recognize situations where conflict of interest may arise due to their subordinate role within the organizational power structure.[117] Executive compensation has many grey areas that require ethical judgments because pay standards are not well established, industry practices vary greatly, and actual pay levels based on market data can range immensely, even if one takes into account such factors as company size, geographic area, and qualifications of the executive. The research discussed earlier dealing with distribution of ownership and its effect on executive pay would suggest that these ethical issues are more likely to become paramount in management-controlled firms.

Organizational Strategies and Compensation Committees

In the past, a board of directors has not been aware of an organization's strategic orientation.[118] Lacking information on business goals and objectives, directors often failed to develop compensation systems that adequately reflect these goals or to appraise and reward executive performance with any accuracy. For boards of directors and compensation committees to strengthen their control over setting, administering, and monitoring the pay process, members must be fully informed of a firm's strategy and how well an organization is accomplishing its mission.

If a board of directors and the compensation committee actively participate in the strategic process and thoroughly understand the short- and long-term goals required of management, then committee members can institute a process to evaluate the effectiveness of current rewards policies. A universal formula that each firm can use does not exist; rather, each evaluation process should reflect the unique goals of a firm's strategy.

As discussed below, a compensation committee needs expert advice from tax specialists, accounting professionals, and legal counsel in order to consider changes in these arenas when evaluating the current system. The board should also evaluate the performance of the compensation committee, which, again, requires knowledge of the strategic goals of the overall business and of the compensation program. The appropriateness of the overall company strategy, as well as the ability of the rewards program to meet this strategy, should also be assessed from time to time.

Accounting and Tax Considerations

Designers of executive compensation programs must consider a barrage of IRS rules that constantly change and fluctuate.[119] The Tax Reform Act of 1986 is seen by some analysts as a major force that will change every facet of executive compensation. At the same time, these experts anticipate that many aspects of the act will be revised. For example, most tax professionals expect that the current maximum personal income tax rates of 28 percent (in some cases 33 percent) will increase. Therefore, a corporation that immediately reacts to tax code changes might find itself in a quandary the following year when additional changes are enforced.

Rather than revising compensation plans in response to every piece of legislation or IRS ruling, HR managers should seek to understand how changing laws, accounting standards, and tax codes so impact the reward system and how to use these changes to pursue their organization's specific, desired objectives. Unfortunately, consultants and tax accountants often overlook strategic concerns and focus on "getting the most for the buck" with the IRS. A recent review found that changes in the CEO compensation plans of the top 100 industrial firms coincided perfectly with changes in tax rules during the 1960s and 1970s.[120] A 1987 survey likewise found that 18 percent of the firms contacted had already changed their executive compensation plans in response to TRA 1986, and an additional 37 percent were considering amendments in their programs.[121] If other corporations follow the lead of these firms, the resulting executive compensation plans will likely be completely out of line with their strategic business needs.

One analyst of TRA 1986 has suggested that lower income tax rates for individuals combined with the raising of the capital gains tax to 28 percent should make employees indifferent to the type of income they receive.[122] But is this indifference shared from the corporate viewpoint? Executive compensation should be linked to successful job performance, and each form of compensation has specific goals for employee development. For example, firms commonly provide stock ownership in an effort to give employees a personal vested interest in the organization's success. Cash rewards will not elicit this same commitment, even though cash is part of an organization's assets. Research indicates that equity ownership motivates key executives more than lower-level employees and this vested interest has a positive effect on shareholder wealth. Therefore, compensation designers should carefully weigh the motivational effect of changes in pay mix before amending an executive compensation package.[123]

Sensitivity to accounting and tax changes is essential, but corporations that blindly follow the crowd will not gain a competitive advantage. As one observer has noted, business places too much emphasis on accounting considerations and should instead view tax laws as a technical issue, not as a goal.[124] This overreliance on tax ramifications prompted corporations to pay executives less in perquisites after the SEC instituted new disclosure requirements and the IRS began to enforce taxation of perquisites in 1978. As a result, many of these firms may have lost an important tool for recruitment and retention.

Executive Compensation Laws and Regulations

A variety of constantly changing state and federal laws, tax regulations, and accounting standards must be weighed when designing executive compensation programs. The following review provides an introduction to the issues that should be taken into account.

Reasonable Compensation

From a legal standpoint, the issue of reasonable compensation raises two concerns. Employers that pay executives in excess of what the IRS considers reasonable compensation may find their allowable tax deduction for payroll expense questioned.[125] The issue of "reasonableness" is also essential for maintaining reliable stockholder relations since state laws allow stockholders to sue a corporation if they consider the rewards allocated to the executive team to be excessive.

To avoid these problems, designers of executive compensation packages should examine two issues: (1) whether the compensation is reasonable in relation to the services provided, and (2) whether payment is actually made for services rendered.[126] If the IRS considers payment to an executive to be a dividend rather than salary, the corporation will not be allowed to deduct the expense and the employee will pay personal income tax. The IRS has incentive to define pay as a dividend rather than salary because, in effect, the government will collect double taxes—from the employer and employee. To diminish any suspicions that compensation is merely a distribution of profit and not payment for services, the rewards package should always be negotiated at the beginning of the fiscal year rather than at the end of the year.

Although the IRS has not strictly defined "unreasonable" compensation, it does commonly inspect certain areas in determining reasonableness.[127] Salary history is reviewed to determine if the dollars awarded to the executive(s) in question suddenly changed. The dividend history of the company is also reviewed for any sudden change, particularly a lack of consistent dividend payments. In addition, the IRS examines the level of compensation of other employees for extreme deviations from expected hierarchical norms. Competitive salary structures within the industry and similarly sized firms may be reviewed. The IRS may also compare the employee's qualifications against the job's requirements and salary. Finally, the IRS may study the employee's contribution to corporate success.

Employers can avoid problems with the IRS by specifying what type of performance will be rewarded and under what conditions the money will be distributed prior to negotiation of a pay package. The board of directors should be able to spell out the contingencies of the compensation package, how it relates to the firm's goals, and exactly how the executive team contributes to achieving those goals. For instance, golden parachutes that appear unreasonable on the surface may be justified as delayed compensation to an executive who takes the job under risky circumstances, such as when a company faces the threat of hostile takeovers.[128] Adequate recordkeeping is a must for everyone involved.

Disclosure Laws

The Securities and Exchange Commission (SEC) requires disclosure of all forms of compensation for the five highest paid employees who earn a salary in excess of $60,000. The Employee Retirement Income Security Act also requires reporting and disclosure of employee welfare and pension plans.

Age Discrimination in Employment Act

Individuals ages 40 and older are considered a protected class under the Age Discrimination in Employment Act. In addition, state laws governing age discrimination might be more restrictive than the federal regulations. Mandatory retirement of most employees became illegal as of January 1, 1987, and antidiscrimination laws also require that older employees receive health care plans identical to those of other company employees. However, the act does exempt bona fide executives and high-level policy-making employees from its retirement provisions. In other words, a mandatory retirement age may be established for these groups.

Effect of the Tax Reform Act of 1986

In general, TRA 1986 lowered the personal income tax of employees (maximum of 28 percent), increased the maximum capital gains tax to 28 percent from 20 percent, and lowered corporate income tax rates.[129] For the first time in history, personal income tax rates are lower than corporate income tax rates.

Stock-based programs, particularly the previously popular incentive stock options, have been affected by TRA 1986. The act also made several changes in qualified retirement plans, effectively lowering the maximum benefit available to executives and expanding antidiscrimination rules. These plans are discussed in more detail in the next section.

Executive Compensation Tools

Once organizational strategy has been delineated, HR managers should determine which components of the executive pay package will prove most conducive to meeting the firm's goals. The following review of the various vehicles for delivering rewards considers the advantages and disadvantages each method may have in inducing various types of executive behavior.

Direct Compensation

Base salary and bonuses for top executives rose 8 percent during 1987, a decline from the 18 percent raise given during 1986.[130] A salary and bonus package tends to reflect an executive's relative status within an organization and will normally be highest for the chief executive officer. While salaries usually increase with position in a company, total compensation need not necessarily follow the corporate hierarchy.[131] For example, if a corporation's strategy calls for greater emphasis on research and development, scientists and engineers may earn greater awards than the CEO. This phenomenon seems more likely to occur in small to mid-sized high-technology firms.

Base Salary

While many companies use formal job evaluation procedures to set base pay,[132] these methods do not always work for positions not easily defined in a job description (as in the case of most top executives). Job evaluation methods emphasize internal equity and often fail to reflect the difficulty of recruiting and retaining top executives. Instead, market data, or external equity, is often a more appropriate determinant of base pay for executives. Salary surveys should be utilized to evaluate the average market rate for top positions, and data specific to the industry is most relevant. Base pay for executives generally forms between 40 percent and 80 percent of their total compensation package and is an important determinant of the executive's status.[133]

Base pay represents the fixed component of a pay package; it tends to remain fairly stable over time, with minimal downside risk to the incumbent. From a strategic perspective, organizations should avoid relying heavily on base pay in the compensation mix so as to retain the flexibility needed to deal with contingencies such as changes in goals and market conditions. Furthermore, executives generally take base pay for granted, thus reducing its motivational value.

Bonuses

A recent trend appears to be toward increased use of bonuses within all industries.[134] Bonuses are short-term incentives linked to specific annual goals. A recent survey of 500 large employers, reported by the Commerce Clearing House, shows that 91 percent of the corporations surveyed had an annual bonus plan in effect for management employees.[135] Pharmaceutical companies were the highest providers, with 100 percent of the businesses utilizing bonus plans. The average bonus award equalled 27 percent of base salary, with senior managers receiving an average of 35 percent of base salary and CEOs earning an average of 59 percent of base salary during 1987.[136]

The trend toward higher bonuses appears to come at the cost of lower salary increases. This finding poses some interesting strategic implications since executives will likely maximize whatever criteria trigger the bonuses. If fulfilling the bonus criteria causes executives to neglect other crucial performance dimensions (such as customer relations, investments in plant and equipment), or directs executives' attention to short-term objectives, CEO bonuses may have dysfunctional consequences for organizations.

The variable nature of bonuses of course, presents higher risks to executives than base salary. The amount of risk incurred depends on the kind of measurement system utilized and the goals that executives must attain to acquire the bonus. Commonly used criteria include rate of return, dividends, sales, costs, stock price, and net profit. In addition, organizations can make bonuses contingent upon meeting concrete, qualitative goals specified in advance, such as successfully concluding a joint-venture agreement overseas.

Corporations vary as to whether they impose a ceiling on the annual bonus. Some observers recommend against use of a bonus ceiling since no similar limit exists on the amount of shareholder wealth that an executive can create.[137] On the other hand, boards and compensation committees must consider the issue of reasonable compensation and the impact that short-term bonuses may have on achievement of an organization's long-term strategic objectives.[138] A limit on bonuses also allows adequate cash flow planning.

Long-Term Incentive Plans

Organizations can choose from a variety of long-term incentive plans (see Figure 1). Each method has advantages and disadvantages that should be considered in the context of a corporation's goals and objectives. These plans can fall into three categories: those that provide employee ownership through transfer of corporation stock, those that use only cash rewards, and those that provide the flexibility to distribute either cash or stock to executives.

Stock Ownership Plans

A number of firms feel that an effective method of linking the executives' and stockholders' interests is to provide incentives that reward the top management team with corporate stock. In these cases, the executives share ownership in the company, and their actions will affect the wealth of shareholders in addition to their own personal estate.

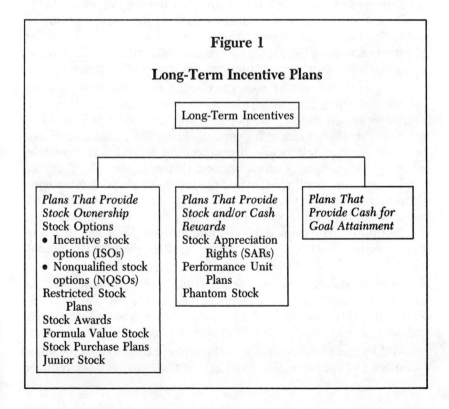

Figure 1

Long-Term Incentive Plans

Long-Term Incentives

Plans That Provide Stock Ownership	*Plans That Provide Stock and/or Cash Rewards*	*Plans That Provide Cash for Goal Attainment*
Stock Options • Incentive stock options (ISOs) • Nonqualified stock options (NQSOs) Restricted Stock Plans Stock Awards Formula Value Stock Stock Purchase Plans Junior Stock	Stock Appreciation Rights (SARs) Performance Unit Plans Phantom Stock	

Stock Options. Stock options allow an executive to purchase a predetermined amount of stock at a set price. The period during which an executive may exercise stock options is almost always restricted in the contract. When exercising the option, an executive can either retain the stocks to enjoy the benefits of ownership or sell them on the open market for cash. Most executives find that they need to sell at least a portion of the stocks to recover the cash spent to purchase the options.

Companies that employ stock options usually allow themselves flexibility in choosing between either incentive stock options, sometimes called statutory or qualified stock options, or non-qualified stock options, often called nonstatutory stock options.

Incentive or qualified stock options were created in 1950 when Congress enacted legislation to promote their use. These options allowed both executives and employers to receive favorable tax treatment if they met a set of IRS restrictions governing such items as the option price and amount of time that the stock options must be held before the employee could exercise the options.[139] Qualified stock options proved extremely popular during the 1950s and 1960s. While Congress tightened the regulations for these options in 1964,[140] a tax advantage remained that resulted in their continued use (the maximum long-term capital gains tax rate was 25 percent while the maximum personal income tax rate was 75 percent).

Use of these options began to decline following enactment of the Tax Reform Act of 1969. This act raised the maximum long-term capital gains tax rate to 35 percent and lowered the maximum personal income tax rate to 50 percent. For many executives whose personal income fell below the maximum tax rate, the relative advantage of obtaining stock options that met these lengthy tax regulations was negligible. After use of these stock options continued to decline, the Economic Recovery Tax Act of 1981 reintroduced qualified stock options under the form of incentive stock options. However, TRA 1986 might have the same negative impact as the 1969 legislation by eliminating favorable tax treatment and retaining existing regulations.[141]

Non-qualified stock options have obtained their name because they do not meet the set of requirements delineated by the IRS. Favorable tax treatment is relinquished in order to issue options that are not governed by the restrictions of the tax code.

Table 2 summarizes some of the current distinctions between incentive and non-qualified stock options. Incentive stock options

Table 2

Differences Between Incentive and Non-Qualified Stock Option Plans Under the Tax Reform Act of 1986

Incentive Stock Options (ISOs)	Non-qualified Stock Options (NQSOs)
—Executives taxed only when stock is sold.	—Executives taxed twice: *at exercise of option *when stock is sold
—Exercise price must be at least equal to fair market value when option is granted.	—Exercise price can be less than or equal to fair market value at time of grant.
—No tax deduction for the employer.	—Employer can deduct the difference between option price and fair market value at time of exercise.
—$100,000 grant limitation replaced by $100,000 exercise limit.	
—Favorable capital gains treatment lost.	
—Sequential exercise rule repealed effective 12/31/86. Do not need to exercise in order to be granted.	—No minimum holding period.

currently offer several disadvantages to employers. Companies do not receive a tax deduction when executives exercise their stock options. In addition, employers lose flexibility in negotiating stock prices because the option price must be at least equal the fair market value of the stock on the date of the grant. In other words, TRA 1986 has made incentive stock options more costly to employers than non-qualified stock options, and continued use of incentive stock plans might be difficult to justify.[142]

Non-qualified stock options are currently favored because employers receive a tax deduction (although there is no impact on cash) and the stock option price is not regulated. Employers are free to discount the stock price in any way deemed appropriate.

The capital gains deduction previously allowed for incentive stocks was repealed on January 1, 1987, and employees now pay personal income tax rates for any gains.[143] Non-qualified stock options result in two liabilities for executives. Taxes are imposed at the time of purchase on the difference between current fair market value and the option price, and again when the executive sells the shares on the increase in fair market value (gain). This taxation often promotes a buy-sell behavior on the part of executives.

The Financial Accounting Standards Board is currently considering expensing stock options for the computation of book net income. The prevailing view is that many compensation committees, not feeling the immediate impact on cash or net income of stock options, are too generous in distributing options without considering the consequences. If accounting regulations do change, the result would reduce employers' reported net income on the balance sheet.[144]

Stock Purchase Plans. Stock purchase plans are more restrictive than stock options because of the narrower time period in which an executive can decide whether to buy company stock. The stock purchase decision usually must occur in a one- or two-month period, whereas executives often have a ten-year time window in which to exercise stock options. Executives can purchase stocks at a price either less than or equal to fair market value. Most companies extend stock purchase plans to all employees.

Participation in a stock purchase plan is not a particularly impressive offer to executives. Their rewards tend to be more customized, and involvement in this type of program is generally seen as a mere entitlement rather than an incentive to perform at an exceptional level. In addition, these plans promote a shorter-term orientation than other plans.

Restricted Stock. These plans grant executives stock either at no cost or for a very nominal cash outlay. The restrictions applied to these stocks allow the grantors to devise incentives for executives to remain with the organization. Restricted stocks are a common tool of start-up firms that intend to go public at some point. These stocks provide a mechanism to recruit talented individuals into a new venture and to retain them at least until the firm has successfully completed its initial public offering. The typical restricted stock contract requires an executive to remain with the firm for three to five years before gaining ownership of the promised stock. If employment is terminated before the stocks are awarded, the executive forfeits any right to the stock. Restricted stock can be placed under a vesting program which awards portions of the stock over a series of years. This method allows employers to utilize restricted stock as continual reinforcement and an incentive for executives to remain with the firm.

Restricted stock provides executives with partial ownership in a firm. As far as this ownership induces executives to maximize some measure of corporate performance, restricted stock promotes the goal of linking corporate goals to executive performance. If, instead, executives simply maximize the market price of the stock right before gaining ownership (e.g. by raising cash dividends) and does so at the expense of other important strategic goals, use of restricted stock may prove detrimental to an organization.

Creative Stock Programs

Creative stock plans tend to be utilized on an individualized, ad hoc, customized basis for executives. In most cases, they constitute a contract between an executive and an employer. Use of these tailor-made agreements has clearly risen in recent years. While this section will provide a brief introduction to the primary use, advantages, and disadvantages of creative stock programs, this arena is constantly changing and readers should consult tax, benefits, and accounting specialists before devising such a plan. These specialists can provide administrative advice, but only individuals familiar with the ultimate goals of an organization can effectively determine the best fit between incentives and business strategy.

Stock Awards. Stock awards resemble cash bonuses except the form of payment is in stock. Recruiters often use stock awards as an up-front bonus that does not interfere with the established compensation program or internal consistency. Since an executive does not pay for the stock, these awards in effect constitute a stock purchase plan with a 100 percent discount.[145] Although the executive owns the stock, an employer may place restrictions on transferring or selling the stock, thus providing an incentive for employees to consider the long-term value of the award. During the time that the stocks are restricted, many organizations provide the executive with rights to dividends and associated voting privileges.

Formula Value Stock. Formula value stock provides the designers of executive compensation plans with a unique opportunity to customize criteria for rewarding top management. The value of this new class of stock is derived by a pre-determined formula rather than marketplace pricing. Unlike many stock plans, this approach recognizes that many variables outside the control of the top management team can affect the market value of an organization's stock.

Under these plans, businesses often use book value as the criterion for payment. Employees who purchase the stock when book value is low and who remain with the firm as the stock's book value increases (presumably as a result of executives' performance) will find that the value of their original stock has increased. This appreciated stock can then be sold to the organization or converted into common stock.

Every formula utilized to value the stock will send a different message to an executive team. For instance, employing book value might motivate behavior that will reduce dividends paid to stockholders because lower dividends will increase the resulting book value of the organization. However, some observers have suggested that companies currently fail to use formula value stock as creatively as they might, given that these stocks could help promote a variety of corporate goals.[146]

Junior Stock. This class of stock is separate and subordinate to the organization's common stock, and its recipients have limited voting and dividend rights. Junior stock is not commonly used for rewarding executives because the accounting treatment results in large reductions to net earnings. Junior stock has less value than common stock, which allows an executive to spend less cash up front to purchase the stocks. Executives can then convert their shares to common stock upon achievement of specific performance goals.

Junior stock was initially utilized by many established high-technology firms, particularly those in Silicon Valley which had smaller growth in their stock value. Junior stock provided these companies with a method to compete with start-up organizations that could offer large increases in wealth if they were successful. Unfortunately, the combination of poor accounting treatment and loss of tax incentives has made this alternative less viable for organizations.

Plans That Provide Cash Only

As a result of TRA 1986's lowering of personal income taxes for executives, plans that provide executives with cash today may become more attractive than those that defer income to a later date when tax rates might be higher. Employers can reward executives for goal attainment by providing one-time cash awards. The amount can vary and need not be pre-determined by the board. The bonus can be tied to specific financial performance measures or be more subjective, based on non-financial results. As a one-time award, the bonus is treated as a variable expense that may be funded out of future expected revenues. For example, First Chicago Corporation is providing its managers with bonuses based on improved customer service.[147] According to author Tom Peters, "There are ways to measure what was once thought to be unmeasurable [i.e., quality of service]."[148] In the high-technology industry, cash bonuses are widely used to direct managerial behavior in ways consistent with firm goals.[149] Cash awards in this industry are tied to such criteria as meeting a project deadline, prompting a technological break-through, patenting a new process, or releasing a new and innovative product to the market.

Plans That Award Cash and/or Stock

These plans allow employers to defer the decision on method of payment until the time of the award. The employer then has flexibility to take advantage of revised tax laws and accounting treatment in addition to considering the specific needs of the incumbent. The three major plans under this rubric are discussed below.

Stock Appreciation Rights. Stock appreciation rights provide the grantee with cash or stocks equal to the difference between the value of the stock when awarded and its value when the stock is exercised. The executive is rewarded for the increased value of the stock although no stock was actually granted by the firm.

Stock appreciation rights are commonly used in conjunction with stock options to alleviate the cash burden placed on executives who incur tax liability when exercising their options. If used independently, they are very similar to performance units (discussed next), in that the market value of the stock determines the payment awarded executives.

Performance Plans. Performance plans come in two types: performance units or performance shares. Performance units refer to a contract between an executive and organization that specifically stipulates the dollar amount of the reward that the executive will receive for each share owned. The value of each share is tied to a measure of financial performance, which is flexible and preferably linked to the strategic needs of the firm. For example, under a earnings-per-share plan, an organization might provide $100 per unit share owned by an executive for every percent increase in earnings. Therefore, if earnings per share increase by 3 percent, an executive would receive $300 for each share owned. Payment may come in the form of cash or common stocks.

In a performance share plan, the number of stocks provided to the executive is generally based on profitability figures using a predetermined formula. The actual compensation per share depends on the market price per share at the end of the performance or award period. Employers commonly place a cap on the amount of money that can be earned in performance share programs.

Performance plans provide designers of executive compensation programs with considerable flexibility in choosing the performance criteria and method of payment. They are particularly useful in combining both accounting and "stockholder's welfare" dimensions of performance, thereby reducing the pitfalls associated with either measure, as discussed earlier in this chapter. Performance plans have some additional advantages, as the following discussion demonstrates:[150]

> First, performance plans have a longer time period for accounting performance evaluation (e.g., three to six years) than the typical short-term plan which provides a bonus based upon yearly accounting performance. Second, performance plans are similar to other long-term plans in that any expected compensation associated with the performance plan is deferred until some future date and is usually forfeited if the executive leaves the corporation during the award period. Third, the performance targets or goals are explicitly stated in terms of growth in accounting-based measures over an award period. This contrasts with say, stock option plans where performance (and compensation) depends [exclusively] upon increases in market price per share.

Phantom Stock. Phantom stocks pay bonuses proportional to the performance of company stocks rather than to the performance of company profits. Phantom stock is only a bookkeeping entry; a company does not distribute actual stock. Instead, executives receive a number of shares of phantom stock in order to track the cash reward that will be received upon attaining performance objectives.

Book value is a common performance criteria used by firms employing phantom stock plans. An employee earns a specific amount of "shares," whose value is determined by, for example, present book value (assets minus liabilities, divided by the number of outstanding shares). When book value increases, the employee receives the net increase, in cash, based on the number of "shares" awarded.

The result of the process is that the executive receives a cash award for increasing a specific financial measure of corporate performance. Awarding phantom shares allows corporations to motivate executives by establishing a close linkage between pay incentives and agreed-upon performance criteria. It also allows corporations to differentiate between executives by awarding more phantom shares to those who are more likely to have an effect in meeting those objectives.

Phantom stocks provide executives with an opportunity to earn wealth if the corporation's stock gains value. These plans pose no downside risk to executives because they do not invest cash to purchase actual shares of the corporation's stock.

Strategic Uses of Long-Term Incentives

Table 3 summarizes several important strategic choices associated with long-term incentives. Careful consideration of those issues on the part of compensation committees and thoughtful insight into the types of behaviors required to support a firm's strategic goals are crucial to the eventual success or failure of any executive pay program. If an organization's objective is to make executives partial owners of the corporation through a stock ownership plan, then the company should consider what decisions will maximize gains under the plan. For instance, if firm growth in sales or market share form the criteria for providing stocks in a performance share plan, then executives may be encouraged to expand the company's merger and acquisition activities, even if these decisions prove inefficient. If stock options are utilized but the firm does not provide the executive with access to cash for covering the expected tax liability, the executive will likely sell at least part of the stocks in the marketplace in order to cover the tax burden. The process of selling stocks will dilute the executive's ownership, possibly to a level less than that desired by the board of directors.

Designers of compensation plans should also consider how often the executive receives rewards or incentives under the plan. Is continuous reinforcement, such as that provided by a stock purchase plan, important or will a lump-sum payment, as in a stock award or annual cash bonus, suffice?

The marketplace determines the value of common stock, and these stocks can be traded in the open market. In a sense, the value of common stock is similar to that of cash in that executives can negotiate with the stocks outside of the organization. On the other hand, plans such as formula value stock or phantom stock consist of

Table 3

Strategic Choices Associated With Long-Term Incentives

Strategic Choice	Compensation Options
1. Pay Mix	Cash, stock, or combination.
2. Degree by which firm encourages ownership in the business.	Choice of stocks that induce market trading vs. retention for long period of time.
3. Schedule of payment.	Frequent and reoccuring bonuses or awards vs. lump sum payments.
4. Mix of rewards that have value outside vs. inside the corporation.	Use of stocks that can be openly traded vs. those that only have value within the firm.
5. Amount of incentive.	Use of a ceiling for incentive plans vs. unlimited earning potential.
6. Criteria for stock value.	Market price vs. customized financial criteria.
7. Performance criteria.	Business unit, division, or corporate.
8. Degree of uniformity.	Corporate-wide plan vs. customized at the business unit or division level.
9. Source of funding.	Corporate vs. division accounting criteria.
10. Restrictions for payment.	Seniority vs. goal attainment.
11. Time horizon.	Definition of long- and short-term (e.g., 3, 5, or 10 years).
12. Basis for payment.	Profitability, growth, stock prices, or a combination.
13. Layers of management included in the plan.	CEO, top five executives, division managers, etc.

"paper money" that can only be redeemed within the organization. More liquid items give executives a greater sense of financial freedom, but stock whose value is determined within the organization gives the firm more leverage in retaining executives (e.g. by establishing some minimum tenure) and pegging the award to desired objectives.

Incentives vary as to whether a cap exists on the amount an executive can earn or whether the potential payment is unlimited. A board can have a variety of reasons for providing either type of incentive to an executive. In some instances, a compensation plan with unlimited rewards may be necessary to lure a prospective executive. In other cases, a board may prefer to assure reasonable compensation and to maintain a trusting relationship with stockholders by capping executives' rewards. For instance, performance unit shares provide an organization with extremely specific guidelines, and the compensation committee can communicate to any interested parties the maximum cost of the plan. Cash bonus systems that are open ended or stock awards can have unlimited ceilings.

A large firm might wish to design a plan that considers the performance of a business unit or of an individual in addition to overall corporate performance. Cash bonuses can be used to reward individual performance, irrespective of an organization's financial results. This method might prove desirable, particularly for an organization whose poor financial data can be turned around by performance of a few key individuals. Formula value stock can be particularly useful to develop customized compensation plans based on the performance of specific business units or divisions.

Compensation designers should also consider issues covered elsewhere in this chapter, such as long- versus short-term time horizons and accounting versus stock-based performance measures. Every compensation program signals that a certain type of performance is desired and rewarded. Designers of compensation programs must look beyond the obvious and ask themselves what type of behavior is most likely to result from the set of rewards under consideration. In addition, HR managers must constantly monitor compensation plans to determine whether the expected results are transpiring or if unexpected forces are interfering with the program's success.

Executive Benefits

The effects of TRA 1986 will most likely spur innovative thinking in the area of executive benefits. Sweeping non-discrimination rules will also eliminate or reduce many executive benefits since these rules require taxation of any benefits not provided to all employees.[151] Tax reforms have limited the level of benefits that executives can receive from most qualified retirement plans. When plans are qualified, proceeds are kept in a trust fund and an employee is not taxed until the money is withdrawn. The 401(k) plans were revised under TRA 1986 so that the $30,000 limit on qualified annual contributions per person has been reduced to $7,000. Employers who actively used 401(k) plans as part of their executive benefit program find themselves in need of securing new, creative methods to maintain the same level of after-tax benefits.

Vesting rules were also changed under the 1986 tax reforms. Beginning in 1989, employers must offer either full five-year vesting or an alternative seven-year plan that provides gradual vesting to employees starting at three years. [152] Those employers who previously relied on ten-year vesting as a mechanism to retain key employees will need to revise their strategy because this tool has lost its potential power to achieve that goal.

The hottest perk appears to be membership in health clubs. A recent survey indicates that the number of companies providing this benefit rose to 17 percent during 1986, up from 1 percent in 1982. [153] During the same period, organizations dropped membership in luncheon clubs by 10 percent. Other perks that have lost support include country club membership and corporate aircraft, while golden parachutes are increasing in popularity.

The amount of dollars spent on benefits and perquisites are staggering for many corporations. To utilize those dollars effectively, designers of executive compensation packages should consider the alternatives in light of their strategic goals. Health club membership contributes to employees' well-being while providing a relaxed place for executives to discuss business. Luncheon and dinner clubs also provide places to meet, but drinking is common, and the risk of alcohol abuse is not desirable by most employees and employers.

Conclusion

The past has been rich with change in executive compensation, and the future will likely be no different. Employers should expect that this area will continue to evolve, and increasingly complex tax, legal, and accounting regulations will greatly affect the relative advantages and disadvantages of various executive pay programs. The best preparation for any future changes is to think strategically about executive compensation.

Boards should be fully informed about strategic goals so that they can improve their ability to design and administer executive compensation programs. Employers will demand plans that provide flexibility. Flexibility is needed not only to respond to the regulations that affect executive compensation but also to motivate the new breed of executives who are entering the work place. This new breed, according to some observers, will feel less loyalty to a firm than executives of the past.[154] Hostile takeovers, mergers, and downshifting have resulted in the loss of many executive positions, and top brass no longer feels that their company will "take care of them." This shifting loyalty makes creative compensation for executives a critical concern for many organizations.

♦

Notes

1. Taylor, p. 30.
2. McComas.
3. Kerr and Bettis; Murthy and Salter; Crystal (1988b).
4. Amend; Williams.
5. Tosi and Gomez-Mejia.
6. Toppel.
7. CPA Journal, p. 80.
8. Miller.
9. Byrne.
10. Brindisi and Friedman.
11. Patton.
12. Connelly.
13. Balkin and Gomez-Mejia (1984).
14. Crystal (1988b).
15. Brickley, Bhagat and Lease, p. 116.
16. Simon, R.
17. Rappaport; Alexander.
18. Brindisi and Friedman; Blair and Kaserman.
19. Taussig and Barker.
20. Deckop (1987b).
21. Baumol.
22. Roberts; McGuire, Chiu and Elbing.
23. Lewellen and Huntsman.
24. Posner, B.; Deckop (1988).
25. Masson; Murphy (1985); Couglan and Smith.
26. Kerr and Bettis.
27. Loomis; Kerr and Bettis.
28. Smyth, Boyes and Peseau; Hirschey and Papas; Dyl.
29. Ciscel and Carroll.
30. Crystal (1988a).
31. Berle and Means, p. 65.
32. For reviews, see Eisenhardt; Hoskisson, Hitt, Turk, and Tyler.
33. Fama; Fama and Jensen (1983a), (1983b); Demsetz.
34. Santeer and Neun; McEachern; Dyl; Gomez-Mejia, Tosi and Hinkin.
35. Blair and Kaserman; Firth; Brindisi and Friedman; Kroll, Simmons and Wright.
36. Grossman and Hart.
37. Bhagat, p. 310.
38. Peck.
39. Ungson and Steers.
40. Murthy and Salter.
41. Pitts (1974).
42. Roche.
43. Agarwal.
44. Deckop (1988).
45. Ungson and Steers.
46. Luthans.
47. Tosi and Gomez-Mejia.
48. Ungson and Steers, p. 318.
49. Mintzberg (1973).
50. Ungson and Steers.
51. Simon, H.A.
52. Mahoney.
53. Peck.
54. Id.
55. E.g., Prasad.
56. Pearce, Stevenson, and Perry.
57. Pfeffer and Salancik.
58. Hall.
59. Lambert; Murphy (1986).
60. Black and Scholes; Kerr and Bettis.
61. Antle and Smith.
62. Benston; Lewellen.
63. Gomez-Mejia, Tosi and Hinkin.
64. Deckop.
65. Dodd.

66. Mintzberg (1979).
67. Balkin and Gomez-Mejia, in press; Broderick; Butler, Ferris, & Napier; Gomez-Mejia and Balkin, in press; Gomez-Mejia and Welbourne; Hambrick and Snow; Milkovich; Pitts (1976); Schuler and Jackson; Tichy, Fombrun and Devanna.
68. Milkovich.
69. Salter.
70. Sethi and Namiki.
71. Rappaport.
72. Murthy and Salter.
73. Id.
74. Bureau of National Affairs.
75. Hymowitz.
76. Ochsner.
77. Carroll.
78. Pfeffer and Salancik.
79. Eaton and Rosen.
80. Rappaport, p. 82.
81. The term "abnormal market rate returns" refers to a rate of return on the company's stock which is greater than that of other firms in the industry during the same time period.
82. Gomez-Mejia, Tosi and Hinkin.
83. Bickford; Ellig; Rick and Larson.
84. Weiner and Mahoney.
85. Gomez-Mejia, Tosi and Hinkin.
86. Id., pp. 59–60.
87. Cheeks.
88. Roche.
89. Stata and Maidique.
90. Rappaport.
91. Verespej.
92. Schlesinger.
93. Ungson and Steers.
94. Stonich.
95. Rappaport.
96. Stonich.
97. Kerr; Balkin and Gomez-Mejia (1984).
98. Salscheider.
99. Hambrick and Snow.
100. Kerr and Slocum.
101. Id.
102. Lawler.
103. Burg and Smith.
104. Murthy and Salter.
105. Verespej.
106. Hambrick and Snow; Carroll.
107. Salter.
108. Gomez-Mejia, Balkin, and Welbourne.
109. Andrews.
110. Cook.
111. Sethi and Namiki; Williams.
112. Geneen, p. 29.
113. Murthy and Salter.
114. Allen; Herman; and Pfeffer. For review of this literature, see Mizruchi.
115. Murphy (1986).
116. See Miller.
117. Tosi and Gomez-Mejia.
118. Bacon and Brown.
119. A thorough review can be found in *The Business Lawyer*, November 1987, V43, N1. Executive Compensation: A 1987 Road Map for the Corporate Advisor.
120. Hite and Long.
121. Posner, M.
122. Walter.
123. Bhagat, Brickley and Lease.
124. Levine.
125. Cheeks.
126. Cohn and Lindberg.
127. Id.
128. Knoeber.
129. Walter.
130. Byrne.
131. Cohn and Lindberg.
132. Id.
133. Kerr and Bettis.
134. Peck.
135. Commerce Clearing House.
136. See Compensation and Benefits Review.
137. Cohn and Lindberg.
138. Cheeks.
139. IRC §424.
140. IRC §422.
141. IRC §422A.
142. The Business Lawyer.
143. Rubin.
144. CPA Journal.
145. Ellig.
146. Poster.

147. Peters.
148. Peters, p. 81.
149. Gomez-Mejia and Balkin (1985).
150. Larcker, p. 8.
151. Toppel.

152. Posner, M.
153. Compensation and Benefits Review.
154. Crystal (1988b).

◆

References

Agarwal, N.C. 1981. "Determinants of Executive Compensation." *Industrial Relations* 20 (Winter): 36–46.

Alexander, C.P. 1988. "Trade: Getting Back into the Game." *Time* (October 17): 28–31.

Allen, M.P. 1974. "The Structure of Interorganizational Elite Cooptation." *American Sociological Review* 39: 393–406.

Amend, P. 1987. "Annual Compensation Survey." *Inc* (September): 50–53.

Andrews, K.R. 1980. "Directors' Responsibility For Corporate Strategy." *Harvard Business Review* (November-December): 30–42.

Antle, R. and A. Smith. 1985. "Measuring Executive Compensation: Methods and an Application." *Journal of Accounting Research* 23(1): 296–325.

Bacon, J. and J.K. Brown. 1973. *Corporate Directorship Practices*. Washington, D.C.: The Conference Board.

Balkin, D.B. and L.R. Gomez-Mejia. 1984. "Determinants of R & D Compensation Strategies in High Tech Industry." *Personnel Psychology* 37(4): 635–650.

––––––. In press. "The Strategic Role of Compensation." *Strategic Management Journal*.

Baumol, W.J. 1959. *Business Behavior, Value, and Growth*. New York: Macmillan.

Benston, G.J. 1985. "The Self-Serving Management Hypothesis: Some Evidence." *Journal of Accounting and Economics* 7: 67–84.

Berle, A. and G.C. Means. 1932. *The Modern Corporation and Private Property*. New York: Macmillan.

Bhagat, S. 1983. "The Effect of Pre-Emptive Right Amendments on Shareholder Wealth." *Journal of Financial Economics* 12: 289–310.

Bhagat, S., J.A. Brickley, and R.C. Lease. 1985. "Incentive Effects of Stock Purchase Plans." *Journal of Financial Economics* 14: 195–215.

Bickford, C.C. 1981. "Long-Term Incentives for Management, Part 6: Performance Attainment Plans." *Compensation Review* 12(3): 14–29.

Black, F. and M. Scholes. 1973. "Pricing of Options and Corporate Liabilities." *Journal of Political Economy* 81: 637–654.

Blair, R. and L. Kaserman. 1983. "Ownership and Control in Modern Organizations: Antitrust Implications." *Journal of Business Research* 11: 333–344.

Brickley, J.A., S. Bhagat, and R.C. Lease. 1985. "The Impact of Long-Range Managerial Compensation Plans for Shareholder Wealth." *Journal of Accounting & Economics* (April): 115–129.

Brindisi, L.J., Jr. and S. Friedman. 1988. "Are U.S. Managers Overpaid?" *Management Review* 77(3): 60–62.

Broderick, R.F. 1986. *Pay Policy and Business Strategy—Toward a Measure of Fit.* Unpublished doctoral dissertation. Cornell University.

Bureau of National Affairs (BNA). 1988. *Changing Pay Practices: New Developments in Employee Compensation.* Special Report. Washington, D.C.: The Bureau of National Affairs, Inc.

Burg, R.H. and B.J. Smith. 1988. "Compensation Management in Practice. Restructuring Compensation and Benefits to Support Strategy, Part 1: Executive Compensation." *Compensation and Benefits Review* 20(4): 15–22.

The Business Lawyer. Subcommittee on Executive Compensation of the Commission on Employee Benefits and Executive Compensation. 1987. *Executive Compensation: A 1987 Road Map for the Corporate Advisor* (November 1987): vol. 43, no. 1.

Butler, J., G. Ferris, and N. Napier. 1989. *Strategic Human Resource Management.* Cincinnati, OH: Southwestern Publishing Co.

Byrne, J.A., 1988. "Who Made the Most—and Why." *Business Week* (May 2): 50.

Carroll, S.J. 1987. "Business Strategies and Compensation Systems." In *New Perspectives on Compensation,* eds. D.B. Balkin and L.R. Gomez-Mejia. Englewood Cliffs, NJ: Prentice-Hall, pp. 343–346.

Cheeks, J.E. 1982. *How to Compensate Executives,* 3rd ed. Homewood, IL: Dow Jones-Irwin.

Ciscel, D.H. and T.M. Carroll. 1980. "The Determinants of Executive Salaries: An Econometric Survey." *Review of Economics and Statistics* 62: 7–13.

Cohn, T. and R.A. Lindberg. 1979. *Compensating Key Executives in the Smaller Company.* New York: AMACOM.

Commerce Clearing House. 1988. *Executive Compensation* (January): 4201–4304.

Compensation and Benefits Review. 1988. Currents in Compensation and Benefits (January-February): 1–3.

Connelly, M. 1988. "Iacocca's High Pay Dulls Offer to Union." *Automotive News* (April 25): 1.6.

Cook, F.W. 1981. "The Compensation Director and the Board's Compensation Committee." *Compensation and Benefits Review* 13(2): 37–41.

Couglan, A.T. and R.M. Smith. 1985. "Executive Compensation Management Turnover and Firm Performance—An Empirical Investigation." *Journal of Accounting and Economics* (April): 43–66.

CPA Journal. 1987. 57(2): 62.

Crystal, G.S. 1988a. "The Wacky, Wacky World of CEO Pay." *Fortune* (June 6): 68–78.

————. 1988b. "Executive Compensation: Challenges in the Year Ahead." *Personnel* 65(1): 33–36.

Deckop, J.R. 1987a. "Top Executive Compensation and the Pay-For-Performance Issue." In *New Perspectives on Compensation*, eds. D.B. Balkin and L.R. Gomez-Mejia. Englewood Cliffs, NJ: Prentice-Hall, pp. 285–294.

————. 1987b. "Twenty Years of Executive Compensation Research." Paper presented at the Southern Academy of Management Meetings, New Orleans, LA.

————. 1988. "Determinants of Chief Executive Officer Compensation." *Industrial and Labor Relations Review* 41(2): 215–226.

Demsetz, H. 1983. "The Structure of Ownership and the Theory of the Firm." *Journal of Law and Economics* 26: 375–390.

Dodd, P. 1980. "Merger Proposals, Management Discretion and Stockholder Wealth." *Journal of Financial Economics* 8: 105–137.

Dyl, E.A. 1988. "Corporate Control and Management Compensation: Evidence on the Agency Problem." *Managerial and Decision Economics* 9(1): 21–25.

Eaton, J. and H. Rosen. 1983. "Agency, Delayed Compensation, and the Structure of Executive Remuneration." *The Journal of Finance* 23(5): 1489–1505.

Eisenhardt, K.M. 1989. "Agency Theory: An Assessment and Review." *Academy of Management Review*, January (in press).

Ellig, B.R. 1984. "Incentive Plans: Over the Long-Term." *Compensation Review* 16(3): 39–54.

Fama, E.F. 1980. "Agency Problems and the Theory of the Firm." *Journal of Political Economy* 88(2): 288–307.

Fama, E.F. and M.C. Jensen. 1983a. "Agency Problems and Residual Claims." *Journal of Law and Economics* 26: 327–349.

————. 1983b. "Separation of Ownership and Control." *Journal of Law and Economics* 26: 301–324.

Firth, M. 1980. "Takeovers, Shareholder Returns, and the Theory of the Firm." *Quarterly Journal of Economics* 94: 235–239.

Geneen, H.S. 1984. "Why Directors Can't Protect the Shareholders." *Fortune* (September 17): 28–32.

Gomez-Mejia, L.R. and D.B. Balkin. 1985. "Managing the High Tech Venture." *Personnel* (December): 31–37.

————. In press. "The Effectiveness of Aggregate and Individual Incentives for R&D Employees." *Industrial Relations*.

Gomez-Mejia, L.R., D.B. Balkin, and T.M. Welbourne. 1988. "The Influence of Venture Capitalists on Human Resource Management Practices in the High Technology Industry." *Proceedings of the 1988 High Technology Conference at the University of Colorado*, Boulder. pp. 26–29.

Gomez-Mejia, L.R. and T.M. Welbourne. 1988. "Compensation Strategy: An Overview and Future Steps." *Human Resource Planning* 11(3): 173–189.

Gomez-Mejia, L.R., H. Tosi, and T. Hinkin. 1987. "Managerial Control, Performance, and Executive Compensation." *Academy of Management Journal* 30(1): 51–70.

Grossman, S.J. and O.D. Hart. 1983. "An Analysis of the Principal-Agent Problem." *Econometrica* 51(1): 7–45.

Hall, R.H. 1977. *Organizations, Structure, and Process.* Englewood Cliffs, NJ: Prentice-Hall.

Hambrick, D.C. and C.C. Snow. 1989. "Strategic Reward Systems." In *Strategy, Organization Design, and Human Resources Management,* ed. C.C. Snow. Greenwich, CT: JAI Press.

Herman, E.S. 1981. *Corporate Control, Corporate Power.* New York: Cambridge University Press.

Hirschey, M. and J.L. Pappas. 1981. "Regulatory and Life Cycle Influences on Managerial Incentives." *Southern Economic Journal* (October) 48: 327–334.

Hite, G.L. and M.S. Long. 1982. "Taxes and Executive Stock Options." *Journal of Accounting and Economics* 4: 3–14.

Hoskisson, R.E., M.A. Hitt, T. Turk, and B. Tyler. 1989. "Balancing Corporate Strategy and Executive Compensation: Agency Theory and Corporate Governance." In *Research in Personnel and Human Resources Management* (vol. 7), eds. G.R. Ferris and K.M. Rowland. Greenwich, CT: JAI Press.

Hymowitz, C. 1988. "Stock Options for Middle Managers." *Wall Street Journal* (May 17): 33.

Kerr, J. 1982. "Assigning Managers on the Basis of the Life Cycle." *The Journal of Business Strategy* 2(4): 58–65.

Kerr, J. and R.A. Bettis. 1987. "Boards of Directors, Top Management Compensation and Shareholder Returns." *Academy of Management Journal* 30: 745–664.

Kerr, J. and J.W. Slocum. 1987. "Managing Corporate Culture Through Reward Systems." *Academy of Management Executives* 2(2): 99–107.

Knoeber, C. 1986. "Golden Parachutes, Shark Repellents, and Hostile Tender Offers." *The American Economics Review* 76(1): 155–167.

Kroll, M., S. Simmons, and P. Wright. 1988. *The Determinants of Chief Executive Officer Compensation Following Major Acquisitions.* Unpublished Technical Report, University of Texas at Tyler.

Lambert, R.A. 1983. "Long Term Contracts and Moral Hazard." *The Bell Journal of Economics* (Autumn) 14: 441–445.

Larcker, D.F. 1983. "The Association Between Performance Plan Adoption and Corporate Capital Investment." *Journal of Accounting and Economics* 5(3): 3–30.

Lawler, E.E., III. 1981. *Pay and Organization Development.* Reading, MA: Addison Wesley.

Levine, H.Z. 1988. "Compensation and Benefits Today: Board Members Speak Out." *Compensation and Benefits Review* 20(1): 33–48.

Lewellen, W.G. 1968. *Executive Compensation in Large Industrial Corporations.* New York: National Bureau of Economic Research.

Lewellen, W.G. and B. Huntsman. 1970. "Managerial Pay and Corporate Performance." *American Economic Review* 60: 710–720.

Loomis, C.J. 1982. "The Madness of Executive Compensation." *Fortune* (July 12): 42–51.

Luthans, F. 1988. "Successful vs. Effective Real Managers." *Academy of Management Executives* 2(2): 127–132.

Mahoney, T.A. 1979. "Organizational Hierarchy and Position Worth." *Academy of Management Journal* 22(4): 726–737.

Masson, R.T. 1971. "Executive Motivations, Earnings, and Consequent Equity Performance." *Journal of Political Economy* 79: 1278–1294.

McComas, M. 1986. "Atop the Fortune 500: A Survey of the CEOs." *Fortune* (April 28): 26–31.

McEachern, W.A. 1975. *Managerial Control and Performance.* Lexington, MA: D.C. Heath Co.

McGuire, J.W., J.S.Y. Chiu and A.O. Elbing. 1962. "Executive Income, Sales, and Profits." *American Economic Review* ___: 753–761.

Milkovich, G.T. 1988. "A Strategic Perspective to Compensation Management." In *Research In Personnel and Human Resource Management* (Vol. 6), eds. K. Rowland and G. Ferris. Greenwich, CT: JAI Press.

Miller, E.C. 1976. "How Companies Set The Base Salary and Incentive Bonus Opportunity for Chief Executive Officers and COO: A Comprehensive Review Symposium." *Compensation Review* 8(4): 19–32.

Mintzberg, H. 1973. "A New Look at the Chief Executive's Job." *Organizational Dynamics* 1(3): 20–30.

_____. 1979. "An Emerging Strategy of 'Direct' Research." *Administrative Science Quarterly* 24: 582–589.

Mizruchi, M.S. 1983. "Who Controls Whom: An Examination of the Relation Between Management and Boards of Directors in Large American Corporations." *Academy of Management Review* 8(3): 426–435.

Murphy, K.J. 1985. "Corporate Performance and Managerial Remuneration." *Journal of Accounting and Statistics* 7: 11–42.

_____. 1986. "Top Executives Are Worth Every Nickel They Get." *Harvard Business Review* (March-April): 125–132.

Murthy, K.R.S. and M.S. Salter. 1975. "Should CEO Pay Be Linked to Results?" *Harvard Business Review* 53: 66–73.

Ochsner, R.C. 1987. "The Future of Compensation Management in the United States." Paper presented at a Symposium on Compensation Management, Bureau of Labor Statistics.

Patton, A. 1985. "Those Million Dollar A Year Executives." *Harvard Business Review* (January-February): 56–62.

Pearce, J.L., W.B. Stevenson, and James L. Perry. 1985. "Managerial Compensation Based on Organizational Performance: A Time Series Analysis of the Effects of Merit Pay." *Academy of Management Journal* 28(2): 261–278.

Peck, C.A. 1987. *Top Executive Compensation*, 1987 edition. Research report from The Conference Board.

Peters, T. 1988. "Letter to the Editor." *Inc.* (April 1988): 80–82.

Pfeffer, J. 1972. "Size and Composition of Board of Directors." *Administrative Science Quarterly* 17: 218–228.

Pfeffer, J. and G.R. Salancik. 1978. *The External Control of Organizations*. New York: Harper and Row.

Pitts, R.A. 1974. "Incentive Compensation and Organization Design." *Personnel Journal* (May): 338–344.

———. 1976. "Diversification Strategies and Organization Policies of Large Diversified Firms." *Journal of Economics and Business* (Summer): 181–187.

Posner, B. 1987. "Executive Compensation '87: The Brave New World: The 1986 Tax Reform Act has raised new questions about virtually every compensation tool a company has." *Inc.* 9(7): 63.

Posner, M. 1987. "Prospects for Your Perks (Tax Reform and Fringe Benefits)." *Changing Times* 41(4): 77.

Poster, C.Z. 1985. "Executive Compensation: Taking Long-Term Incentives Out of the Corporate Ivory Tower." *Compensation and Benefits Review* 17(2): 20–31.

Prasad, S.B. 1974. "Top Management Compensation and Corporate Performance." *Academy of Management Journal* 17(3): 554–558.

Rappaport, A. 1978. "Executive Incentives vs. Corporate Growth." *Harvard Business Review* 56(4): 81–88.

Rick, J.T. and J.A. Larson. 1984. "Why Some Long-Term Incentives Fail." *Compensation Review* 16(1): 26–37.

Roberts, D.R. 1959. "A General Theory of Executive Compensation Based on Statistically Tested Propositions." *Quarterly Journal of Economics* 70: 270–294.

Roche, G. 1975. "Compensation and the Mobile Executive." *Harvard Business Review* 53(6): 53–62.

Rubin, I.N. 1988. "After Tax Reform, Part 2, Planning Executive Compensation Programs." *Compensation and Benefits Review* 20(1): 26–32.

Salscheider, J. 1981. "Devising Pay Strategies for Diversified Companies." *Compensation Review* 13(2): 15–24.

Salter, M.S. 1973. "Tailor Incentive Compensation to Strategy." *Harvard Business Review* (March-April): 94–102.

Santeer, R.E. and S.P. Neun. 1986. "Stock Dispersion and Executive Compensation." *Review of Economics and Statistics* (November): 685–687.

Schlesinger, J.B. 1988. *Wall Street Journal* (April 18): 4.

Schuler, R.S. and S.E. Jackson. 1987. "Linking Competitive Strategies with Human Resource Practices." *Academy of Management Executives* (August): 207–219.

Sethi, S.P. and N. Namiki. 1987. "Top Management Compensation and Corporate Performance." *Journal of Business Strategy* 7(4): 37–43.

Simon, H.A. 1957. "The Compensation of Executives." *Sociometry* (March 20): 32–35.

Simon, R. 1986. "Charred Meat." *Forbes* 137(8): 93.

Smyth, D.J., W.J. Boyes, and D.E. Peseau. *Size, Growth, Profits, and Executive Compensation in the Large Corporation.* New York: Holmes and Meier.

Stata, R. and M. Maidique. 1980. "Bonus System for Balanced Strategy." *Harvard Business Review* (November-December): 156–163.

Stonich, P.J. 1981. "Using Rewards in Implementing Strategy." *Strategic Management Journal* 2(2): 345–352.

Taussig, F.W. and W.S. Barker. 1925. "American Corporations and Their Executives: A Statistical Inquiry." *Quarterly Journal of Economics* (November): 1–51.

Taylor, A. (III). 1988. "Tomorrow's Chief Executives." *Fortune* (May 9): 30–42.

Tichy, N., C. Fombrun and M. Devanna. 1984. *Strategic Human Resources Management.* New York: John Wiley & Sons.

Toppel, H.J. "Changes TRA '86 Makes in Executive Compensation." *Corporate Accounting* (Summer) 5: 20–25.

Tosi, H. and L.R. Gomez-Mejia. 1988. "The Determinants of Chief Executive Compensation: An Agency Theory Perspective." Paper presented at National Academy of Management Meeting, Anaheim, CA.

Ungson, G.R. and R.M. Steers. 1984. "Motivation and Politics in Executive Compensation." *Academy of Management Review* 9(2): 313–323.

Verespej, M.A. 1987. "What's Wrong With Executive Compensation?" *Industry Week* (December 14): 43–45.

Walter, D.H. 1987. "An Overview of Compensation Techniques Following TRA '86." *Journal of Corporate Taxation* (Summer) 14, 2: 139–159.

Weiner, N. and T. Mahoney. 1981. "A Model of Corporate Performance as a Function of Environmental, Organization, and Leadership Influences." *Academy of Management Journal* 24: 453–470.

Williams, M.J. 1985. "Why Chief Executives' Pay Keeps Rising." *Fortune* (April 1): 66–73.

◆

Author Index

Authors appearing in this Index appear in the Notes and References at the end of each chapter. The individual authors of the chapters appear here also. Anyone referenced in the body of the text appears in the Subject Index.

Subject Index